FRONT ROW CENTER

Dedicated to
the theatregoing public
and the theatre community
of northern California

No book of this scope could be
completed without the help of friends
and professional colleagues. I want
to note my thanks to them here. It's
not like the cast list in a play
program—not "in order of their
appearance," or even "in alphabetical
order." Nor is it with regard to the
importance or degree of their contributions. It's just as I remember
them, with warm appreciation: Ellen
Ernest Brooks, Mike Timko, Gerald
Karski, Dr. Nadine Payn, Irving "Bud"
Levin, KGO Radio, Devera Kettner,
Russ Riera, Keith Rockwell, the Carbon
Alternative, Kolmar/Raush Associates,
Larry Levin and United Artists Theatre
Circuit, Roberta Blagg, Richard Carreon
(ACT), the Shorenstein-Nederlander
Organization, John Fusco, Nancy
Bernhard, Jacqueline Killeen and
the staff of 101 Productions, and
Jennifer (my daughter who, for the
seventh, eighth, and ninth months of
her life wondered who the strange
man called "Daddy" was), and . . . the
producers, directors, and staffs of
the theatres, production companies,
motion picture chains, city and state
governmental administrative agencies,
and performers represented in this
book. Without their cooperation none
of it would have been possible.

FRONT ROW CENTER

A GUIDE TO NORTHERN CALIFORNIA THEATRES

By Jack Brooks

Theatre sketches by Denise Peach

101 PRODUCTIONS, SAN FRANCISCO

Printed and bound in the United States of America.

Distributed to the book trade in the United States
by Charles Scribner's Sons, New York.

Published by 101 Productions
834 Mission Street
San Francisco, California 94103

Library of Congress Cataloging in Publication Data

Brooks, Jack.
  Front row center.

  Includes index.
  1. Theaters--California, Northern.   2. Moving-
picture theaters--California, Northern.   I. Title.
PN2275.C3B7   792'.09794   81-14069
ISBN   0-89286-193-2   AACR2

Contents

Prologue

Let's begin with a quiz—they're always fun. Where can you:
- see sex, violence, and radical politics in a Methodist Church basement?
- see the original cast of a hit Broadway musical?
- pay New York ticket prices to see that musical?
- see Shakespeare under the stars at a winery or Sam Shepard in a converted Army warehouse on a bay?
- be seated in a theatre built in 1847 or in one designed by Frank Lloyd Wright in the 1950s?

There, I gave it away by saying theatre. All of the above are theatre locations either in northern California or just over the border in Oregon. I'll cover the entire area in *Front Row Center* and acquaint you with one of the most active and exciting stage and screen regions in America—or in the world, for that matter.

Before we go any farther, let's look at that word *theatre*. I'm referring to the actual spelling of the word. It'll come up often in this book.

As you know, the other spelling is *theater*. What we need right off is a rule of thumb, or at least, a rule of index finger. Try this one: The *tre* spelling refers to "live" (or "legitimate") houses of entertainment, dramatic or musical. The *ter* designation, in some people's lexicons, means a movie house "illegitimate"?). I like the foregoing plan, and, since I'm writing the book, that's the one we'll use, unless the theatres themselves prefer the alternate spelling.

In the past decade, the San Francisco Bay Area has become a mecca for actors, actresses, playwrights, musicians, composers, filmmakers, et al. This movement, largely from the East Coast and the Midwest, is based on the myth that there is work for performing artists near the Golden Gate—paying work. By and large, that is, indeed, a myth. But it doesn't seem to matter. The area is so exciting, so adventurous, that the players stay, start their own theatres, apply for government grants, get regular jobs, or go on unemployment, and hope for the best. The result is that, at last count, there were better than 150 operating theatrical companies in the San Francisco-Oakland neighborhoods. Some of these groups have their own buildings to appear in, others are nomadic. Still more disappear after their initial outing.

The proliferation of theatres south of San Francisco, specifically in the Santa Clara, San Jose, Santa Cruz, and Monterey Peninsula areas, has been only slightly less dramatic than in the Bay Area cities. The growth has been most pronounced over the past five years, and the San Jose-Saratoga-Los Gatos cauldrons have been bubbling the most vigorously (metaphorically speaking). The San Francisco Peninsula (San Bruno, San Mateo, San Carlos, Redwood City, Palo Alto, Los Altos, Santa Clara) is active but less rushed in the development of new facilities. Companies are older and more stable than in the community to the south.

San Francisco can be said to contain the best and the worst of northern California theatre. Three commercial houses, operated by the Shorenstein-Nederlander Organization, present Broadway musicals and plays on the way to or touring out of New York. The American Conservatory Theatre operates the Geary for their repertory season, and the Marines Memorial Theatre for attractions that they produce separately or co-sponsor. The Marines is also available to independent producers on a rental basis.

North Beach, home of the famous, or infamous, topless nightclub, is moving slowly but surely toward being the off Broadway of San Francisco. Don't be confused because the street that traverses the area is Broadway. Here you find the smaller-budget attractions, predominantly comedies and musicals, presented with varying degrees of professionalism.

Out in the neighborhoods, and directly on San Francisco Bay in the Fort Mason Center, is the western version of off-off-Broadway. Many of these theatres are politically oriented, some cater to specific ethnic groups, and all are in financially rough straits much of the time.

The East Bay and Contra Costa County boast some of the most stable, and certainly best attended, community and small professional theatres in northern California. The wonderfully restored Paramount Theatre in central Oakland is the home of the Oakland Symphony, the Oakland Ballet, and many major traveling attractions. It is the epitome of what a rescued, recycled movie palace can become with community help. Suburban Concord, Walnut Creek, and Lafayette each have permanent theatres with full, year-round schedules.

The Bay Area isn't short of outdoor facilities for balmy nights of entertainment. The biggest moonlighter is the Concord Pavilion with its nationally known musical stars. Oakland has Woodminster Amphitheatre for summer musicals (semiprofessional) and John Hinkel Park Amphitheatre for Shakespeare under the stars. On San Francisco's busy Nineteenth Avenue (stretching from Daly City to the Golden Gate Bridge) is Stern Grove. Sunny summer Sunday afternoons and free admission jam this eucalyptus grove with thousands of comfortably casual fans of local and national orchestras, opera companies, and Dixieland groups. In Marin there's Mount Tamalpais mountain theatre. Guerneville has the lovely Armstrong Grove stage in the redwoods.

Since Marinites are notoriously loath to leave their home turf, that county is rapidly growing its own crop of creditable theatres. Most companies are housed in cozy, rustic playhouses that used to be something else. For the bigger shows, and an occasional grand opera, there's Marin Veterans' Memorial Theatre close by the Frank Lloyd Wright–designed Civic Center complex.

Sacramento can best be characterized as taking its local theatre seriously and with a consistent amount of attention. Many of its actors and directors are hometown-educated and -nurtured artists. Some theatre plants date from Gold Rush days, others are of a more modern and recent vintage and design. The state capital also hosts California's only arena theatre in a tent.

Little-theatre groups, made up of secretaries, business executives, nursery school owners, and milkmen, perform with stage, screen, and television stars in public auditoriums designed by star architects. Barns and carriage houses of formerly private estates ring with laughter at the punch lines of Neil Simon or hum along with the tunes of Stephen Sondheim (no mean feat) or Richard Rodgers (much easier). In wooded glens and flowered meadows there are picturesque outdoor amphitheatres. Hardly a hamlet doesn't have a Hamlet.

Every major urban center and assorted rural areas boast giant auditoriums (newly created or recently restored landmarks). These present touring New York shows, TV stars, concert favorites, rock bands, and travelogue programs extolling the glories of Rome (Italy or Georgia), or just general roamin'.

Finally, complexes of movie houses (or cinemas, depending on your financial and/or intellectual strata) serve the millions of northern Californians with varying degrees of courtesy, cleanliness, and professional pride in what and how the films are presented to the public. While not looking into individual movie theaters (*ter* ending), except maybe one or two, I will tell you who owns the bulk of these entertainment emporiums and to whom to address your praise and/or complaints.

Two sections in this book are devoted to special events that command international attention: the Oregon Shakespearean Festival in Ashland, Oregon (a place that should be declared an honorary part of northern California), and the San Francisco International Film Festival. Both of these happenings are covered in detail because of the interest they generate.

Front Row Center is presented as a guide to the vast treasure that is housed in the theatres *and* the theaters of northern California. I have used the criteria of longevity, visibility, and prominence, and in some cases, uniqueness and charm of setting, in my selection of those locations included. Naturally, I will have overlooked a very important theatre or two, and I may have left out your pet cinema. My apologies in advance. I'll make every effort to correct any such errors in future editions. Until then, pull up your chair to a position approximately *Front Row Center.* Or, by using the seating charts provided in this book, you can sit just about anywhere you please and make that choice well in advance of queuing up at the box office. Be sure to check in advance in all cases as to days of performance and curtain times. You won't find those details in *Front Row Center.* They're subject to change too frequently to keep up with. That said . . . right this way, please!

Carmel-Monterey Peninsula

CALIFORNIA'S FIRST THEATRE, MONTEREY

Given the natural beauty of the Carmel–Monterey area and the massive tourist influx year-round, it's no wonder that several theatres have a fairly long history, and one is, in fact, the oldest theatre in California. Add to these the college facilities, and we find a vigorous performance schedule in this, the first of our *Front Row Center* areas of discussion.

Granted, other than theatrical events hold the national limelight in Monterey. There's the Laguna Seca Raceway for car buffs and the Mon-terey Jazz Festival for those who want their scat-singing in the sunshine. Duffers flock to Pebble Beach for the annual Bing Crosby Golf Classic, and readers of Steinbeck and those who've never heard of him rub shoulders on Monterey's Cannery Row.

Still, local theatre thrives. It varies from Moliere to melodrama, from *Oklahoma!* to *Ah, Wilderness*. Some of it is outdoors, some in dinner-theatre settings, and there's even a cozy upstairs arena on Old Fisher-man's Wharf.

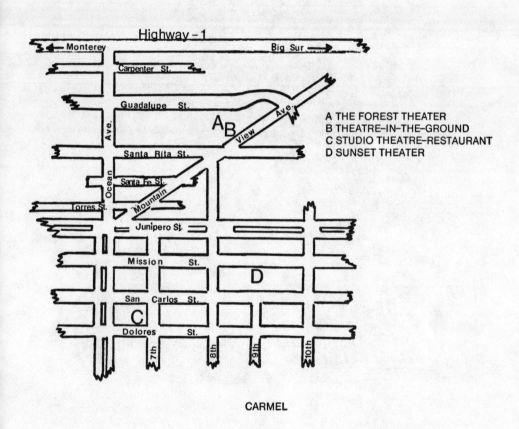

A THE FOREST THEATER
B THEATRE–IN–THE–GROUND
C STUDIO THEATRE–RESTAURANT
D SUNSET THEATER

CARMEL

SUNSET THEATER

733 seats (reserved or non-reserved depending on event).

LOCATION San Carlos and Ninth streets (between Eighth and Tenth streets), Carmel.

BUSINESS-BOX OFFICE ADDRESS
Sunset Center
P.O. Box 5066
Carmel-by-the-Sea, CA 93921.

BOX OFFICE TELEPHONE (408) 624-9892.

BUSINESS TELEPHONE (408) 624-3996.

GENERAL DIRECTOR Richard Tyler.

HANDICAPPED ACCESS Entry to the theatre by wheelchairs is possible through the entrance behind the box office. The restroom facilities, however, present a real problem. The men's room is on the first floor but wheelchair access is almost impossible.

The Sunset Center began life a half century ago as the Sunset School, an elementary-level facility. It was converted to general public use for the arts and cultural activities in 1964. The theatre auditorium had always been used by local presenters, musicians, and performers. The Sunset Community Cultural Center (its official full name) is entirely owned and operated by the city of Carmel, along with the Forest Theater, an adjunct of the operation.

The large stage (33 feet by 52 feet) can be expanded by adding a portable unit forward of the permanent apron. There is ample height (31 feet floor to grid), and an adequate sound and lighting system is part of the house. The proscenium arch opening measures 28 feet wide by 17 feet high. There are dressing room areas on the floor below the theatre, and a green room backstage.

Touring shows and musical groups use the Sunset Theater on a semi-regular basis, although local events have preference. Interested parties can rent the facility for $100 a performance (a like security bond must be posted along with a valid public liability insurance policy in the amount of $500,000) and the obligatory stage manager gets $7.50 an hour for his time. The rental base is computed against 10 percent of the gross, and the Center charges whichever is greater. All in all, it's a good deal for a lovely theatre if you wish to be seen in Carmel.

Community-sponsored groups that appear at the Sunset on a regular basis include the following:
● The Monterey County Symphony, which gives six concerts a year with soloists.
● The Carmel Music Society, which presents six concerts and sponsors the California Young Artists' Competition as well.
● The Chamber Music Society, which presents a half dozen concerts and an annual Ensemble Competition.
● The world-renowned Carmel Bach Festival, which is held each summer, with concerts and a youth program featuring works of the master and his period.
● The Carmel Festival of Dance, which presents four concerts with major dance companies.
● The Hidden Valley Music Seminars, which bring together young vocal and orchestral musicians for five concerts and master classes.
● A ten-tilm theatrical Film Festival, which searches for important artistic advances in filmmaking.
● The Carmel Classical Guitar Festival, which features art exhibits in addition to recitals.
● The Festival of Firsts Playwriting Competition, in which the city of Carmel gives a $2,000 prize for the best new play and retains the right of first refusal on the initial presentation of the winning work.

As if all of the above weren't enough to occupy the theatregoer's time, add barbershop quartets, school bands and orchestras, a ballet or two, and the annual Christmas-in-Carmel festivities and you have a theatre utilized to the maximum for the public's gratification. Call the numbers at the beginning of this section for dates and details about the above events.

The beauty of this theatre is derived from the cathedral-like style of the architecture. Soaring arches frame the entire auditorium and direct the focus to the stage. A small balcony is located in the rear. Ornate chandeliers offer soft, dramatic lighting to the room, and a plush combination of rich reds and golds adds a regal tone to the hall.

There is parking for 200 cars within the Center for theatre patrons or visitors to any of the various social and educational sessions always taking place here. The theatre is centrally located near the picturesque Carmel shopping district. From Highway 1, follow Ocean Avenue west to San Carlos and turn left to Ninth Street.

THE FOREST THEATER

600 seats (outdoor amphitheatre; nonreserved)
LOCATION AND BOX OFFICE
Mountain View Avenue and Santa Rita Street
Carmel, CA 93921.
BOX OFFICE TELEPHONE (408) 624-1531.
BUSINESS INFORMATION TELEPHONE (408) 624-3996.
ADMINISTRATION City of Carmel-Forest Theatre Guild.
ARTISTIC DIRECTOR Guest directors.
HANDICAPPED ACCESS There's an easy grade from the parking lot to the seating area. Space at the ends of the rows or forward of the front row is available for wheelchairs. Restroom facilities are also accessible.

When Herbert Heron came to Carmel in 1908 it struck him that the area needed a place for poets and actors to present their talents to the local citizens. It may have struck him thus because Heron was a poet and a dramatist. Whatever his motives, the Carmel Development Company, which owned most of the town, turned a site at Mountain View Avenue and Santa Rita Street over to Heron's organization, the Forest Theater Society. The donors not only didn't charge rent, they also gave funds for the building of a stage and a seating area. The Forest Theater opened officially on July 9, 1910.

From that first day until 1935 the theatre was in operation every summer. Dramatic readings, poetry conclaves, musicales, and plays continued under the aegis of the Society. The theatre was in need of work, however, and to accomplish this, the deed for the property was handed over to the city of Carmel to make it eligible for renovation by the WPA. You'll run into other outdoor theatres that owe their existence to this agency throughout the book.

The stage and seating as it now exists came into being in the thirties. Newer to the theatre is the presentation of Shakespeare. That was inaugurated in 1972 with a production of *Twelfth Night*. The summer program isn't restricted to the Bard of Avon. Musicals and American dramas and comedies are also mounted on the broad, wooden stage. The city presents a free Sunday afternoon concert series during the months of July and August.

The Forest Theater Guild, under the guidance of its board of directors, selects independent producers and directors on a one-season-at-a-time basis. The average season consists of three or four shows.

As at many other theatres of this type, the seating is bare lumber and the evening air is often cool, or

THE FOREST THEATER

downright chilly. It's always good advice to bring a pillow for your underside and a blanket for your upper side. The soaring redwoods all around make a natural windbreak and provide a scenic backdrop unattainable by any set designer. If the elements are too brisk, the stone-fronted platform sports two huge fireplaces, one stage right, one stage left, to take the nip out of the air. The restrooms are located to the right side of the theatre as you face the stage, and the box office is just below.

Summer shows in the Forest Theater are presented on Thursday, Friday, Saturday, and Sunday evenings. Tickets are under five dollars and there is plenty of free, lighted parking.

To get to the Forest Theater, take Highway 1 to Carmel. Turn west on Ocean Street, past Carpenter and Guadalupe streets to Santa Rita Street. Turn left on Santa Rita to the intersection of Mountain View Avenue and you're at the entrance to the Forest Theatre in Carmel-by-the-Sea.

STUDIO THEATRE-RESTAURANT

120 seats (reserved).
LOCATION East side of Dolores Street between Ocean and Seventh Street in central Carmel.
BOX OFFICE-BUSINESS ADDRESS
P.O. Box 3591
Carmel, CA 93921.
BOX OFFICE TELEPHONE (408) 624-1661.
BUSINESS TELEPHONE (408) 624-8688.
MANAGING DIRECTORS Connie Curtis, Robert Tidwell.
ARTISTIC DIRECTOR Marina Curtis.
HANDICAPPED ACCESS Not accessible to wheelchair-confined persons.

A dinner theatre in every sense of the term. The Studio Theatre-Restaurant, with its mini-Elizabethan facade and its multitiered auditorium, has been in existence since 1958. It's currently a family-run, year-round operation that presents commercially oriented plays and musicals. The stage limitations dictate small-cast ventures, and the emphasis is heavily on light comedy and thriller mysteries.

The dinner portion of the presentation gives patrons a choice of two entrées, salad, dessert, rolls, and an assortment of beverages including beer and wine.

There's nothing fancy about the theatre itself, but it has a quaintly intimate feeling about it that makes for a relaxed evening. After passing through a small foyer that contains display cases of posters and photos of past shows, you enter a long hallway that is a showcase area for production photographs on the right, with a food table on the left. As you pass through you can make a mental note of what you will order when the waiter asks you later at your table. Once inside the auditorium you'll be politely ushered to a table on one of several levels. Candles and checked tablecloths give the setting a comfortable feeling, as do the canvas directors' chairs you sit in. The rear and right side walls are covered with large posters representing the plays and musicals that have filled the Studio's stage throughout its history. The general lighting is provided by simple white opaque globes suspended from the rather low ceilings. Across the back elevation are barstool-height directors' chairs for those wishing to attend the show only.

Dinner and show combinations are about $16 per person, or you can skip dinner and just see the show for $7. The food is good, however, and I recommend the combo.

Productions usually play Thursday through Sunday, with each show getting an eight-week run.

STUDIO THEATRE–RESTAURANT

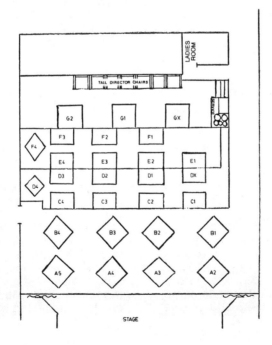

THEATRE-IN-THE-GROUND
THE CHILDREN'S
EXPERIMENTAL THEATRE
THE STAFF PLAYERS
REPERTORY COMPANY

60 seats (non-reserved).
LOCATION Mountain View Avenue and Santa Rita Street, Carmel.
BOX OFFICE-BUSINESS ADDRESS
CET/Staff Players Repertory Company
P.O. Box 3381
Carmel, CA 93921.
BOX OFFICE TELEPHONE (408) 624-1531.
BUSINESS TELEPHONE (408) 375-6555.
GENERAL DIRECTOR
Marcia Gambrell Hovick.
HANDICAPPED ACCESS There is a ramped approach from the parking area to the wooden deck that serves as the entrance to the theatre. The same restrooms serve this theatre as those for the Forest Theater. Call ahead for special arrangements.

Most areas under stages are used for dressing rooms, scenic workshops, or storage space. Not so the space under the stage of the Forest Theater. It houses another theatre, aptly called the Theatre-in-the-Ground. This facility is in operation from September through May and the same producing company has been in residence for over two decades.

The Children's Experimental Theatre was founded by Marcia Gambrell Hovick for the purpose of training young actors for either a career in the theatre or for an avocation to expand their life's experiences. CET has done that job so well that many of the actors connected with the adult wing of the group began as child acting students. All the CET work culminates in a public performance of the plays that have been the subject of the instructional ses-

sions. The youngsters may also appear with adult actors, either in CET presentations or in those of the other facet of The Theatre-in-the-Ground's resident group, the Staff Players Repertory Company.

The Staff Players came to be when the teachers of CET felt the need to tread the boards themselves. The Staff Players are just that, members of the staff of CET, plus other adult thespians of the Carmel community who wish to participate in this nonprofessional troupe devoted to the classics including Moliere, Ibsen, and Shaw. They pride themselves in being the Monterey Peninsula's only theatre company so committed.

This is an intimate house, totally lacking in stuffiness or pretension. Intermissions may be spent on the wide outside deck in the open air or in the small but comfortable lobby. If you're in the mood for a snack between the acts, there is usually a simple table set up to serve apple juice, brownies, coffee, hot chocolate, and the like for a modest fee. Speaking of a modest fee, ticket prices are under five dollars, and, with a choice of subscription plans, the savings are even more economical.

The decor is mainly devoted to photo displays of the current cast and show for both companies and a photographic record of the productions that have gone before. There's a feeling of a cozy living room about the lobby, enhanced further by a bookcase that divides the lobby from the auditorium. Draperies separate the dressing area to the far end of the lobby. A table near the door serves as the box office.

The platforming that supports the padded stack-chairs elevates the tiny seating area so that the sight lines are unrestricted from any location. The small stage is utilized to the maximum by cleverly designed, easily manipulated sets. Because of the limitations imposed by the facility itself, extra attention is given to lighting and costuming. The cramped space also requires the use of the lobby for exits and entrances (there is virtually no wing space to the sides of the stage) and the device of bringing players through the audience.

The color motif carried throughout the Theatre-in-the-Ground is a blend of earth tones in browns and beiges. Carpeting adds to the general warm feeling of the house.

To get to this Carmel beehive of artistic activities, follow the same directions as are noted in the section on the Forest Theater.

THE WHARF THEATER

110 seats (reserved).
LOCATION AND BOX OFFICE
Old Fisherman's Wharf
Monterey, CA 93940.
BOX OFFICE-BUSINESS TELEPHONE
(408) 372-2882.
OWNER-PRODUCER Angelo DiGirolamo.
MANAGING DIRECTOR Chuck Thurman.
HANDICAPPED ACCESS Wheelchair access is difficult. There is a long stairway up to the second-floor auditorium, then tiered seating. The chairs are canvas directors' chairs, so they are

easily removed to accommodate wheelchairs once several strong backs have gotten the wheelchairs up the stairway.

This lovely indoor amphitheatre shares its location with art galleries and an old radio tapes and memorabilia shop. It's just steps away from Monterey's famous seafood restaurants, the nearest being owned by the theater owner and named for him: Angelo's. He also owns the art gallery in the theater lobby. (You may note that we are using the *ter* spelling. That's at this establishment's request.)

The original Wharf Theater was housed in a fish-packing shed not far from the present site. It opened in 1950 and carried on until 1959, when fire ended its career. The intrepid company moved to the Old Opera House on Alvarado Street, but it just wasn't the same. In 1963 the opera house fell to urban renewal. The current building, constructed of old lumber from demolished Army barracks, opened in 1976.

The art gallery, which you encountered at the top of the entry stairway and in the outer lobby, continues into the auditorium. Paintings adorn the wooden walls (originally the roofing of the demolished barracks)

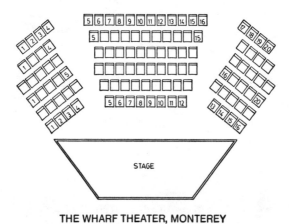

THE WHARF THEATER, MONTEREY

and are sometimes similar in subject matter with the theme of the current play or musical. The highly elevated tiered seating area is divided into three sections: a center and two sides created by aisles. The seating is on multicolored directors' chairs. The stage floor is nonelevated. There are upper playing areas above the main floor. The color scheme is tied together throughout by a burnt-orange carpet.

The entertainment fare here is intended for both community and tourists. Musical comedies figure heavily in the scheduling, followed by light comedies and an occasional drama. It's a year-round operation utilizing nonprofessional casts. From October through June, performances run Friday through Sunday. July through September a Thursday opus is added. There are three ticket prices, all under ten dollars. Take the Munras Avenue exit off Highway 1 and follow it all the way to the Fisherman's Wharf parking lot, park, and walk out on the pier.

THE WHARF THEATER

CALIFORNIA'S FIRST THEATRE

134 seats.
LOCATION AND BOX OFFICE
Scott and Pacific streets
Monterey, CA 93940.
BUSINESS ADDRESS
c/o Marabee Boone
1118 Piedmont Avenue
Pacific Grove, CA 93950.
BOX OFFICE-BUSINESS TELEPHONE
(408) 375-4916.
ARTISTIC AND MANAGING DIRECTOR
Lavern Seeman.
BUSINESS MANAGER Marabee Boone.
HANDICAPPED ACCESS Wheelchairs may
enter on the sides of the building,
where there are three low steps to
be negotiated. Once inside, there is
no problem in the placement of
chairs. There are no restroom facilities
for the handicapped in the theatre.
There are, however, facilities one
block to the east in the Pacific
House Memory Garden (Scott and
Oliver streets).

California's First Theatre is just that.
Located a seashell's throw from the
Presidio of Monterey and Old Fisherman's Wharf, the building is a state
historical landmark. It was built in
1847 by an English sailor of Scots
heritage, named Jack Swan. It was
his intention that it should be a
home away from home for his brother
seamen: a kind of a combination
saloon and lodging house. No sooner
did he get it built than some bored
soldiers from the Presidio, up the
block, asked if they could stage
theatricals on the premises. Swan
agreed, and California had its first
playhouse. Came the Gold Rush of
'49 and everyone, audience and all,
headed north. The playhouse was
no more.

Then, in 1937, a group called the
Troupers of the Gold Coast got
permission to reopen the delapidated
hall. It was renovated and rejuvenated,
and it's been operating ever since.

A prerequisite for plays performed
by the nonprofessional company is
that the work date from before
1900. That means that you get
mostly melodramas, followed by
musical olios to fill out the evening.
The Drunkard is a perennial favorite,
along with *Ten Nights in a Bar
Room,* and the show that reopened
the house in 1937, *Tatters, the Pet
of Squatter's Gulch.*

The auditorium's front two-thirds is
cabaret tables and chairs. The last
section is benches, each one its
own riser. Although the building is a
little rickety, the sight lines are
good. Historical memorabilia fill the
small, charming, fireplaced lobbies.

Performances run Wednesday
through Sunday, and for the summer
season two different plays alternate
on the schedule. Call for titles and
curtain times. Tickets are scaled at
$4 for adults, $3 for children 13
through 17, and $2 for children 12
and under. Coming from north or
south on Highway 1, take the Downtown Monterey-Fisherman's Wharf
exit to Del Monte, then left to Scott
and Pacific. There is a parking lot
directly across from the theatre.

Salinas-San Juan Bautista

MISSION SAN JUAN BAUTISTA

Before heading to the north along the coast, let's take a side trip to the east into the Salinas Valley. The Salinas Valley area boasts two major theatre facilities. One is relatively new, while the other is a firmly established entity with an international reputation. The latter, unfortunately, is like the prophet with no honor in his own country. El Teatro Campesino, headquartered in San Juan Bautista and housed in a recently acquired larger facility, is very possibly America's best-known theatre company abroad, particularly in Europe. Many northern Californians have never heard of it. We'll look at the newer facility in Salinas first.

HARTNELL THEATRE
THE WESTERN STAGE

499 seats main theatre; 125 to 150 seats studio theatre.
LOCATION AND BOX OFFICE
156 Homestead Avenue
(on the Hartnell College campus)
Salinas, CA 93901.
BOX OFFICE TELEPHONE (418) 758-1221.
BUSINESS TELEPHONE (408) 758-8211.
GENERAL MANAGER Stanley Crane.
MANAGING-ARTISTIC DIRECTOR
Ronald Danko.
HANDICAPPED ACCESS. The Hartnell Theatre is accessible for wheelchairs, and the main theatre has space for approximately five standard chairs or three motorized chairs. The small studio setting is also easily reached.

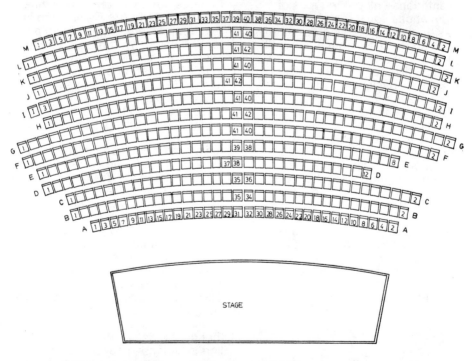

HARTNELL THEATRE

The Performing Arts building of Hartnell College actually houses two theatres. One is the 499-seat, Continental-arranged, main-stage theatre. It is typical of modern theatre design and was built in 1973. The second, smaller facility is the 125- to 150-seat Studio Theatre. Based on the "black box" concept, its walls are movable black drapes, and the size and shape of the playing space can be changed, along with the size of the audience area, as the needs of the play dictate.

Salinas has several little-theatre groups, and the Hartnell Theatre is made available to them on a limited basis. This relieves the city's problem of no other adequate performance spaces.

During the regular college year, the theatres at Hartnell are used for concerts, college theatre-department presentations—all of the types of performances you'd expect—plus an occasional one-person, star-name touring show. Then, from June until September, the Western Stage takes over, and summer stock (on a semi-professional basis) fills both stages with over a hundred performances of a half dozen or more plays and musicals.

Tickets are scaled in several price categories, but all seating is under ten dollars per ducat. There is almost unlimited free parking in the well-lighted parking lot a few steps from the main entrance.

Hartnell College and its theatre are located twenty-five miles east of Monterey-Carmel, with access on Highway 68. From the north or south, take the Main Street exit from Highway 101. The theatre is just north of the center of Salinas.

EL TEATRO CAMPESINO

175 to 250 seats in a flexible arrangement (nonreserved).
BOX OFFICE ADDRESS
705 Fourth Street
San Juan Bautista, CA 95045.
BUSINESS ADDRESS
P.O. Box 1278
San Juan Bautista, CA 95045.
BOX OFFICE-BUSINESS TELEPHONE
(408) 623-4505.
GENERAL MANAGER Andreas V. Gutierrez.
ARTISTIC DIRECTOR Luis Valdez.
HANDICAPPED ACCESS There is ramped access to the theatre and easy placement of wheelchairs. The restrooms are accessible and equipped for the handicapped.

The primary cause for northern Californians not being on a first-name basis with El Teatro Campesino is that, until recently, it has been a touring company. It has played on special occasions and at Christmas in the Old Mission San Juan Bautista (circa 1797) and in various places around this historic community. If you've never visited this restored nineteenth-century California town, you should. It will be even more rewarding if you happen to be an antiques buff. Some of the finest shops in the state are on the main street. You won't be disappointed with the restaurants, either.

Latino-Chicano theatre has gained world renown through the efforts of El Teatro Campesino. They've won an Obie Award in New York and have been cited for excellence by the Los Angeles Drama Critics' Circle. Clive Barnes and Peter Brook have sung their praises. Not bad for a theatre that began with farm-workers (hence the name) walking a picket line in Delano in 1965.

Several works have brought this theatre group and its dynamic artistic director, Luis Valdez, to the fore.

Many have seen the Christmas folk opera, *La Pastorela,* either live at the mission or in its televised version. *Zoot Suit,* after taking Los Angeles by storm, became the first play by a modern Latino author (Valdez) to make it to Broadway. Hollywood likewise succumbed. Next came *El Fin del Mundo,* a twentieth-century Chicano mystery-miracle play.

The recently completed theatre and cultural center will allow expanded scheduling and is a permanent base of operations and presentation. El Teatro Campesino is fifteen minutes from Gilroy and twenty minutes from Salinas. Hollister is seven minutes to the east.

The large lobby is left free for comfortable lounging, as the box office is located on the front porch, to the right of the main entrance. The restrooms are off the lobby, with the actors' entrance and green room-dressing rooms on the opposite side of the large building (formerly a produce warehouse). The auditorium is long and wide, and the seating areas are elevated on wooden platforming. The chairs are colorful directors' chairs. The entire arrangement can be shifted to change the playing area's shape and location. The scenic and costume workshops are located to the rear. There is a small parking area in front of the building and another to the side on the west. The wheelchair ramp is on this side and leads to the wooden veranda that fronts the simple but attractive facade.

Looking south from the town one can see a luscious hillside with cattle serenely grazing on it. If current plans are followed, a Latino cultural and art center will fill the forty-odd acres owned by El Teatro Campesino before many more years have passed. By that time, many more northern Californians and visitors from around the nation and the world will be aware of this theatre.

Whether you're coming up or down Highway 101 or approaching San Juan Bautista from the east, use Highway 156, the main access to San Juan Bautista and Hollister. Exit at either of the San Juan Bautista turnoffs.

EL TEATRO CAMPESINO

Santa Cruz-Scotts Valley
Los Gatos

BARN THEATER, SANTA CRUZ

Traveling north on Highway 1 from Monterey you'll pass through Moss Landing. If you're an antiques enthusiast, spend a few hours browsing in the many shops and warehouses. But don't be late for curtain time in Santa Cruz, Scotts Valley, or Los Gatos. These are our next three stops.

Santa Cruz is a rejuvenated city with a famous boardwalk, an amusement park, and beaches. It also has one of the two barn theatres that I'll cover in this section. Like San Francisco, Santa Cruz has more than its share of cabarets that feature comedy-satirical groups reminiscent of the improvisational groups of the sixties, such as the Committee. Other small theatrical groups surface and fade from production to production. College productions are plentiful, but there is a dirth of performance space for groups who wish to become permanent and grow. One tenacious theatre has been successful in both of these endeavors.

BARN THEATER
BEAR REPUBLIC THEATER

180 seats (reserved).
LOCATION AND BOX OFFICE
Bay and High streets
Santa Cruz, CA 95061.
BUSINESS ADDRESS
115C Harvey West Blvd.
Harvey West Park
Santa Cruz, CA 95061.
MAILING ADDRESS
P.O. Box 1137
Santa Cruz, CA 95061.
BOX OFFICE TELEPHONE (408) 425-1703.
BUSINESS TELEPHONE (408) 425-1725.
MANAGING DIRECTOR Andy Griggs.
ARTISTIC DIRECTOR Michael Griggs.
HANDICAPPED ACCESS The theatre is fully ramped, with wheelchair accommodations inside. Specify needs when ordering tickets.

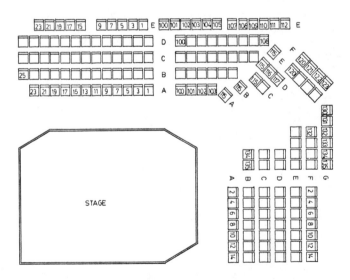

BARN THEATER

This rustic edifice is at the entrance to the University of California at Santa Cruz campus. Owned by the university, it is rented by the Bear Republic Theater, primarily for the presentation of their summer schedule. That schedule includes a broad representation of standard modern repertory classics such as Lope de Vega's *Fuente Ovejuna* and Shaw's *Misalliance,* and new works and recent Broadway and off-Broadway plays. Special late-night and off-schedule dates allow for a varied program of theatre groups from other parts of the country, along with one-person shows and children's theatre presentations.

The Bear Republic Theater began nearly a decade ago as a purely summer operation. Now the professional and semiprofessional staff and casts engage In year-round production: summers in the barn and the balance of the season in locations around Santa Cruz and in their studio, where workshops and classes ensure that the company will be around for another decade.

The ticket scale seldom gets above the six-dollar mark, and you can choose from three separate seating areas in the rather unorthodoxly designed Barn Theater.

If you're traveling on Highway 1, you'll notice that it becomes Mission Street in Santa Cruz. Follow it to Bay and turn left (from the north) or right (from the south). Coming from the San Francisco area on Highway 280, pick up Highway 17 south in San Jose and take it to Santa Cruz, then north on Mission to Bay and turn right to the Barn Theater.

SANTA CRUZ CIVIC AUDITORIUM

1,100 fixed seats (capacity increases to 1,952 seats when temporary chairs are added to the main floor; reservation policy at discretion of renting presenter).
LOCATION AND BOX OFFICE-BUSINESS ADDRESS
307 Church Street
Santa Cruz, CA 95060.
(Tickets are sold per event at announced outlets or at the time of performance at the theatre.)
BUSINESS TELEPHONES (408) 429-3779, (408) 429-3757.
SUPERVISOR OF FACILITY Don Ricker.
HANDICAPPED ACCESS There is wheelchair access to the main floor. This is Santa Cruz's all-purpose hall. It's 2-1/2 blocks northwest of the center of town (Pacific Avenue Mall) at Church and Center streets, adjacent to City Hall and the Public Library.

Relatively few theatrical events are booked into this auditorium due to the limitations of the stage. Ballet, a rare touring opera, and assorted rock concerts grace the building, along with sporting events and rummage sales.

The auditorium is a nonprofit operation with a staff of seven or so. Renters provide everything else.

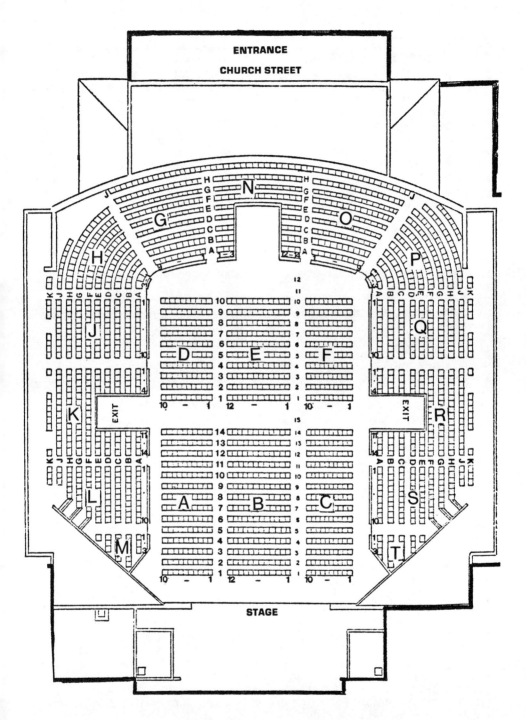

SANTA CRUZ CIVIC AUDITORIUM

ART CENTER THEATRE

85 seats (nonreserved).
LOCATION AND BOX OFFICE
1001 Center Street
Santa Cruz, CA 95060.
MAILING ADDRESS
P.O. Box 1502
Santa Cruz, CA 95060.
BOX OFFICE-BUSINESS TELEPHONE
(408) 429-1188.
MANAGING DIRECTOR Patty Oblath.
ARTISTIC DIRECTOR Varies with presentation.
HANDICAPPED ACCESS The theatre is wheelchair accessible and has a restroom equipped for the handicapped. Many productions by local groups are signed for the hearing impaired.

If it were not for the large sign on the roof, from the street you might not recognize the Arts Resource Center for what it is. India Joe's Restaurant occupies the front of this all-wooden building, which was originally a warehouse. The multiwindowed structure contains, in addition to the restaurant, art galleries, a glass blower, artists' studios, and the small theatre in the rear of the complex. There is no lobby, and a small booth serves as the box office just outside the playhouse entrance.

Inside the recently renovated theatre, most everything, from the rugs to the theatre seats to the walls, is red. This color scheme is broken by black drapes over the windows along the outside wall. The seating area is elevated, with the front two rows at floor level. You enter from the rear of the room, and an aisle separates the rows of ten seats into sections of six- and four-seat combinations. There is no stage curtain, and the performance area is painted black. Modern spotlights,

mounted in the ceiling, provide the house lighting.

Presentations here are professional and nonprofessional, providing valuable playing space for local theatre groups, musicians, and artists. Plays, musicals, and concerts are the usual offerings. Some of the productions are sponsored by the nonprofit organization that operates the building, while other shows are independently produced by entrepreneurs who rent the hall. The facility has a busy, year-round schedule.

From Highway 1 or Highway 17, take the Central District off-ramp and head for the Pacific Avenue Mall. Signs are plentiful along the way. When you pass the picturesque town clock, turn left on Center Street for one block. That brings you to the Arts Resource Center. The theatre is located in the rear of the building.

HOLIDAY BARN DINNER THEATER

Seats 150 persons at tables of 10 each (advance reservations strongly recommended).
LOCATION AND BOX OFFICE
100 Santa's Village Road
Holiday Host Travel Park (on the grounds of Holiday Host Travel Park)
Scotts Valley, CA 95066
BOX OFFICE-BUSINESS TELEPHONE
(408) 438-1601.
PRODUCER-OWNER Claire Hodgin.
MANAGING DIRECTOR Chuck Largent.
ARTISTIC DIRECTORS Chuck Largent and Nanci Irwin.
HANDICAPPED ACCESS Access is difficult for wheelchairs. There are fewer than ten steps leading into the "hayloft" portion of the barn, with no ramping available.

HOLIDAY BARN DINNER THEATER

For the first thirty-five–odd years of its life, this 1914-built barn led a respectable life with cows on the first floor and hay on the second. In the late 1940s, the Scotts Valley Community Club bought the barn, and basketball took the place of bovine bells. In the sixties the barn went psychedelic, and the counter-culture filled it with folks like Ken Kesey *(One Flew Over the Cuckoo's Nest),* Led Zeppelin, Janis Joplin, and the Grateful Dead. From the demise of that era to early 1979 the barn was a Christian school, a church, a dance hall, a community center, and a wedding-reception facility.

For about fifteen dollars per person you can have dinner in the theatre and see the show, which is usually a Broadway musical, but occasionally there's a revue instead. The year-round operation plays on Friday and Saturday evenings and utilizes a nonprofessional cast from the area and sometimes guests from the San Francisco scene. The staff is professional. Due to space limitations the orchestra is usually limited to a piano or two or a simple trio.

Because of the wide-open space afforded by a dairy barn's hayloft, the Holiday Barn Dinner Theater has the luxury of placing tables, chairs, and stages anywhere it pleases. Lighting currently is of a rudimentary nature, so there are no problems with rearranging massive pipe grids. Tables, utilized for dining before the show, can be placed in conventional rows, with an elevated platform at one end of the hall or the other. More imaginatively, stages are set at both ends and one in the center opposite the entrance. The wooden floor in the center is left unencumbered for stage action and dancing, and the audience is placed the length of the room on both sides. This gives a grand feeling of being involved in the action of the musical or of having the biggest number of the revue sung just to you. Unfortunately, somewhere in its checkered past the barn ceiling got itself plastered with that awful glittery stuff that you see on the ceilings of some apartments. Try not to notice and it will soon fade from your view.

There is usually cabaret entertainment presented downstairs in the restaurant after the main show. See it for a glimpse of some good, young talent and even a few more songs from members of the show cast from upstairs. They call it, appropriately enough, Act IV. I know, musicals are normally done in two acts. At the barn, they're done in three to give you an additional stretch break. Smart move.

The food offered by the dinner theatre is always a full-course affair. There are salad, beverage, meat or poultry, accompanying vegetables and garnishes, and dessert. Kids under twelve get the dinner and show combo for half price.

I would be remiss if I failed to mention the Holiday Barn Kitchen Restaurant, on what used to the cow level of the barn. For exceptionally reasonable prices you can have a family-style country dinner in a charming and friendly setting. Traditions include Sunday morning pancake breakfasts and a Friday fish fry. It's a real good spot.

The barn is part of the Holiday Host Travel Park, operated by Dave and Claire Hodgin. This recreational-vehicle oasis is situated just below the summit of Highway 17's path through the Santa Cruz Mountains. It's next to Santa's Village, a venerable and easily spotted landmark. From the north, exit at Scotts Valley and Santa's Village Road, turn left on Scotts Valley Drive, then left over the freeway overpass to a stop sign. Then cross Granite Creek Road to Santa's Village Road and you're there. From the south, take Granite Road exit and take the first left onto Santa's Village Road.

OLD TOWN THEATRE

410 seats (reserved).
LOCATION AND BOX OFFICE ADDRESS
TheaterWest,
50 University Avenue, No. 1
Los Gatos, CA 95030.
BOX OFFICE TELEPONE (408) 395-5434.
BUSINESS TELEPHONE (408) 395-3529.
MANAGING DIRECTOR Armand Plato.
ARTISTIC DIRECTOR Armand Plato and guest directors.
HANDICAPPED ACCESS There is wheelchair access on the south side of the theatre, utilizing the ramps leading into the Old Town shopping complex. Wheelchairs are positioned at row ends on the main floor. Restrooms equipped for the handicapped are located outside the theatre.

The first elementary schoolhouse on this historic wooded site was built in 1881. The new University Avenue Elementary School was constructed in 1923, and the Old Town Theatre building was the school auditorium. It continued to function as such until 1961, when it was closed as an educational facility forever. Enterprising developers bought the property from the city of Los Gatos in 1964, and in 1969, following the lead of other restoration shopping centers around

OLD TOWN THEATRE

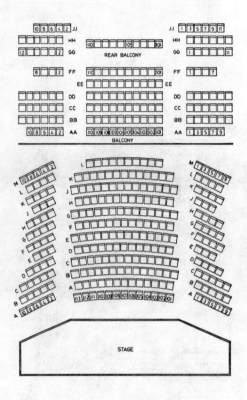

OLD TOWN THEATRE

the nation (Ghirardelli Square in San Francisco and Gaslight Square in St. Louis), Old Town emerged. The theatre space has been used as a Shakespearean festival site, a home for the Los Gatos Community Players, and, most recently, the long-term house for the South Bay's first professional Actors' Equity company, the California Actors' Theatre (CAT, now defunct). If word games your forte you've already noted that CAT falls right in line with Los Gatos, Spanish for, yep, "the cats."

At this writing, the Old Town Theatre is under the operational management of TheaterWest. It's a semiprofessional group that runs the show gamut from drama through comedies and musicals. Some of the top talent in the area is employed here, and the attractive indoor theatre plays year-round, with an emphasis on lighter material in the summer months.

The ticket prices, all under ten dollars, make this entertainment trip an even more attractive recommendation for those willing to spend some time getting to a charming locale for a few hours' diversion.

It's an easy trip to Old Town on Highway 17 from the coast or from San Francisco or San Jose, exiting at the Los Gatos-Saratoga-Highway 9 cutoff. There are many fine places to get a snack, a leisurely drink or a full-course meal, either in the Old Town complex or in nearby downtown Los Gatos, just a block or two away. There's ample parking.

Saratoga-Campbell
Cupertino-Sunnyvale

Though there are several well-established theatre groups in the Saratoga area, performance space is at a premium, the Saratoga Civic Theatre being the one facility available for rental to most of these nonprofessional organizations. The city of Saratoga, which also uses the building for council chambers, sponsors none of the theatrical ventures and maintains no box office at the theatre facility. For the purposes of this guide I will simply describe the theatre and list the organizations most often using it.

The Saratoga scene has two other activities that I will describe in detail, and the Campbell and Cupertino theatres will have listings of their own in this section.

THE SARATOGA CIVIC THEATRE

300 seats.
LOCATION
13777 Fruitvale Avenue, Saratoga, CA 95070.
BUSINESS TELEPHONE (408) 867-3438 (for rental information only).
HANDICAPPED ACCESS There is wheelchair access through the ground-level doors, and two ramplike slanted aisles to the lobby. Wheelchairs are placed at row ends. There are no special restroom facilities for the handicapped.

The theatre is reached by taking the Saratoga Avenue exit off Highway 280 and proceeding to the civic center on Fruitvale Avenue. Located in the Saratoga City Hall, it's directly across from the West Valley College Campus.

Theatre production groups using the facility are:

SARATOGA DRAMA GROUP
P.O. Box 182
Saratoga, CA 95070
Telephone (408) 255-0801

COMMUNITY PLAYERS
OF LOS GATOS-SARATOGA
P.O. Box 704
Los Gatos, CA 95030
Telephone (408) 224-0681

WEST VALLEY
LIGHT OPERA ASSOCIATION
P.O. Box 779
Los Gatos, CA 95030
Telephone (408) 268-3777

EL CAMINO OPERA COMPANY
P.O. Box 5081
San Jose, CA 95150
Telephone (408) 252-8942

GILBERT AND SULLIVAN
SOCIETY OF SAN JOSE
P.O. Box 6741
San Jose, CA 95150
Telephone (408) 267-1200

SARATOGA CHAMBER THEATRE

99 seats (reservations recommended).
LOCATION AND BOX OFFICE
12378 South Saratoga Road
Saratoga, CA 95070.
BOX OFFICE TELEPHONE (408) 252-6510.
BUSINESS TELEPHONE (408) 996-8777.
MANAGING DIRECTOR Wes Finlay.
ARTISTIC DIRECTORS Wes Finlay, Ross Nelson.
HANDICAPPED ACCESS Poor access, due to the seating arrangement and limited space.

This relatively new theatre can only be described as a "jewel box." The stage and backstage areas are larger than the auditorium, but none of them can be called big. The seating, nicely elevated, is accomplished with what must be categorized as padded church pews. The appointments of the theatre, from the front door all the way through, are tasteful and old-world in feeling, with the accent on wood. It is a pleasant, intimate atmosphere.

Though technically not a dinner-theatre, you couldn't ask for a closer choice of restaurants. The Auld World Inn shares the playhouse's lobby, and the La Bohème is just a few steps away.

Productions at the chamber theatre are in keeping with the size and mood of the surroundings, varying from semiprofessional presentations of Moliere, contemporary comedies, chamber operas, mini-musicals and revues, to chamber music concerts on a Sunday afternoon played on a beautiful Bösendorfer grand piano. The place is also available week-days for meetings and seminars. All in all, a lovely little spot. Ticket prices hover in the six-dollar-per-person range, subject to change.

Getting there is as easy as falling off the freeway. Take the Saratoga-Sunnyvale Road exit and head west. Between Cox and Prospect roads you'll find the Azule Crossing Mall next to a set of railroad tracks. There's plenty of parking adjacent to the Detuer Building, which houses the Saratoga Chamber Theatre.

CARRIAGE HOUSE THEATRE

299 seats (unreserved).
LOCATION Montalvo Road off High-way 9, Saratoga (Saratoga-Los Gatos Road).
BOX OFFICE ADDRESS
P.O. Box 715
Saratoga, CA 95070.
BOX OFFICE TELEPHONE (408) 867-3586.
BUSINESS TELEPHONE (408) 867-3421.
EXECUTIVE DIRECTOR Patricia Oakes.
HANDICAPPED ACCESS There is wheel-chair access, and the restrooms are equipped for the handicapped.

Though this has been leased by local community theatre groups on a continuing basis in the past, it is presently available to programers on a one-time basis. Part of the Montalvo Center for the Arts, projects are submitted to the Montalvo Drama Committee for approval.

Built in 1912 as the private home of San Francisco Mayor, and later Senator, James D. Phelan, the 168-acre estate went into public trust in 1930 as per the terms of Phelan's will. The carriage house was converted into a playhouse in 1960, and it's seen everything from Shakespeare to musical recitals and melodramas in the ensuing years.

The Carriage House Theatre is adjacent to the Montalvo Mansion, a Mediterranean-styled gem that has formal gardens accented with a sphinx and an obelisk, and an outdoor amphitheatre that is also available for fair-weather performances. There is an artist-in-residence program, and art displays in the mansion proper. Parking is no problem, and the view from the sprawling front lawn is spectacular.

Getting to Montalvo is no problem at all. Take Highway 280 to the Saratoga-Sunnyvale exit. Go to the center of Saratoga, pick up Highway 9, and follow it west for about a quarter of a mile. You'll see the sign for Montalvo Road. Follow it upward through a mile and a half of beautiful homes and lush countryside. When you get to the top of the hill, you're there.

PAUL MASSON
MOUNTAIN WINERY

1,000 seats (unreserved).
LOCATION Pierce Road off Big Basin Way, Saratoga.
BOX OFFICE ADDRESS
P.O. Box 97
Saratoga, CA 95070.
BOX OFFICE TELEPHONE (408) 725-4275.
BUSINESS TELEPHONE (408) 257-7800.
MANAGING DIRECTOR Bruce Labadie.
HANDICAPPED ACCESS Access for the handicapped and aged is extremely well provided for in this mountain-side setting. Wheelchairs can move easily down the gentle slope to the seating area from the parking lot. Restrooms are equally accessible, with plenty of winery staff available to render aid.

This is a summer series that started in 1957. The Paul Masson Winery concerts are the granddaddy of all such winery offerings. This one is unique in the variety it offers. In its beginnings it offered such jazz artists as Jon Hendricks. Now, under the title of "Vintage Sounds," it hosts the biggest names in that genre, plus some blues artists. "Music at the Winery" is the general heading for the classical music concerts, and Shakespeare plays have recently been added to the series.

Most ticket sales are through the Mountain Winery box office, but tickets are also available through major ticket outlets in the South Bay and in the San Francisco Bay Area.

The Shakespeare program is presented by the Saratoga-based Valley Institute of Theatre Arts (VITA). Under the direction of Judith Lyn Sutton and Bill Peck, a semiprofessional company of players presents a mid-summer night's (and a few afternoons') scene. Professional actors from top regional theatres are added to the local thespians. VITA also provides ongoing training for aspiring performers in area school facilities, and at Christmastime presents a touring theatrical season's-greeting called An Old-fashioned Christmas.

Many of the musical events are held in the afternoon, so the winery provides free sunhats and umbrellas to the patrons who don't arrive early enough for seats under the trees that punctuate the grounds. Seating is on padded folding chairs. To make it all more comfortable and enjoyable, free wine or champagne is served at intermission.

A brief historical note. The facade of the concrete winery building that backs the stage is covered in ancient-looking stone. It is, in fact, from a twelfth-century Spanish church. It came "around the Horn" in 1900 and was incorporated into St. Patrick's Church in San Jose. The 1906 earthquake leveled St. Pat's, and Paul Masson bought the rubble to face his winery. The price he paid for the debris was sufficient to rebuild the devastated church.

To get to the Mountain Winery, take the Saratoga Avenue exit off Highway

280, not the Saratoga-Sunnyvale turnoff. You'll see the Paul Masson Winery on your left as you follow Saratoga Avenue toward Saratoga. After you go through Saratoga, the street name will change to Big Basin Way (Highway 9). About a mile or so beyond the city limits, you'll come to Pierce Road on the right. Turn right and follow the road to the sign that announces the Paul Masson Mountain Winery. Turn right and follow the road to the parking lots.

GASLIGHTER THEATER

196 seats (reservations recommended).
LOCATION AND BOX OFFICE ADDRESS
400 East Campbell Avenue
Campbell, CA 95008.
BOX OFFICE TELEPHONE (408) 866-9852.
BUSINESS TELEPHONE (408) 866-1408.
MANAGING-ARTISTIC DIRECTORS Richard, Mark, and Peggy Gaetano.
HANDICAPPED ACCESS Accessible to wheelchairs. Wheelchairs are placed in the front or the rear of the main floor. The restroom facilities are cramped but accessible.

Booing, hissing, and cheering are all encouraged in this 1922-vintage theatre. The only type of presentation is the melodrama, and there's free popcorn for all. A semiprofessional cast presents an hour and a half of "olios" (songs, dance, and vaudeville) plus an hour-long melodrama play. Tickets are currently set at $5.50, with a dollar off for kids.
   This historic building began its public life in 1922 as the Grower's National Bank. It stopped being a financial institution with the stock market crash of 1929. It reopened its doors ten years later as a movie house with a screening of *Gone with the Wind*. Motion picture patrons continued to visit what was then called the Campbell Theater until 1963, when the doors were once

again locked. Live melodrama took occupancy in 1967 and has called the building home ever since.
   The box office has moved inside and shares the lobby bar area. The decor is done in pinks and burgundies, and that color scheme continues into the auditorium. The standard theatre seats are covered in brocaded fabric. The floor is raked to the footlighted stage, and the side walls feature shadow boxes displaying antique clothing. There is a balcony for those who wish more lofty accommodations.
   Coming north or south on Highway 17, take the Hamilton Avenue exit and proceed to Bascom Avenue. Take Bascom to Campbell, turn right on Campbell to Central, take another left on Central to Campbell again and turn left—you're there.
   If you're looking for a place to take the family for plain old-fashioned entertainment with a lot of audience participation, try the Gaslighter.

FLINT CENTER FOR THE PERFORMING ARTS

2,571 seats (reserved).
LOCATION AND BOX OFFICE
21250 Stevens Creek Boulevard
Cupertino, CA 95014.
BOX OFFICE TELEPHONE (408) 257-9555.
BUSINESS TELEPHONE (408) 996-4820.
OTHER TICKET OUTLETS BASS, Ticketron.
EXECUTIVE ASSISTANT Joan Carlson.
HANDICAPPED ACCESS There is wheelchair access into the well-ramped theatre. There are also restroom facilities for the handicapped.

The Flint Center for the Performing Arts is not only one of the newest (1970) of the northern California theatres but certainly one of the most active. It is in constant use, with touring Broadway shows making it their temporary home, along with

STAGE

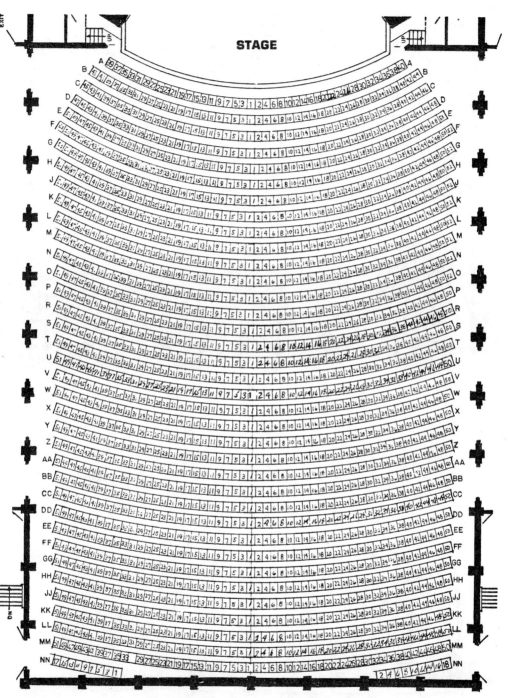

FLINT CENTER FOR THE PERFORMING ARTS

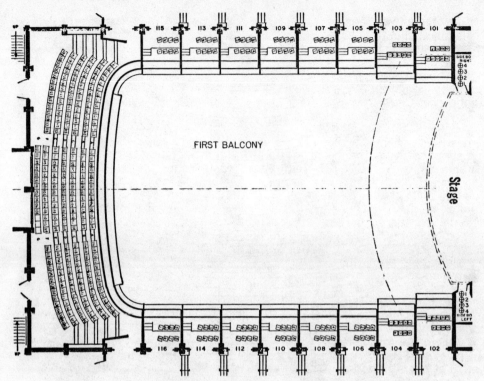

FLINT CENTER FOR THE PERFORMING ARTS

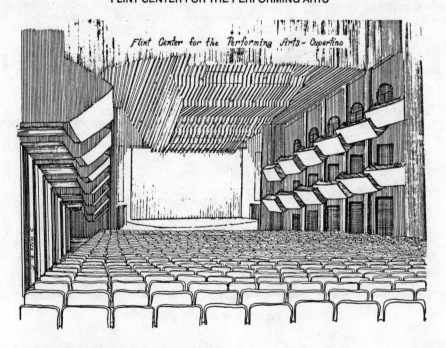

Flint Center for the Performing Arts~Cupertino

major symphony orchestras, world-acclaimed ballet troupes, and the biggest names in show business and the concert field.

The theatre is also available for rental by local groups and independent promotors and is operational on a year-round basis.

The Flint Center is one of the most attractive and comfortable of the super theatres. The interior color scheme makes for a feeling of warmth, and the exterior landscaping makes you feel that you are farther away from an urban center than you actually are. The facility is a favorite stopping point for national touring companies, and there are many people in northern California who, given a choice of theatres in which to see the same attraction, will choose this Cupertino landmark.

Located on the DeAnza College campus, it is one of the easiest theatres to find. Just take the Stevens Creek exit off Highway 280, and you're at the front door. There's unlimited parking. The top ticket prices usually fall around ten dollars, but that can change based on the attraction.

THE SUNNYVALE PERFORMING ARTS CENTER

200 seats (unreserved).
LOCATION 550 East Remington Drive, Sunnyvale.
BOX OFFICE-BUSINESS ADDRESS
P.O. Box 60607
Sunnyvale, CA 94088.
BOX OFFICE TELEPHONE (408) 733-6611.
BUSINESS TELEPHONE (408) 738-5521.
MANAGING DIRECTOR Susan L. Manning.
ARTISTIC DIRECTOR Each tenant has its own.
HANDICAPPED ACCESS The theatre has room for just four wheelchairs per

performance. The restroom facilities for the handicapped are located in the building next door, which is open at show times.

The Sunnyvale Performing Arts Center is centrally situated between Santa Clara and Mountain View and boasts better than 400 presentations a year. This includes appearances by six "in residence" local performing troupes as well as visiting touring companies and single acts from around the state. South Bay residents can, for instance, see the One Act Theatre Company of San Francisco or the Old Globe Theatre of San Diego without leaving Sunnyvale.

It's an intimate theatre with good production facilities and comfortable Continental seating. The proscenium stage isn't large, but it can accommodate dance programs and moderate-sized casts of musical comedies.

Among the regulars at the Center are the community-based Sunnyvale Community Players. They do an average of three musicals a year, a teen show in the summer, and a couple of children's shows during the school year. An adult company of professional actors, the California Young People's Theatre, performs children's shows on a regular basis October through June.

Also headquartered in the Sunnyvale facility is the Sunnyvale Mime Company, professionals who rehearse here, tour the county, and return for one major showing a year. Ensemble International, a professional folk dance company, does the same, but their touring takes them all over the United States in the fall and spring.

Two other musical groups round out the cast of companies: the Sunnyvale Singers, a semipro adult choir, and the Sunnyvale Music Association, a nonprofessional aggregation of musicians that presents recitals twice a month. How's that for a busy hall?

If you're coming in off Highway 101, take the South Fair Oaks Avenue exit. From Highway 280, swing up to Sunnyvale on the Sunnyvale-Saratoga exit. On El Camino, Remington Drive and the Community Center are about a mile south of Sunnyvale's Civic Center.

KING DODO PLAYHOUSE

162 seats (unreserved seating in an arena setting. Reservations are accepted, but no specific location is guaranteed).
LOCATION AND BOX OFFICE
176 East Fremont Avenue
Sunnyvale, CA 94087.
BOX OFFICE TELEPHONE (408) 366-6060.
BUSINESS TELEPHONE (408) 867-1933.
MANAGING-ARTISTIC DIRECTOR
Jaleen Holm.
HANDICAPPED ACCESS There is easy entrance for wheelchairs, with good positioning for up to ten chairs in the auditorium. The restrooms are accessible to wheelchairs.

The dodo bird that dominates this theatre's logo is no relative of Alice's acquaintance in Wonderland. The theatre's first home, better than twenty years ago in 1959, was in the old Hawaiian Gardens in San Jose. On the men's room door was a crude sign proclaiming "This room is a dodo"—hence the name. A cartoonist from the Walter Lantz organization was in an early audience and created the King Dodo bird logo.

On top of being northern California's oldest year-round, self-supporting acting company, the King Dodo was probably, in its original digs, America's first dinner theatre, predating even New Jersey's Meadowbrook Dinner Theatre. In its present home, opened in 1980 in Sunnyvale, it is that rare bird, a theatre designed exclusively as an arena performance space. With the demise of legitimate shows at Circle Star in San Carlos, it is certainly the only fulltime theatre-in-the-round (or oblong or square) on the Peninsula. Alameda has the Altarena, but we'll get to that one later.

The King Dodo Playhouse used to be a bank. With a long-term lease in their pocket, the owners turned it into a showplace, with the accent on forest colors. Dark-brown see-through drapes accent the lobby, which features a custom-built box office, a wine bar, and a coffee bar. Green carpeting leads you through burnt-umber drapes into the theatre itself. There are three levels of comfortable theatre seats around the dusty-rose-carpeted playing area in the center of the room.

The Sondheim lyric in *A Funny Thing Happened on the Way to the Forum* happily states, "Bring on the lovers, liars, and clowns! Tragedy tomorrow, comedy tonight!" But the nonprofessional casts at King Dodo do only comedies, and not just one at a time. Each weekend, forty-seven weeks a year, they present two or three different light-hearted plays on Friday, Saturday, and Sunday. Many of the offerings run well over a year.

Take Highway 280 to the Sunnyvale-Cupertino exit. Travel north to Fremont Avenue. Turn right on Fremont, and a half a block farther on the right is the King Dodo Playhouse.

San Jose

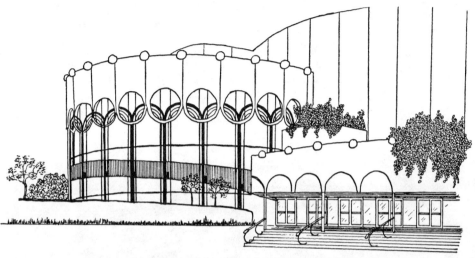

SAN JOSE CENTER FOR THE PERFORMING ARTS

SAN JOSE CENTER FOR THE PERFORMING ARTS

2,701 seats (reserved).
LOCATION AND BOX OFFICE
255 Almaden Boulevard
San Jose, CA 95113. (Box office
open only on day of event.)
BOX OFFICE TELEPHONE (408) 279-1414.
EVENTS INFORMATION TELEPHONE
(408) 288-7469.
BUSINESS TELEPHONE (408) 277-5277.
OTHER TICKET OUTLETS All major
agencies.
MANAGING DIRECTOR John Popovich.
ASSISTANT MANAGER George Brodeur.
HANDICAPPED ACCESS There are spe-
cial parking available, complete access
ramping in the building and audi-
torium, and wheelchair seating spaces.
There are also special restroom
facilities for the handicapped.

This Frank Lloyd Wright showplace
opened in 1972. After some unfor-
tunate structural problems with the
roof—it collapsed—the house closed,
was repaired, and reopened in 1975.
There have been some additional
repairs, and all seems to be in order
at this writing. It's a stunning theatre
with fountains—illuminated at night—
at the main entrance, and a glass
wall allowing the arriving audience
to view the interior of the lobby from
the outside. A graceful circular ramp-
way takes the place of stairs, and
elevators are available for the upper
seating areas.

The seats give an impression of a
sea of blue as you enter the gigantic
cavern of the auditorium. The stage
is fronted by a deep orchestra pit,
which is actually an elevator floor. It
can be raised to stage-floor level to
act as an apron that brings the show
on stage closer to the patrons. The
acoustics are aided, when properly

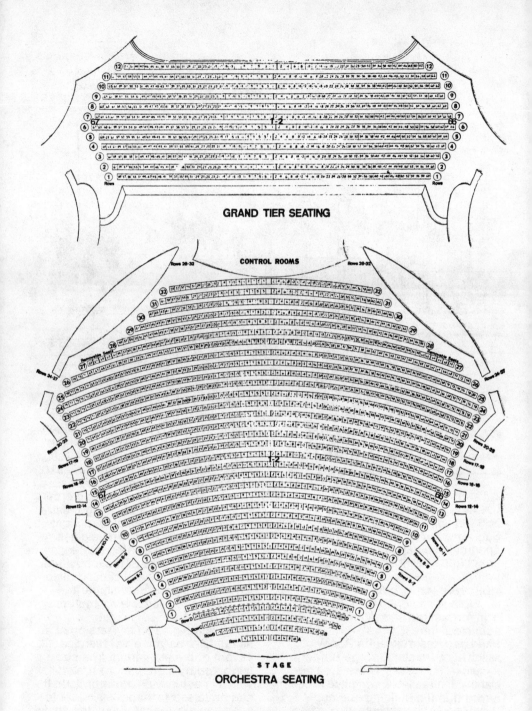

GRAND TIER SEATING

ORCHESTRA SEATING

SAN JOSE CENTER FOR THE PERFORMING ARTS

supervised, by a sound system whose giant speaker box is suspended above the stage.

The Performing Arts Center is available as a rental facility only. The hall has no resident company and sponsors no events itself. The main tenants are touring Broadway musicals, dance companies, orchestras, and individual concerts. There is a community group, the San Jose Civic Light Opera, that performs regularly at the center. I'll talk about them as soon as I give you directions to the hall.

The easiest way to the Park and Almaden location is to take the Vine-Almaden exit off Highway 280, turn left to Almaden, and go the four blocks or so to Park.

SAN JOSE CIVIC LIGHT OPERA
BUSINESS-BOX OFFICE ADDRESS
18 Paseo de San Antonio
San Jose, CA 95113.
BOX OFFICE TELEPHONE (408) 286-6841.
BUSINESS TELEPHONE (408) 297-8811.
OTHER TICKET OUTLETS Major South Bay outlets; some San Francisco area outlets.
GENERAL MANAGER Stewart Slater.
ARTISTIC DIRECTOR Changes with each production.

In 1935, the year Gershwin's *Porgy and Bess* was premiering in New York and Nelson Eddy and Jeanette MacDonald were first teamed in *Naughty Marietta,* the San Jose Civic Light Opera Company was created to perform operettas on the local level. The original company sang Gilbert and Sullivan and Sigmund Romberg on the second floor above a clothing store. By the early 1950s it had adopted a broad-based casting policy and was doing bigger shows, and more modern ones, at the Montgomery Theatre (see next section).

With the opening of the new San Jose Center for the Performing Arts in 1972, SJCLO took another big step. It was among the first tenants of the facility and produced *South Pacific* with a star, Enzo Stuarti. After the roof problems at the Performing Arts Center, SJCLO returned to the Montgomery Theatre and temporarily abandoned the star system.

From 1976 until the present, the cast has been semiprofessional, with a small number of Actors' Equity Association members working with the local volunteer singers, dancers, and actors. The stars are back and the stage of the Performing Arts Center is once again alive with the sound of music. Tickets are in the $8 to $15 range, depending on performance day and seat location. Weekends get the top tariffs.

MONTGOMERY THEATRE

529 seats (reserved).
LOCATION AND BOX OFFICE
145 West San Carlos Street at Market
San Jose, CA 95113.
BOX OFFICE TELEPHONE (408) 277-4468.
BUSINESS TELEPHONE (408) 277-5277.
MANAGING DIRECTOR George Rakis.
HANDICAPPED ACCESS There are locations for six wheelchairs per performance. These spots are reached by ramped approaches. The restroom facilities are up to current codes, and there are specially marked parking spaces. Please call ahead for additional aid.

Before the new Performing Arts Center was built, the Montgomery Theatre was the community-theatre facility. It is still much in use by local organizations, and a professional repertory company has taken up residence (see next section). The Spanish flavor of San Jose is faithfully retained in this adobe building. There is an enclosed courtyard leading to the main entrance and a

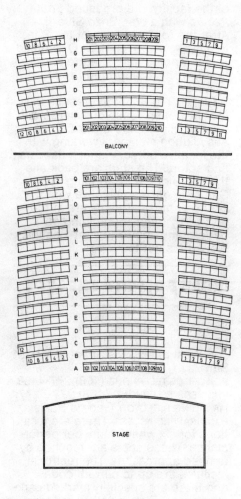

BALCONY

STAGE

MONTGOMERY THEATRE

fountain in the center of the yard. Once inside, the foyer of antique-looking white and beige plaster contains the box office and the restrooms. The entrance to the auditorium is centered in the opposite wall. Spanish tile is everywhere.

You'll enter the seating area just about in the center. The balcony entrance is by the stairs at the far end of the lobby. The purple-hued stage drapes complement the gold-cushioned standard theatre seating. The stage is a proscenium-arched platform, and the main floor features stepped, elevated sections of seats. The side aisles are carpeted. The feeling is intimate, and the theatre is well suited to dramas and comedies. The acoustics lend themselves to the spoken word.

The Montgomery Theatre is one block from the San Jose Performing Arts Center. You can use those directions from Highway 280. Or, take Highway 17 south off of Highway 101 and turn off at Coleman Avenue. Travel east on Coleman until it becomes Market Street. Continue on Market to West San Carlos and the theatre. The Montgomery, by the way, is a fine example of early thirties' California architecture and design. The Montgomery Theatre is housed in a much larger facility that constitutes the San Jose Civic Center Complex. This includes a convention center-exhibition hall, meeting rooms, an outdoor plaza, and a small outdoor amphitheatre.

SAN JOSE
REPERTORY COMPANY

LOCATION Montgomery Theatre,
preceding.
BOX OFFICE ADDRESS
P.O. Box 9584
San Jose, CA 95157.
BUSINESS ADDRESS
372 South First Street
San Jose, CA 95157.
BOX OFFICE TELEPHONE (408) 294-7572.
BUSINESS TELEPHONE (408) 294-7582.
OTHER TICKET OUTLETS Major San Fran-
cisco and South Bay outlets.
EXECUTIVE PRODUCER James P. Reber.
PRODUCING DIRECTOR David Lemos.

This young (1980) professional company holds residency in the Montgomery Theatre from September
through June. It is presently the
Santa Clara County area's only resident Equity troupe. It presents a
yearly average of five comedies and
dramas, with subscriptions and group
rates available. There are also special
ticket plans for students and senior
citizens. Each opening night is treated
as a gala, and there are low-priced
Thursday night previews before each
official opening. Ticket prices range
from $5.50 to $12.50. The San Jose
Rep is a nonprofit California corporation.
   Another innovative function that
the Rep is also spearheading is a
Theatre Resource Service for the
entire South Bay theatre community.
This not only pools physical stage
furnishings such as costumes, set
pieces, and props, but is also a
reservoir of knowledge, ideas, and
personnel. Too often theatre groups
jealously guard their autonomy to a
point of total noncooperation. San
Jose Rep intends to improve com-
munications and break down the
walls that hamper the growth of the
arts.

THE SAN JOSE BLACK THEATRE
WORKSHOP
MAILING ADDRESS
3445 Cunard Court
San Jose, CA 95132.
TELEPHONE (408) 251-9162 or
(408) 277-8299
EXECUTIVE DIRECTOR David Piper.
ARTISTIC DIRECTORS Mark Fee, Vierra
Whye, Ann Mitchell.

Founded in 1972 by David Piper,
this growing ensemble is also a
regular tenant of the Montgomery
Theatre. The plays presented are
selected from the library of black
ethnic works and have included *For
Colored Girls Who Have Considered
Suicide/When the Rainbow Is Enuf,
No Place to Be Somebody,* and *Day
of Absence.* It is the only black
theatre group currently operating in
Santa Clara County, and auditions
are open to interested actors and
technicians. In addition to their own
presentations, the actors of the San
Jose Black Theatre Workshop are
often called upon for productions of
other South Bay theatre organizations.

San Francisco Peninsula

PALO ALTO COMMUNITY THEATRE

Professional, higher-priced theatre has not been historically successful, for any length of time, on the San Francisco Peninsula. Witness the careers, as legitimate theatres, of the Circle Star (San Carlos), the Hyatt Music Circus (Burlingame), and the California Actors' Theatre (at the Fox Theatre in Redwood City). After a few seasons of respectable business doing either Broadway musicals or major plays, the audiences faded away and the rooms became single-act showcases (Circle Star), a movie house (Hyatt), and a bankrupt, defunct company (CAT). The case of CAT is particularly sad, as it had built its well-deserved reputation of excellence in an area totally lacking professional theatre.

Community theatres, that is to say nonprofessional groups, thrive on the Peninsula. It is as difficult to pinpoint the reasons for their success as it is to define the causes of the demise of the pros. Ticket prices? Surely. The cost of productions in these times of inflation? Certainly. But even if it's significantly cheaper to mount an amateur show, you still must fill the seats.

One of the answers must be perseverance. The longevity of several of these groups makes them local institutions—Hillbarn in Foster City, for instance. Loyalty must be another big plus: Their audiences are personally involved with the theatres as well as with the casts. Since making a bundle of money isn't a primary motivation, theatre is a cause rather than a business.

Finally, and all of this is not limited to Peninsula community theatre but applies to community theatre in general, there is pride. Whether their talent is wonderful or horrendous, nonprofessional players burn with a pride amazing to behold. Almost nothing can overcome their collective momentum.

There are several academic theatre facilities on the Peninsula that sometimes host noncollegiate presentations. At Stanford University in Palo Alto there are Dinkelspiel Auditorium and the Memorial Auditorium. Within the Memorial Auditorium Building is the Little Theatre. Dinkelspiel has 720 seats; Memorial Auditorium, 1,694 seats; and the Little Theatre, 168 seats. One phone number, (415) 497-4317, serves all these theatres. The box office is located in the Tresidder Union Building. For general public events all of the major ticket agencies usually handle off-campus reservations.

Foothill College, at 12345 El Monte Road in Los Altos Hills (zip code 94022) has a 971-seat auditorium. Ticket information for shows may be obtained by calling (415) 948-4444. Some presentations are handled by the ticket agencies. The College of San Mateo Little Theatre, 1700 West Hillsdale Boulevard (zip code 94402) has 412 seats, sometimes reserved, sometimes not. That box office number is (415) 574-6208.

In the Redwood City-Woodside area, many nonprofit theatre groups avail themselves of the Cañada College Theatre at 4200 Farm Hill Road, just off Highway 280. This attractive indoor amphitheatre has 550 seats and a fully equipped stage. For information and tickets call (415) 364-1212, extension 271.

Just over the Peninsula-South Bay Area line is the Louis B. Mayer Theatre on the campus of the University of Santa Clara at Lafayette and Franklin streets in Santa Clara. Its seating plan is flexible and can vary with each production. There are 390 permanent seats, but that number can be raised to 575 by changing the wall configuration. The stage can be a proscenium with an orchestra pit or a thrust stage with no pit. Ticket and programing information can be had by calling (408) 984-4015.

Even though Circle Star Theatre

on Industrial Road in San Carlos stopped doing musicals years ago, you may want to catch one of the headliners doing a musical turn on the big revolving stage of this arena theatre. To make reservations or to find out who's playing, call (415) 364-2550 if you live in San Mateo County and to the south, or (415) 982-6550 if you're in San Francisco or to the north. Tickets are also available at all major agencies. The general manager is Jack Medlevine. The seating capacity of Circle Star is 3,900. Take Highway 101, north or south, and watch for the big reader board with the revolving star in a circle above it. Exit on the Redwood City-Whipple Road turnoff.

LOS ALTOS CONSERVATORY THEATRE

---

100 seats (reserved).
LOCATION 97 Hillview Avenue, Los Altos.
BOX OFFICE ADDRESS
P.O. Box 151
Los Altos, CA 94022.
BOX OFFICE TELEPHONE
(415) 941-LACT (5228).
BUSINESS TELEPHONE (415) 941-5146.
OTHER TICKET OUTLETS
Stanford Barn Box Office, Los Altos Chamber of Commerce, and CAPA Box Office (Palo Alto).
GENERAL MANAGER Steve Kaplowitz.
ARTISTIC DIRECTOR Doyne Mraz.
HANDICAPPED ACCESS Entrance to the theatre is easy, with wheelchair positions on the main floor level. The restroom situation is less suitable: It's a short journey to an adjacent building to get to the bathrooms.

This community-based, semiprofessional theatre has made its quarters in an abandoned city-owned warehouse, originally part of the Los Altos School District's administrative center. The other buildings in the center were demolished because of earthquake code deficiencies, and the prefab metal shell stood empty. The Los Altos Conservatory Theatre needed a home, and this was it. They also got a great rental arrangement: With stipulations regarding upkeep and usage, it's free.

There are few of the frills that you might expect in a neighborhood house. The emphasis is on making the facility work as good theatre. There's no lobby. You enter behind the last row of seats. The walls are partially draped, and in some areas you can look at a pictorial record of L'ACT's past productions. The stage is elevated, as are the standard theatre seats.

L'ACT offers plays forty-eight weeks a year. They operate as a self-sustaining nonprofit corporation. Group sales and subscriptions add to the stability that has prevailed since 1974. They've been the recipient of a Hewlett Foundation grant for playwrights in residence, and they're one of a growing number of resident theatres that offer a student-rush admission break.

If you buy tickets at the box office (located in a separate booth outside the theatre building) you'll pay anywhere from $5.50 to $7.00 for a seat. You'll see, if you come often, a full range of theatre fare: from Agatha Christie to Tennessee Williams, with Shakespeare, Moliere, Chekov, and Kurt Weill (they do some smaller musicals) not far behind.

If you are approaching Los Altos on Highway 101, exit on the San Antonio Road ramp. Travel to downtown Los Altos and turn left on Hillview. In half a block you're there. From Highway 280 there are a few more turns. Take the El Monte exit to Los Altos, then make a left on the Foothill Expressway. Take the first right onto San Antonio, then a right onto Hillview. The same half block gets you to the front door.

PALO ALTO COMMUNITY THEATRE

428 seats, main theatre; 200 seats, children's theatre; reservation policy is at the discretion of the presenting organization.

LOCATION AND BOX OFFICE
1305 Middlefield Road
Palo Alto, CA 94301.

BOX OFFICE TELEPHONE (415) 329-2623.
BUSINESS TELEPHONE: (415) 329-2652.
MANAGING DIRECTOR City operated.
ARTISTIC DIRECTOR Differs with each community-based group using the facility.
HANDICAPPED ACCESS There are wheel-chair accommodations for theatre entry, auditorium positions, and rest-room facilities.

The Palo Alto Community Theatre provides a home base for several local theatre groups as well as a space for touring shows and special one-time presentations. It's in opera-tion all year and is an integral part of the city-operated Lucie Stern Community Center. It is one of the most complete operations of its kind on the Peninsula, offering not only a stage and auditorium to the theatre community, but support services as well.

The entrance to the theatre takes you through a garden area onto an archway-framed patio. The box office is located on this tiled veranda, which ultimately leads into the foyer and then the auditorium. There is an old-world feeling to it all. There's a concession area for refreshments and plenty of stretching room for intermission relaxation. Benches pro-

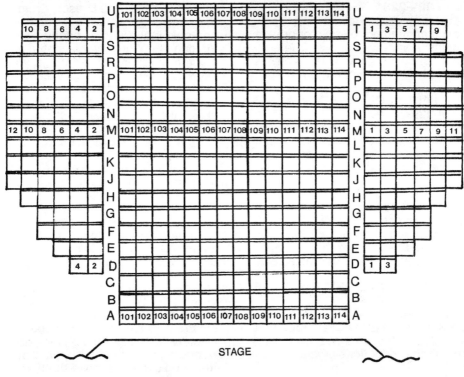

STAGE

PALO ALTO COMMUNITY THEATRE

vide additional comfort. The auditoriums utilize standard theatre seating. The sight lines and acoustics are good.

To reach the Palo Alto Community Theatre from Highway 101, take the Embarcadero West off-ramp. After about a mile, you'll be at Middlefield Road. Turn right for one block and you're at the Community Center. From all other points, find Middlefield Road and head in the appropriate direction. It's easy to find.

Ticket prices vary according to the type of production and the company presenting the show. A children's theatre production may be just 50¢ and an opera ticket $8.50. The average price is somewhere in the $3.50 to $5.00 range.

Among the groups utilizing the theatre are:

THEATREWORKS
(415) 329-2281
ARTISTIC DIRECTOR Robert Kelly
Four summer and four winter presentations: A variety of shows. The fourth show of the summer is always an outdoor Shakespeare offering.

PALO ALTO COMMUNITY PLAYERS
(415) 329-2319
ARTISTIC DIRECTOR: David Motroni
They've passed their fifty-year mark, and present six plays a year, September through June.

WEST BAY OPERA
(415) 321-3471
ARTISTIC DIRECTOR: Maria Holt
With over a quarter of a century behind it, this lyric-theatre group performs three major operas a year.

PALO ALTO CHILDREN'S THEATRE
(415) 329-2216
ARTISTIC DIRECTOR: Patricia Briggs
Boasting an international reputation for its work, this organization presents ten productions a year.

MANHATTAN PLAYHOUSE

99 seats (unreserved).
LOCATION AND BOX OFFICE
Manhattan Avenue and West Bayshore Boulevard
Palo Alto, CA 94303.
BOX OFFICE-BUSINESS TELEPHONE
(415) 322-4589.
MANAGING-ARTISTIC DIRECTOR
Judith Dresch.
HANDICAPPED ACCESS Getting into the theatre is easy, and there are fully equipped restroom facilities for the handicapped. Those with sight or hearing problems may request a specific location. Wheelchairs are positioned in the front row.

There is a decidedly European flavor to the Manhattan Playhouse. That is chiefly due to the influence of its driving force, Judith Dresch. From the moment you enter the purple and gold lobby with its chandeliers, Victorian furniture, marble statue and columns, and French paintings, you know that you are in a highly theatrical setting. Even the floors have been given a parqueted look. The large white stucco building, with its wrought-iron window trim and its name in large letters, is easily seen from Highway 101.

The auditorium features elevated seating with padded folding chairs. The stage is of an Elizabethan thrust design with platformed levels on either side. Dressing rooms occupy a second floor. The stage sets for the predominantly period and costume presentations are detailed and authentic.

Versatility is evident in the semi-professional production schedule that operates year-round. Russian theatre is well represented, especially Chekov. Musical offerings include operettas and chamber operas, and the good acoustics make the theatre

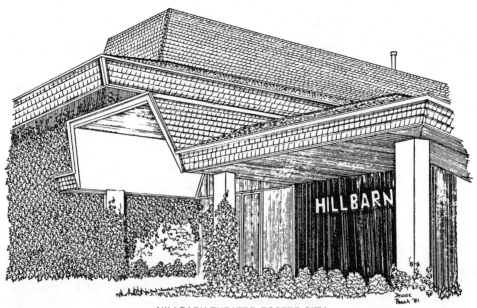

HILLBARN THEATRE, FOSTER CITY

a fine place for chamber concerts, which are usually given on Sunday afternoons.

From Highway 101 take the University Avenue exit west for one block, turn right, and you'll see the theatre on the Bayshore fence line.

HILLBARN THEATRE

196 seats (reserved).
LOCATION AND BOX OFFICE
1285 East Hillsdale Avenue
Foster City, CA 94404.
BOX OFFICE TELEPHONE (415) 349-6411.
BUSINESS TELEPHONE (415) 349-6412.
MANAGING DIRECTOR: Jane S. Keyston.
ARTISTIC DIRECTOR Robert Brauns.
HANDICAPPED ACCESS The ground-floor-oriented plan throughout the building, with the exception of the elevated auditorium seating sections, allows for wheelchair access. The restrooms, though not specially equipped, can be used by wheelchair-confined patrons. Make your needs known when calling for reservations.

Hillbarn Theatre actually started in a barn on a hill. That was in Belmont in 1941. A move took it to the Borel Chapel in San Mateo, where Highway 92 met El Camino Real. That was destroyed to make room for a freeway. The bell, however, was saved, and in the present theatre signals curtain times for one of the most stable and substantial of the Bay Area's community theatres.

The nonprofessional casts are directed by a professional fulltime director, and the shows include comedies fresh out of New York, originals by area writers, classic dramas, and old and new musicals. The all-year season starts in September and ends in August. Subscriptions are sold to an amazing number of patrons, and cast members and audiences exhibit a higher-than-usual degree of loyalty.

The exterior of the Hillbarn Theatre bears little resemblance to a traditional barn: the barnlike quality is expressed in a modern architectural mode. There is a large parking lot to the rear of the facility, and entrance to the lobby is through glass doors in the ivy-covered facade. To the right, as you enter, is the box office, with the administrative office behind it. The entrance to the auditorium is to the left, and there is a courtyard patio beyond the lobby. The green room, dressing rooms, and workshops occupy the rear of the building. The interior of the auditorium is decorated in natural burlap, and the platform stage has no permanent proscenium arch. Seating is located on platformed elevations, making every seat a good one.

There's much to be said for longevity in theatre, especially resident nonprofessional theatre. The quality of the shows is usually proportionate to the experience and age of the troupe. Hillbarn's consistently high-quality work attests to that theory.

Hillbarn is San Mateo County's oldest community theatre and one of the oldest established permanent nonfloating theatre groups in the state (apologies to Frank Loesser).

Take the Hillsdale Boulevard exit east toward Foster City off Highway 101 or, from Highway 280, take Highway 92 to Foster City, turn off at the Hillsdale Boulevard exit, and head east to the theatre. There's ample free parking. The tickets are scaled into three categories, and none will set you back more than $6.50.

SAN MATEO PERFORMING ARTS CENTER

1,605 seats (reservation policy depends on company using facility).
LOCATION AND BOX OFFICE
600 North Delaware
San Mateo, CA 94401.

BOX OFFICE-BUSINESS TELEPHONE (415) 348-8243.
OTHER TICKET OUTLETS Bass, Ticketron, other major agencies.
MANAGING DIRECTOR Ross Williams.
HANDICAPPED ACCESS The theatre is completely ramped for wheelchair access, and all restroom facilities are equipped for handicapped patrons.

The San Mateo Performing Arts Center is the largest public theatre between Cupertino's Flint Center and San Francisco's War Memorial Opera House. Owned and operated by the San Mateo High School District, it is geared toward mid-Peninsula organizational use. It's available for plays, musicals, ballets, symphony orchestras, special film events, and large-scale ceremonies. Though it has no resident tenants, it is used extensively by performing groups.

The stage facility is one of the largest in the Bay Area and is equipped to handle a wide variety of theatrical endeavors. Because of the diversity of the groups producing in the center, the ticket scale goes from zero to a top of around fifteen dollars. Both pros and nonpros provide the offerings, and you have to depend on local advertising to know what's going on, or you can call the box office for schedule information.

The theatre is located between Peninsula and Poplar avenues, three blocks off Highway 101. From the south take the Peninsula Avenue turnoff, from the north, the Poplar Avenue exit.

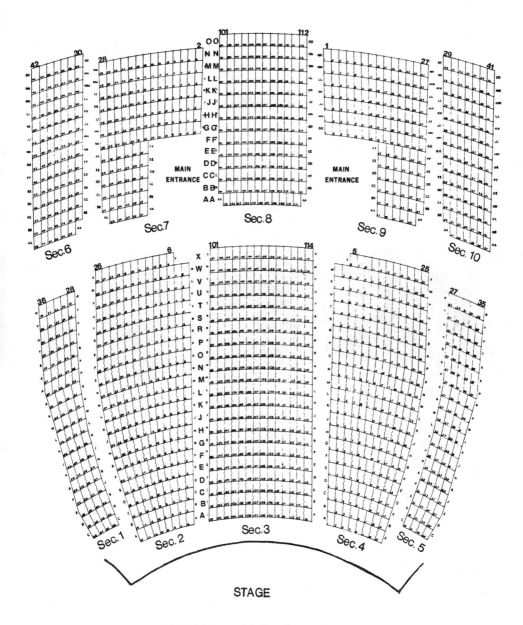

STAGE

SAN MATEO PERFORMING ARTS CENTER

San Francisco

GEARY THEATRE

From the days of the fabled Gold Rush until the present, San Francisco has always been regarded as "a theatre town." The Junius Brutus Booths, Senior and Junior, lived and worked here in the 1850s and '60s. Son and brother John Wilkes Booth made a notorious name for himself elsewhere.

Lotta Crabtree, first as a child star (a "lilliputian prodigy") and then as a sensuous adult queen of song, won the hearts of nineteenth-century theatregoers. Today, perhaps because singers and water cannot be long parted, the drinking fountain she built for her city still stands where Kearny, Geary, and Market streets meet.

A lady named Adah Menken scandalized an era not easily shocked by playing the male lead in *Mazeppa*, astride a live horse and clad in skin-colored tights. Lola Montez undulated in her provocative "Spider Dance," and Lillian Russell made her San Francisco musical comedy debut in a show descriptively titled *Horrors*. That was in 1875. Two years later William F. Cody (Buffalo Bill) appeared at the Bush Street Theatre in *Scouts of the Prairies*. Sarah Bernhardt was here and so were Ellen Terry and Henry Irving. Ambrose Bierce, critic for the *Examiner*, hated him, loved her. The Irving-Terry company's manager was Bram Stoker; he later wrote *Dracula*.

As the new century came, new stars arose in the East and traveled to the West. When the 1906 earthquake hit, Enrico Caruso was on the scene for a production of *Carmen*. Grand opera wasn't new here; California's first complete opera had been staged in 1851 in San Francisco. That was *La Sonnambula*, presented by Signor and Signora Pelligrini. Success was quick because the price was right: $1 to $4 a ducat.

Many years later, in a newer, bigger opera house, the world's greatest stars would appear. It's sad to note that when Jeanette MacDonald graced that very hall, the critics were less than kind to her efforts— even after she made that nice film and sang that stirring song about their town.

Al Jolson, Sophie Tucker, Eddie Cantor, Bing Crosby, John Barrymore, Helen Hayes, Isadora Duncan, Frank Sinatra, Rudolf Nureyev, Yul Brynner, Katharine Hepburn, Emlyn Williams, Vincent Price, and legions more would grace San Francisco stages as the years progressed, not to mention the thousands of local talents that stayed and worked, or stayed and gave up, or left to become stars on other stages in other places.

Theatre names came and went as rapidly as the buildings themselves. The demise of these structures had less to do with lack of business than with more natural causes, such as fire and earthquake.

The first makeshift San Francisco theatre was on the second floor of Washington Hall. In 1850, Doc D. G. Robinson and Tom Maguire opened a real theatre, not a public hall, and called it the Dramatic Museum. That was on California Street. Early major houses included the American and the Metropolitan. There was also the Jenny Lind, named for a singer who never sang there.

Later, new names appeared. Some of them would endure, others disappear: the Californian, the Baldwin, the Alhambra, the Alcazar, the Fischers, the Orpheum, the Tivoli, the Central, and the Chutes, and still later, the Golden Gate (for movies and vaudeville), the Geary, and the Curran.

Great plays filled the theatres: Shakespeare, Moliere, Shaw, Coward, and so on. Great showmen cut their teeth by San Francisco before heading for the Hudson River: the Frohman Brothers (Gustave, Charles, and Daniel), David Belasco, Oliver Morosco. Florenz Ziegfeld sent his Follies to

San Francisco as early as 1911. Broadway hits were a regular staple of the scene even earlier. *The Merry Widow* wowed the town in 1909, , and *Babes in Toyland* was packing them in at the Columbia on the evening before April 18, 1906.

The pattern has changed little since then. Hit plays and musicals play the Bay Area while the originals are still on Times Square. And Sam Shepard writes plays that appear on postage-stamp–sized stages in San Francisco the year before they win prizes (including the Pulitzer) in New York.

One final note about a subject that will have to be covered in a later volume: the San Francisco cabarets. They grew up with the city and many are still going strong. Boomtown saloons, such as the Bella Union, had showrooms for the girlie shows and the raw-humor comics. The Barbary Coast had variety music halls and "melodeons" (named for the reedy organs that provided the accompaniment). Ned Harrigan and Eddy Foy, Jr., started up the show business ladder in these bawdy, rowdy Pacific Street establishments.

Yes, San Francisco has seen it all, and there's still more to come, I'm sure. Seven-year-old Anna Maria Quinn played Hamlet in the early 1850s, and don't be surprised if someone promotes a white Labrador Retriever as Othello next week. San Francisco theatre, like everything else in town, has never been timid or unimaginative.

An explanation about a term that will pop up in regard to San Francisco and East Bay theatres: *Equity waiver house.* Actors' Equity is the labor union (AFL-CIO) that represents stage actors in musicals and plays. In large metropolitan areas union performers are supposed to work in union contract productions only. Because work is so hard to come by, Equity allows its members to work with nonunion casts in nonunion houses. It's a kind of a dispensation. The theatre can have no more than ninety-nine seats to get the OK. I'll designate those houses as we go. It means that, though the company may be nonprofessional, you may well be seeing professional actors at work. That's the meaning of an Equity waiver house.

DOWNTOWN THEATRES

San Francisco's downtown theatre "district" is about as indefinable as the San Francisco theatrical "season." For the purposes of this section, we'll draw an imaginary line around the area that contains the large commercial playhouses, the Civic Center arts complex, and several smaller professional and semiprofessional houses.

We'll begin a few steps north on Mason Street off Geary. Just beyond the San Francisco Experience (a multimedia screen program about the city in what used to be the Stage Door Theater) we come to the Showcase Theatre, currently the home of the One Act Theatre Company of San Francisco. Next door, in a Congregational Church basement, is their second playhouse, the Playwright's Theatre. A block and a half up the hill, at Sutter and Mason, is the Marines Memorial Theatre.

Coming back down to Geary, we cross the street and turn right. In a few steps we're in front of the Geary and then the Curran Theatre. A couple of blocks west, on the opposite side of the street between Leavenworth and Jones, is the Alcazar. From there we proceed to Van Ness Avenue and turn left to the Performing Arts Center of San Francisco at Civic Center. There are the side-by-side matching facades of the Veterans Memorial Building, housing the Herbst Theatre, and the War Memorial

Opera House. Across Grove Street is the new Louise M. Davies Symphony Hall. Turning left on Grove, past the Civic Auditorium at Polk Street, we continue on across Larkin and, at Hyde Street, cross to Market Street at the intersection. A large marquee, built flush with the face of the building, announces the Orpheum Theatre.

Three long blocks east, down Market Street to Taylor, brings us to the entrance of the Golden Gate Theatre. Up Taylor to Geary and right on Geary to Mason, and we're ready to visit these theatres.

As long as I have you here at the corner of Sixth and Market, let's take a short walk east to 982 Market Street. That's the location of the Warfield Theatre. Not strictly a legitimate playhouse, you might find occasion to get tickets for a rock concert, a touring musical revue, or a star's one-person presentation. The Warfield opened on May 13, 1922, as a flagship of the Loew's chain of vaudeville-movie palaces. It was designed by G. Albert Lansburgh, who, with Arthur Brown, Jr., later designed the War Memorial Opera House (see San Francisco Performing Arts Center). Marcus Loew named it for a native San Franciscan who began as an usher and achieved stardom in the theatre, David Warfield, a personal friend of Loew. Like all Market Street houses, after dropping the live acts, it went to a continuous "grind" policy of first- and second-

SAN FRANCISCO DOWNTOWN THEATRES

1 SHOWCASE & PLAYWRIGHT'S
2 MARINES MEMORIAL
3 GEARY
4 CURRAN
5 ALCAZAR
6 HERBST
7 WAR MEMORIAL OPERA HOUSE
8 DAVIES SYMPHONY HALL
9 ORPHEUM
10 GOLDEN GATE

run films. (In movie vernacular "grind" means showing films over and over throughout the day without a break; one, two, three, or more features run back-to-back. The idea is to get as much play time and as many people into the house as possible. Most grind houses provide more shelter for vagrants than entertainment for the general public.) The house went from Loew's management to Fox West Coast operation. Finally, in 1978, the lease was taken over by Mike Thomas Theatres, and the building was refurbished, cleaned up, and reopened as a special-product movie house. In late 1979 and 1981, Thomas sublet the facility to Bill Graham Productions. Graham is famous for making the "San Francisco sound" in rock music a world-wide phenomenon. The Warfield contains 2,400 seats, nearly always sold on a reserved basis. For schedule information you can call (415) 775-7722. Reservations can be made by calling (415) 835-4342 or any BASS outlet. The Warfield box office is only open on performance dates and only when tickets are still available for that performance. The actual owner of the Warfield building is a corporation in Taiwan.

THE SHOWCASE THEATRE ONE ACT THEATRE COMPANY

99 seats (unreserved).
LOCATION AND BOX OFFICE
430 Mason Street
San Francisco, CA 94102.
BOX OFFICE TELEPHONE (415)421-6162.
BUSINESS TELEPHONE (415) 421-5355.
OTHER TICKET OUTLETS ASUC,
Emporium, Downtown Ticket Center.
MANAGING DIRECTOR Raffi Del Bourgo.
ARTISTIC DIRECTOR Peter Tripp.
Equity waiver house.

THE PLAYWRIGHTS' THEATRE
60 seats (unreserved).
LOCATION Downstairs next door to the Showcase, in the First Congregational Church basement.
All other information is the same as for the Showcase.
HANDICAPPED ACCESS Neither house has any accommodations for wheelchair access or restroom facilities for the handicapped.

So as not to confuse the reader with a mass of names, I'm going to use the name Showcase Theatre here, the official name of 430 Mason Street. It is also known as the Act I, and the small house next door both as the Playwrights' Theatre and the Act II. Both are the homes of the One Act Theatre Company of San Francisco. As the name implies, they do one-act plays. The troupe claims to be the only company in America (or the world, according to some press releases) devoted to the genre. Whatever the exclusivity of their specialty, they certainly are as good at it or better than anyone I've seen. Usually, three or four plays are combined under an umbrella title.

The Showcase has a truly romantic history. During World War II the basement space of its home, the Native Sons of the Golden West building, was (get ready for a pang of nostalgia) San Francisco's Stage Door Canteen. Most of Hollywood and radio's biggest stars pulled a tour of duty doing "something for the boys." Thus began the performance career of the Showcase. Next, when poetry and guitar music was big, the famous Coffee Dan's occupied the hall.

Before there was the American Conservatory Theatre, there was the Actor's Workshop. Headed by Herbert Blau and the late Jules Irving, some of the Bay Area's finest actors and actresses sparked the ascendance of San Francisco into the ranks of America's active theatrical communities. Now the sign above the front door reads the Encore Theatre. The Actors Workshop flourished until its leaders were tapped to create the repertory theatre for New York's Lincoln Center. After that the Encore saw many independent productions that varied from Rodgers and Hart's *Boys From Syracuse* to America's most famous topless dancer, Carol Doda, starring as Miss Sadie Thompson in *Rain*. Somewhere along the line came the change to the Showcase designation and more independent shows, and then, in 1979, the One Act Company moved in.

The second, smaller house is actually a meeting room with folding chairs and a platform stage. Readings and small mountings of new works are the format in the Playwrights' Theatre (Act II).

Ticket prices for the Showcase (Act I) are under $10.00, most often around $6.50 to $7.00. Prices in the little theatre run from free for some readings to $3.50 to $4.00 for more elaborate stagings. Because of the limited space in both locations, you should phone ahead for a place. The Showcase is nicely elevated, and there's a comfortable lobby-refreshment area alongside the auditorium. What was originally a larger lobby upstairs has been absorbed by the San Francisco Experience operation.

MARINES MEMORIAL THEATRE

640 seats (reserved).
609 Sutter Street at Mason.
LOCATION AND BOX OFFICE
Geary Theatre
415 Geary Street
San Francisco, CA 94102.
(Box office at Marines opens one hour before curtain.)
BOX OFFICE TELEPHONE
(415) 673-6440 (Geary Theatre).

BUSINESS PHONE (415) 771-3880 (ACT).
OTHER TICKET OUTLETS Depending on attraction, most major agencies.
MARINES MEMORIAL CLUB ADMINISTRATION
Colonel William VanZuyen
(415) 673-6672.
ACT ADMINISTRATIVE CONTACT
Ben Moore
(415) 771-3880.
HANDICAPPED ACCESS Elevators are available on the first floor to take wheelchairs and handicapped patrons to the second-floor theatre lobby. For restroom facilities, the handicapped must take elevators to floor 10M. There are locations for wheelchair placement in the auditorium.

The Marines Memorial Theatre puts one in mind of an old-fashioned institutional auditorium facility. The walls are a drab cream color, and the seats offer a minimum of padding and leg space. There's a small orchestra pit, and the proscenium arch has no real decoration. The main curtain is black, with black velour drapes being the only stage adornments. The balcony is shallow and contains seven elevated rows. The main floor is raked slightly. The ventilation in the auditorium allows for little circulation of air. A full house can be a warming experience.

The lobby is inadequate for the number of seats in the house, and it's often advisable to take the flight of stairs down to the first-floor vestibule, or even to go out onto Sutter Street and take the air. There are usually lines waiting to use the small restroom facilities.

If all of the foregoing seems a discouragement to ever attending the Marines Memorial Theatre, don't let it be. There are some very fine theatre pieces presented there. It is just that the Marines Memorial Club was opened in 1927, and the auditorium was never designed to be a major theatre. There has been little or no renovation of the facility, and it

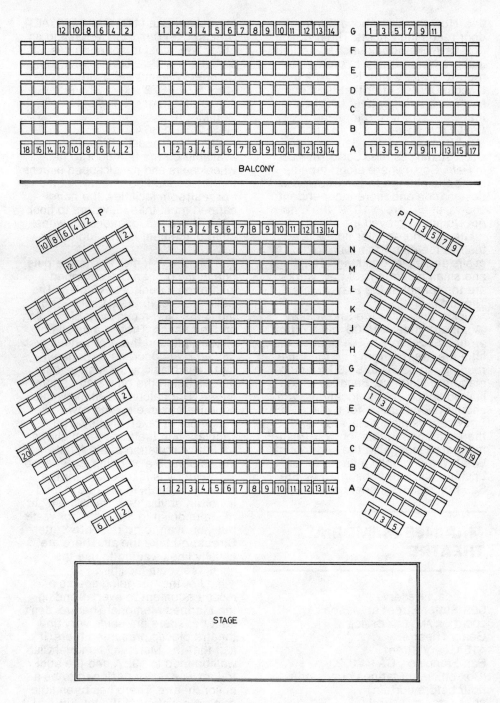

BALCONY

STAGE

MARINES MEMORIAL THEATRE

is feeling its age.

For the past decade the Marines has been operated, on an undisclosed rental deal, by the American Conservatory Theatre. It is known that the maintenance of the theatre is the responsibility of ACT, and that many of the productions that play there are either directly produced or partially sponsored by that company.

The real value of the Marines Memorial Theatre is that it gives medium-sized, moderate-budget plays and musicals, both touring and locally mounted, a chance to survive in the vicious financial world of show business. The union requirements tend to be less stringent here, and the rentals charged for the theatre are reasonable by current standards. All that is needed to make it a more attractive playhouse are some cosmetic changes. A few more hit tenants might make that a distinct possibility.

Rumor has it that in the days of yesteryear, radio broadcasts emanated from this very stage. Names dropped in the story-telling confabs of the old-time members of the club include those of Bing Crosby and Bob Hope.

GEARY THEATRE AMERICAN CONSERVATORY THEATRE

1,354 seats (reserved).
LOCATION AND BOX OFFICE
415 Geary Street
San Francisco, CA 94102.
BUSINESS ADDRESS
ACT
450 Geary Street
San Francisco, CA 94102.
BOX OFFICE TELEPHONE (415) 673-6440.
BUSINESS TELEPHONE (415) 771-3880.
OTHER TICKET OUTLETS BASS and other major outlets.

EXECUTIVE PRODUCER James McKenzie.
GENERAL DIRECTOR William Ball.
EXECUTIVE DIRECTOR Edward Hastings.
ARTISTIC DIRECTOR Changes with each production. Both resident and guest directors are employed.
HOUSE MANAGER Michael Burnor.
HANDICAPPED ACCESS A recent renovation has made the Geary totally accessible to the handicapped. There is wheelchair seating as well as total restroom access. Some performances are signed for the hearing impaired.

The Geary Theatre is a result of the fire that leveled San Francisco's eight downtown theatres following the April 18, 1906, earthquake. In the next eight years, new theatres were built, and San Francisco's live-theatre tradition carried on almost as though nothing had happened. The Geary, designed by Bliss and Faville, was one of the last of these up-to-date theatrical palaces to open. It made its debut on the festive evening of January 10, 1910. The play was *Father and the Boys,* and its star was William Crane. By 1917 all the theatres had abandoned the drama format except for the Geary. As the years rolled by, the cast of greats that graced the stage included Sarah Bernhardt, Isadora Duncan (a hometown girl), Basil Rathbone, the Lunts, and several Skinners.

In 1967 the touring shows lost this venerable old stopping place to a resident theatre company called the American Conservatory Theatre. Founder William Ball had started the troupe two years earlier in Milwaukee, but he liked the looks of the cultural climate in San Francisco and moved the players and the concept here. His instincts proved accurate, and ACT has grown and prospered to become America's strongest and best-regarded regional theatre. The American Theatre Wing confirmed that judgement in 1979 by awarding

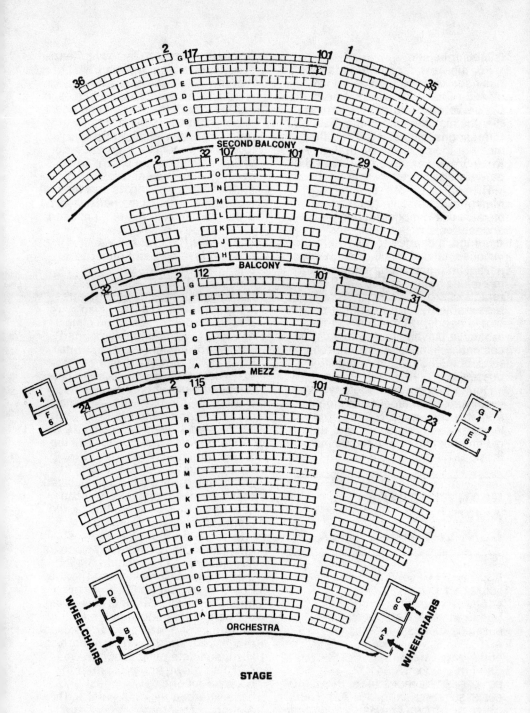

GEARY THEATRE

ACT the coveted Antoinette Perry Award, the 'Tony.'

The Geary gained a new thrust stage with ACT, although the proscenium arch remains. The orchestra pit is gone, and permanent light scaffolds obscure much of the fancy plaster detailing and the tall fluted columns. The main floor is raked, and there is a double balcony arrangement. In keeping with the design of an early–twentieth-century legitimate house, the auditorium is wide, shallow from back wall to stage, and very high. Tall folks may have a little trouble with leg space between rows, but remember that the average American's height has increased since the floor plan was laid out. The stage grand drape is seldom used, and the setting for the play of the evening is in plain sight of the audience as it enters the theatre auditorium.

ACT's season begins in October and continues through May. The repertory is presented in the Continental rotating manner, allowing for a wide choice of plays within any given week. The entire library of world theatre literature is grist for the ACT mill. Contemporary works mingle with Moliere and Shakespeare. Plays fresh off Broadway appear on the playbill with English drawing room comedies from the 1920s. In the summer months the company may tour the United States or the world, and the Geary may house a New York hit, a one-person tour de force, or a touring classic.

Soaring production costs have affected all ticket prices everywhere, whether the theatre be small or large. ACT's Geary Theatre ticket scale is still reasonable by current standards. Tickets are still under the $15 mark, with the top being $14 at this writing. There are half-priced tickets for military personnel and students one hour before curtain time, and wheelchair-confined persons and a guest may purchase ramped box-seat locations for $4. Of course there are group discounts and subscriptions available. The lower end of the scale is around $6, and previews are even better deals.

The combination of a historic theatre plant and excellent theatrical craftsmanship make a trip to an American Conservatory Theatre production at the Geary a double treat. (By the way, it is my belief that ACT performs Ibsen better than anyone else in the world.)

History buffs, please note: The Geary Theatre began life as the Columbia Theatre.

CURRAN THEATRE

1,768 seats (reserved).
LOCATION AND BOX OFFICE
445 Geary Street
San Francisco, CA 94102.
BOX OFFICE TELEPHONE (415) 673-4400.
BUSINESS TELEPHONE (415) 673-1040.
OTHER TICKET OUTLETS All major agencies.
PRODUCER James M. Nederlander.
RESIDENT PRODUCER Carole J. Shorenstein.
GENERAL MANAGER H. Anthony Reilly III.
MANAGER Devera Kettner.
HANDICAPPED ACCESS Wheelchair-confined persons may purchase tickets for the ramped boxes. Handicapped persons must travel to the Geary Theatre to use the restrooms there.

"Hey Cisco!" has nothing, really, to do with the Curran Theatre, except that the opening-night play (September 11, 1934) was *Mike Angelo* starring native son Leo Carrillo— best known for his work in the *Cisco Kid* film series. There was a certain justice in a man whose family had been residents of California for 300 years being the leading player on the stage of California's newest and most beautiful theatre. The opening night was a smash, with the best names in town throwing parties in the plushest hotel ballrooms.

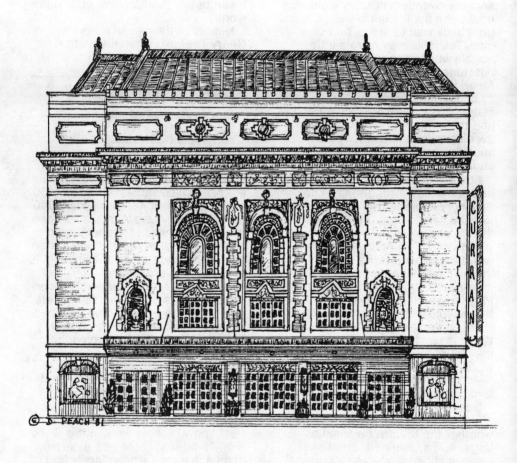

CURRAN THEATRE

Homer Curran spent $800,000 building what was to be the last major legitimate theatre constructed in downtown San Francisco. He loved the theatre to such an extent that when the Depression was closing down other houses around the country he produced shows himself, to keep the lights on. He was a man of many talents. He composed the music for the first operetta (student variety) produced at Stanford. In association with the Wobber Brothers or with Edward Belasco (brother of legendary producer-director-writer David Belasco) he produced some of the West Coast's most memorable and important plays and musicals. The stars who performed, and still perform, on the Curran stage would fill a Who's Who of the theatre.

It should be noted that it was at the Curran, while seated on her grandmother's lap to see Ethel Waters in *As Thousands Cheer* (the people in front were just too tall) that Carol Channing decided to spend her life in show business. She was in the fourth grade at Commodore Sloat School at the time.

How's this for a piece of theatre wonderment? While the Lunts were rehearsing for *Amphitryon '38* (1936), which would have its world premiere at the Curran and then travel to Broadway, they were performing in *Idiot's Delight* next door at the Geary.

The San Francisco Civic Light Opera called the Curran home beginning with its 1939 production of *Blossom Time,* starring John Charles Thomas. By this time Homer Curran was working closely with CLO producer and founder Edwin Lester. That association continued, sending hits to Broadway such as *Song of Norway* until Curran's death in 1952. CLO stayed on until they moved to the Orpheum Theatre on Market Street in May 1977. From then until now the Curran has been controlled by the Shorenstein-Nederlander Or-

ganization, and musicals and plays coming from or headed for Broadway are played under the banner of the Best of Broadway series.

I think that the Curran is my favorite "old" theatre anywhere in the country. It's what a "legit" house should be. The ceiling is dominated by a grand chandelier. The murals by Arthur Mathews are delightfully archaic. The red plush hangings against the gold trim and ivory walls give a feeling of fading opulence. The Grecian feeling of the proscenium arch and the great ornate rose and green front curtain are all what you think of when you think "theatre."

Seating on the main floor is only twenty-two rows deep, and upstairs seating is broken into loge, mezzanine, and lower and upper balcony sections. As the saying goes, there's not a bad seat in the house for sight lines. The audio is sometimes a different matter. The system must often support voices that have not been trained in "grand theatre" projection, and mechanical problems are always a possibility when actors rely on technicians rather than upon themselves. The management of the Curran handles problems quickly and pleasantly, and you'll enjoy attending this handsome theatre.

Ticket prices at the Curran are determined by the attraction on the boards. You probably won't sit in the orchestra for less than $15 ever again, and it can go as high (so far no higher) as $10 above that. The higher up in the seats you go, the lower the ticket prices fall.

It seems odd to describe a theatre of this size as being intimate. But, if there is one word to describe Homer Curran's pride and joy, intimate is that word. There have been renovations and modifications over the years, but the praise that filled the local press after that first night in 1934 regarding the "beautiful new theatre" still applies. The lady has aged gracefully.

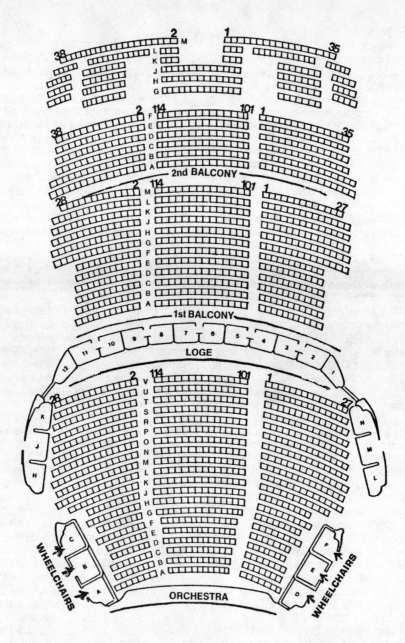

STAGE

CURRAN THEATRE

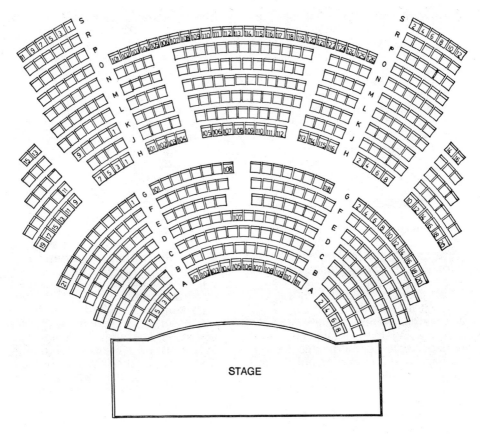

STAGE

ALCAZAR THEATRE

ALCAZAR THEATRE

499 seats (reserved).
LOCATION AND BOX OFFICE
650 Geary Street
San Francisco, CA 94102.
BOX OFFICE TELEPHONE (415) 775-7100.
BUSINESS TELEPHONE (415) 775-1756.
OTHER TICKET OUTLETS Most major
agencies depending on policy of in-
dividual producers.
OWNER CONTACT Keith Rockwell.

HANDICAPPED ACCESS There is an elevator from the lower lobby to the
second-floor theatre site. There are,
however, several steps from the
street level to the first foyer. There
are no special accommodations in
the restrooms.

Depending on which local theatrical
historian you consult, this is either
the fourth or the fifth playhouse in
San Francisco to bear the Alcazar
name. The first one was undoubtedly
opened in the last quarter of the

nineteenth century, and the one before this one was demolished in the mid-1950s. It would be a shame to have a theatre community here without an Alcazar.

The building at 650 Geary Street looks like a mini-mosque. It's true that the Alcazar in Seville, Spain, has much of the Moorish design in it, but it's only by coincidence that the theatre of the same name is Moorish in architectural character. The reason is that it was a Masonic Temple for most of its life, and Shriners tend to lean toward minarets and inlaid-tile designs. In the upper rooms, away from the public portions of the theatre, you can still see pictures of fezed smiling men, long-forgotten members of lodge choruses and softball teams.

This is a rental facility, so the product presented here is of the commercial variety. There have been musicals, Agatha Christie mysteries, drag comedies, and dramatic presentations. The most successful stand was a one-man show starring Dick Shawn. Announced for a short engagement, this superb comic actor packed in the crowds for nearly half a year. Of course, the theatre being what it is, that record could fall at any time.

The builders of this theatre are the same men who created the On Broadway and Little Fox theatres in North Beach; we'll talk about those in another section. The Alcazar is reached by climbing a stairway from the ticket office area in the small street-level foyer. There is not one, but two lobbies on the second floor. One is primarily for the use of the refreshment stand, and the second for milling, visiting, or sitting between acts. Another favorite intermission retreat is out on the outdoor balcony that looks down on Geary.

The entire outer theatre space is decorated in red-flocked wallpaper. The interior of the theatre is red,

and the elevated seats are red. The main level of the floor has slightly stepped levels. The back half of the hall is a steeper stadium-type arrangement, fanning into a three-section mezzanine.

The red continues around the front of the house, with crimson stage drapes framing a thrust platform playing area. There is no proscenium arch, and the lighting is unmasked at the ceiling level.

Because of the second-floor location with its low ceilings, inadequate ventilation can occasionally pose problems for audience comfort in the Alcazar. As the facility gains more tenants and the runs become longer, the owners are returning some of the revenues into improving this newest of midtown's medium-sized theatres.

Parking for the Alcazar can be on the streets surrounding the theatre, depending on your luck finding spaces in the city, or in the parking garage that occupies the first floor of the building. There are also outdoor park-it-yourself lots handy to the playhouse.

SAN FRANCISCO PERFORMING ARTS CENTER

HERBST THEATRE
LOUISE M. DAVIES SYMPHONY HALL
WAR MEMORIAL OPERA HOUSE
BUSINESS OFFICE
Veterans Building
401 Van Ness Avenue, Suite 110
San Francisco, CA 94102.
BUSINESS TELEPHONE (415) 621-6600.
MANAGING DIRECTOR George Matson.
FACILITY-SERVICES MANAGER 864-6850.

I think I'll break form a bit and tell you about this group of facilities collectively, then I'll give you information on each theatre. You'll note that you hear little about the Civic Auditorium or Brooks Hall. You'll get a touch more about Louise M. Davies Symphony Hall. The reason for that is that this is a book about theatres (and theaters). I have religiously avoided the inclusion of public auditoriums, although I may have slipped back there in Santa Cruz. Symphony Hall is just that. You're not likely to see a road company of *Panama Hattie* prancing where the San Francisco Symphony is wont to sit. Come to think of it, before I'm corrected by the powers-that-be, Civic Auditorium isn't part of the Performing Arts Center anyway.

Ground was broken for both the War Memorial Opera house and the Veterans Memorial Building a half century ago, in 1931. This was the WPA granddaddy project of them all. A year later the matching classical buildings, blending nicely with the architecture of City Hall across Van Ness Avenue, were opened to the public.

To wrap up the description of the Performing Arts Center, here are a couple of pertinent facts. It is the second largest center of its type in the United States, with a total of 7,231 seats in the three facilities. Only Lincoln Center in New York is larger. The Kennedy Center in Washington comes in third.

Last, but certainly not least, as any school child can tell you, the War Memorial Opera House holds a singular, nontheatrical, nonmusical place in world history. It was on its stage that the victorious nations, shortly after World War II, signed the United Nations Charter, forming that idealistic world league. Harry Truman signed for the United States, and there is no record that he played the piano afterward.

WAR MEMORIAL OPERA HOUSE
3,252 seats (reserved).
LOCATION AND BOX OFFICE
301 Van Ness Avenue (at Grove)
San Francisco, CA 94102.
BOX OFFICE TELEPHONE (415) 431-1210.
OTHER TICKET OUTLETS Most major outlets.
HOUSE MANAGER John Galindo.
HANDICAPPED ACCESS There is wheelchair access on the Grove Street side of the building. Wheelchair locations are on the main floor, and elevators provide access to the basement-level restrooms.

Opening night for the Opera House was October 15, 1932. Under the sure baton of Maestro Gaetano Merola, the melodious and powerful music of Puccini's *Tosca* resounded in the new home of the San Francisco Opera Company. What a relief it must have been, what a joy for singers, conductor, patrons, orchestra members, everybody, after years in the aforementioned Civic Auditorium, the opera's barnlike digs since 1923. No wonder they didn't include it in the Center. Not that there hadn't been worse. In 1928 they had tried a season in Dreamland Auditorium, née Dreamland Rink, later known as Winterland.

Architects Arthur Brown, Jr., and G. Albert Lansburgh thought nothing of taking liberties with the basic classic lines of the auditorium. Just under the never-used ornate organ loft grills, the cast stone walls suddenly sweep into a flying curve that contains the single-level gold-trimmed private boxes. This is like the rim of a crown looking down on the plush overstuffed seats that fill the orchestra floor. Above this, more or less square-cut at right angles with the wall, are the Grand Tier and the Dress Circle, and above that, two balcony levels. There's plenty of room. The ceiling, with a sunburst

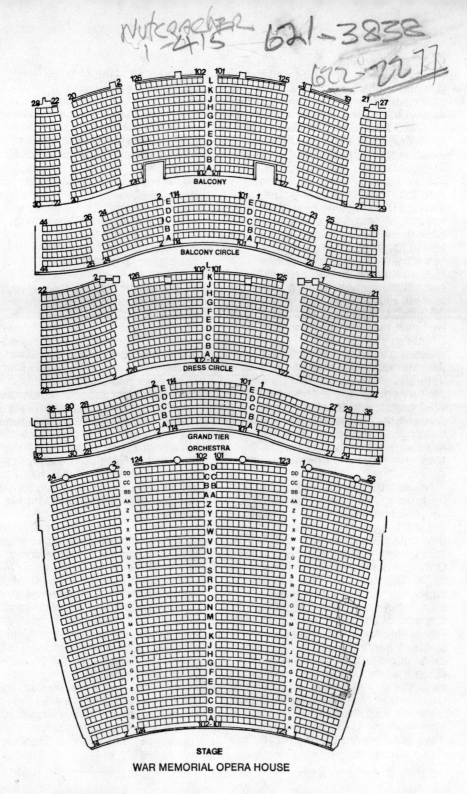

STAGE

WAR MEMORIAL OPERA HOUSE

chandelier that measures twenty-seven feet in diameter, is vaulted and coffered, and the overall hue of buff is accented in gold. The grand drape, with its enormous tassels, completes the golden cascade of color. The mask of Comedy gazes down, stage left; Tragedy on stage right.

The proscenium arch is 52 feet wide by 51 feet high. The gigantic stage it frames is in a stage house that rises 150 feet above the ground. A recent addition is a scenery storage area that was joined to the rear of the building and crafted in such a way to look as if it had been there since 1932.

Entering the house, there is a foyer that contains the box offices to your right. Through glass doors you enter a spacious atrium that spans the width of the building and ends at the staircases leading up to the second floor areas or down into the opera bar and restaurant. A passageway connects this area to the rear of the house under the stage (not open to the public). An in-house nurse is on duty in the refreshment area, just in case the vino or the tenor doesn't agree with you.

HERBST THEATRE
915 seats (reserved).
LOCATION 401 Van Ness Avenue (at McAllister), San Francisco.
BOX OFFICE
War Memorial Opera House
Symphony Box Office
301 Van Ness Avenue
San Francisco, CA 94102.
BOX OFFICE TELEPHONE (415) 431-5400.
OTHER TICKET OUTLETS Most major outlets.
HOUSE MANAGER Chuck Knight.
HANDICAPPED There is total access for wheelchairs through the front entrances. Wheelchair placement is on the first-floor level. Elevators provide access to the basement-level restrooms.

Leaving the Opera House, walk down the front steps, under the awning, and turn left to the Veteran's Memorial Building. There's a mall between the two buildings that occupy the block from Van Ness to Franklin Street. On the Van Ness side is a high, blue-black iron fence with spearpoints on each stave. There are large golden lanterns. It's all very European. So much so, in fact, that some of the commercials you see on television, with the Queen's guard standing in his striped guard box, were probably filmed right there in front of said fence. Ah, the illusion of it all.

There are no sidewalk steps leading to the Veterans Memorial. The foyer isn't distinctive. It just gets you headed where you're going in the building. To the right is an information-ticket booth; to the left, the administrative offices of the Performing Arts Center. Up the stairs, or by elevator, on the second floor is the green room. This is a huge reception hall used for conventions and social soirées.

Back on the first floor, you move through a wide doorway and into the Herbst Theatre lobby. It's a simple room with ornate, palacelike furniture. Stairs on either side take you to a lower lobby-refreshment area and the restrooms. Here, again, elevator service is available. Now, into the theatre auditorium. Renovated in 1978, it is a small theatre with a large feel to it. There are box-type seats running at balcony level along the sides of the house. These are reached by stairs down front, near the stage. Behind these, the regular balcony spans the room. The main floor is raked and the leg room, for taller patrons, is comfortable. The stage is shallow but adequate for

ORCHESTRA

ORCHESTRA PIT

STAGE

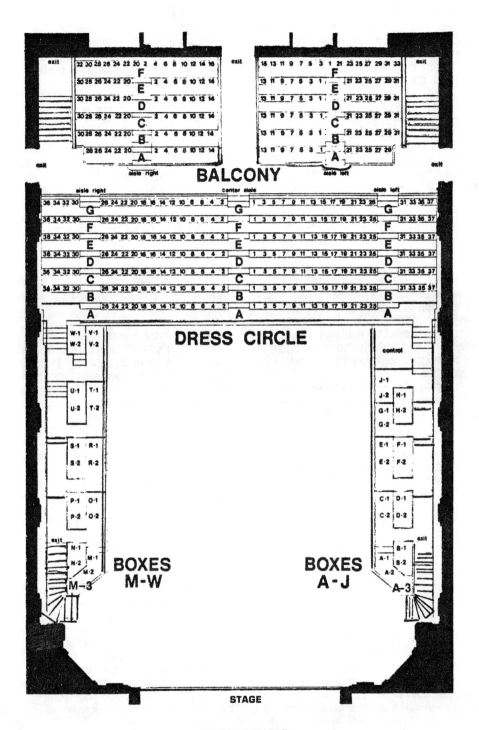

BALCONY

DRESS CIRCLE

control

BOXES M-W

BOXES A-J

STAGE

HERBST THEATRE

moderate-sized plays, musicals, and operas. There's an orchestra pit with a lift-floor that, if no orchestra is needed, can become an extended stage apron.

Acoustics were the biggest problem in the Herbst for years. Renovation cured that: If you take a look toward the ceiling, you'll see round transparent discs hovering in ranks like a fleet of flying saucers. The aquamarine and gold ceiling is coved.

The most prominent feature of the Herbst decor is the colorful Brangwyn murals. These eight paneled paintings once adorned the Court of Abundance at the Panama-Pacific Exposition of 1915 (see Palace of Fine Arts in the San Francisco International Film Festival section). The grand drape is dusty rose with the obligatory gold fringe and tassels. Flat-faced Ionic pilasters adorn the walls at regular intervals. The color scheme is a medium gray, with gold trim and highlights.

You can't tell it from the front of the house, but the Herbst has more dressing room facilities, above the stage and under it, than any of the other theatres in the complex. What you do notice is that the stage lacks wing space, and that there is a minimum of masking available to conceal any off-stage movement. While the Herbst works passably with dance and dramas with small casts, it's at its best when a solo performer is occupying the performance area.

If I didn't mention it on the way in, the second and third floors of the Veterans building are occupied by the San Francisco Museum of Modern Art.

Looking to your left as you head for the main egress, you'll see a room closed off with a tall iron gate. Inside is a display of weaponry that never seems to be open to the public. Perhaps such a display has been thought inadvisable in this age of violence, but it certainly is intriguing. The guard tells me the view of the room is even better from outside in the mall. He doesn't know why it's closed, either. The answer is probably mundane and, besides, would end all the fun of speculation.

LOUISE M. DAVIES SYMPHONY HALL 3,064 seats (reserved).
LOCATION AND BOX OFFICE 201 Van Ness Avenue (at Grove) San Francisco, CA 94102.
BOX OFFICE TELEPHONE (415) 431-5400.
OTHER TICKET OUTLETS Most major outlets.
HOUSE MANAGER Horacio Rodrigues.
HANDICAPPED ACCESS There is total access for wheelchairs, with elevators to all levels and seating areas for wheelchairs.

A full block back past the Opera House and over Grove Street is the Louise M. Davies Symphony Hall, home of the San Francisco Symphony Orchestra and single performances of visiting musicians and dance troupes. The main entrance is about halfway up Grove. There a stainless steel entranceway leads directly into the foyer with its multiple–box office arrangement.

Tickets in hand, you move inside the lower lobby and either climb the carpeted stairs or take one of the shiny steel elevators. The European style of both of the facilities across the way gives way to the Space Age at the Louise M. Davies. The first lobby is impressive, with its brass and steel appointments. The floor is marble, although it was carpeted when the hall premiered in 1980. The walls are peach colored, and the salmon-rose motif that is seen throughout the rest of the building begins here. There are two more lobby levels above, one for each tier, and locations for up to fourteen bars. You can get through some pretty tedious performances with that kind of intermission support, but most of the events here don't need it.

Inside, the main floor decor continues in a salmon-colored flow. The stage is surrounded by a gallery of padded pew-like benches looking down on the open platform. There is a proscenium arch (portable) available for installation at the request of any visiting production. Within the confines of the stage is an elevator floor that drops to orchestra pit depth or all the way to the lower reaches under the stage to transport heavy equipment and instruments to the platform. Mahogony-paneled walls circle the area for ensured resonance.

Looking out at the house you are impressed by the number of levels and size of the seating arrangement. Over it all are the special sound-baffling installations that are constantly being improved upon for the sake of the acoustics. Plexiglass spheres work in concert with adjustable fabric panels that are suspended like venetian blinds from slots overhead. The battle for perfect acoustics never ends in this or any other hall devoted to the playing of classical music.

Looking out of the windows that make up the facade of the hall, you may catch a spectacular sunset providing a mystical backdrop for City Hall at just the right moment of an evening. You can also see the Civic Auditorium a block down Grove but, as promised, I won't talk about that.

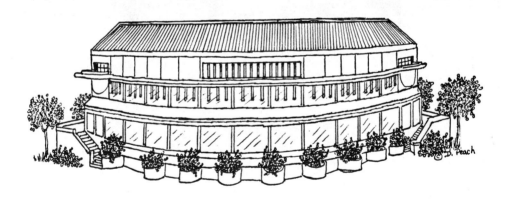

LOUISE M. DAVIES SYMPHONY HALL

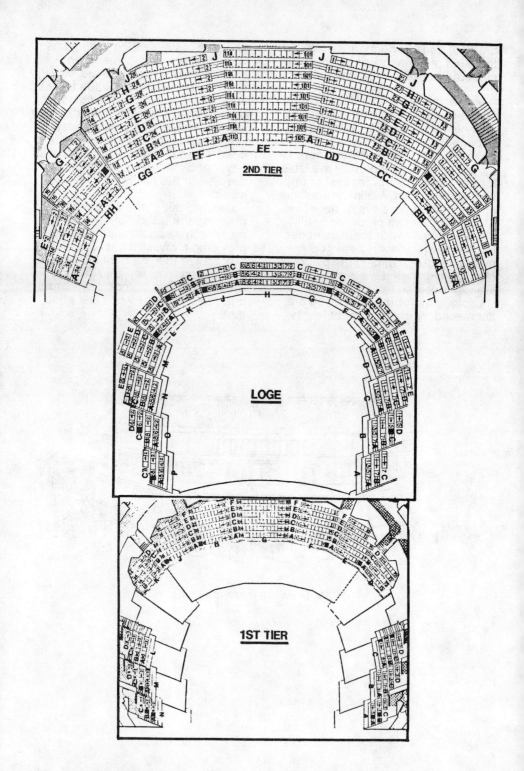

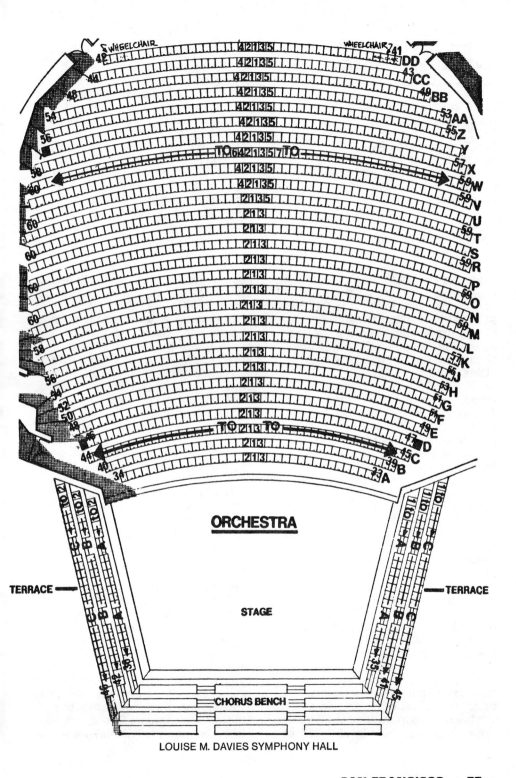

ORCHESTRA

TERRACE —

STAGE

CHORUS BENCH

LOUISE M. DAVIES SYMPHONY HALL

ORPHEUM THEATRE

2,503 seats (reserved).
LOCATION AND BOX OFFICE
1192 Market Street
San Francisco, CA 94102.
BOX OFFICE TELEPHONE (415) 474-3800.
BUSINESS TELEPHONE (415) 552-0155.
OTHER TICKET OUTLETS All major
agencies.
PRODUCER James M. Nederlander.
RESIDENT PRODUCER
Carole J. Shorenstein.
GENERAL MANAGER H. Anthony Reilly III.
MANAGER Robert L. Lazzara.
HANDICAPPED ACCESS Restrooms for
the handicapped are on the main
floor in the outer lobby. The lobby is
at street level with no stairs. A
steady grade leads into the theatre
auditorium. Wheelchairs are placed
beside the rows in the extra-wide
aisles.

If you had been in San Francisco in
February 1926, and among the hoi
polloi of the day's society, you might
well have been invited to the new
Pantages Theatre at Eighth and
Market to see the *Revue of Revues.*
There was also an exciting new film
by that darling of the tail-wagging
set, Rin Tin Tin. Alexander Pantages
had hired top architect B. Marcus
Priteca to make this house the
crowning jewel of his thirty-theatre
chain. Priteca succeeded admirably.
The grandeur of old Spain was
combined with the latest in theatrical
technology. Vaudeville and the new
phenomenon of motion pictures were
presented in one glorious showplace.
  Two years later the bloom was off
the rose, and Pantages sold his
jewel to RKO. They reopened the
theatre in 1929 as the Orpheum,
"the new home of the two-a-day
bills." Historical note: The first
Orpheum Theatre to please San
Franciscans was built in 1876. Since

that date there has seldom been a
time when the city hasn't had an
Orpheum, in one form or another.
  The mid-1930s saw the Orpheum
give up its vaudeville policy and
devote its public hours exclusively
to films. In the fifties the property
containing the theatre and the office
building above it passed into the
hands of Metropolitan Theatres of
Los Angeles. They showed big-screen,
first-fun movies until the Market
Street area deteriorated to a state in
which it was economically unsound
to operate what had become a white
elephant. The Orpheum closed down.
  There are always people in a
community who can't stand to see a
dark theatre. One of these was local
impresario Barnie Gould. He man-
aged to get a lease from Metropolitan
Theatres and open a short-lived
series under the banner of San
Francisco Musicals. It started with a
vaudeville show, then starred Allan
Jones in *Man of La Mancha.* There
were opera presentations on a couple
of Sunday afternoons, but, all in all,
it looked as though the theatre was
doomed.
  Two things happened to change
the complexion of the future. First,
Bay Area Rapid Transit (BART) opened
a station that spilled passengers
right at the Orpheum's front doors.
Second, the city of San Francisco
began a beautification project to
clean up Market Street. The Orpheum
was suddenly the outer edge of
the Performing Arts Center-Civic
Center complex and part of a historical preservation movement. Gould
failed in his effort, but he had
pioneered and prophesied what was
to be.
  In 1970, another significant event
took place. The touring company of
the rock musical *Hair* played the
house. One of the backers was local
moviehouse owner and executive of
United Artists Theatre Circuit, Marshall
Naify. The engagement sold out. It was

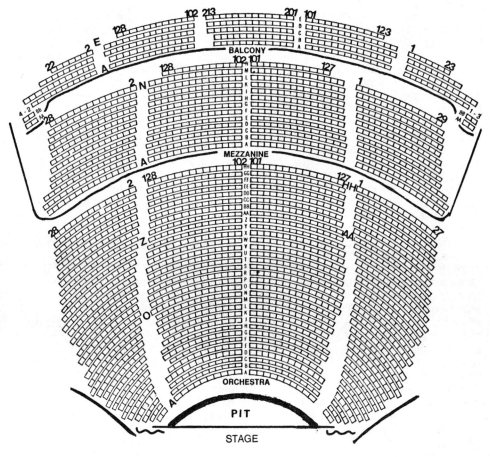

ORPHEUM THEATRE

extended and there were lines around the corner. The old house, once thought hopeless, drew crowds just as it did in the early days.

Meanwhile, the San Francisco Civic Light Opera was feeling a financial pinch based on the limited seats available at its Curran Theatre home. When Edwin Lester went into semi-retirement and Ernest Martin and Cy Feurer became the producing directors of CLO, it was decided to take the massive-capital plunge and refurbish the Orpheum.

On October 1, 1976, the gutting of the interior began. Richard F. McCann of Seattle, a student of Priteca's, (the original Orpheum architect) took over the planning. New stage flies were installed, and all of the electricity and sound, the backstage area, the dressing rooms, the workshops, the auditorium, and the lobbies were rebuilt.

On May 10, 1977, in time to celebrate the eighty-ninth anniversary of Irving Berlin's birth, the new Orpheum opened to the strains of "There's No Business Like Show Business" and a revitalized version of *Annie, Get Your Gun.* Civic Light Opera held out for three more seasons before throwing in the towel and hollering "uncle." A combination of escalating costs and stiff competition from the Shorenstein-Nederlander group sealed

CLO's doom. I also suspect that somewhere along the way the new producers had lost touch with the taste of San Francisco's theatregoers.

In the spring of 1981 the announcement was made that the Orpheum would join the Curran and the Golden Gate as a Shorenstein-Nederlander showplace, giving the downtown area three first-rate theatres presenting America's finest commercial theatre attractions.

The rich earth tones and gold accents of the Orpheum tend to take away some of the "barn" feeling of this cavernous facility. The carpeting and seat fabrics add to the warmth with their deep-red color. Carpets are flecked with black. There are recessed alcoves with statuary behind the gates and soft backlighting to provide an ever-present glow. The proscenium arch is black with gold highlights emphasizing plaster bas relief scenes of characters from a classic Spanish epic. The giant translucent chandelier is surrounded by a permanent ceiling motif of lion's heads, a motif that is evident throughout the theatre. The grand drape is a vibrant red. The ceilings in the upper foyers and in the balcony areas are made up of an engrossing collection of colored tiles. A wrought-iron balcony looks out over the main lobby.

If there is a structural problem with the Orpheum it is the extremely narrow inner lobby leading to the restrooms and the seating sections. It is almost impassable when crowds begin milling in all directions at intermission. Head for a fire exit, usually opened at these breaks, and get fresh air, rather than fight this mass of bodies. Once in the outer lobby you can slip outside to Market Street.

Acoustics have been a persistent bugaboo at the Orpheum. The main culprit for hearing difficulty is the massive balcony overhang. Special speakers have been installed to deliver the voices from the stage to seats under the balcony, but the quality of the sound from this source leaves a little to be desired. Again, acoustics are something that theatres of this size are ever working to improve.

The Orpheum Theatre has seemed through the years to be cursed by being at the wrong place at the wrong time. It will be interesting to see if the curse can be removed in the 1980s. For the entertainment enjoyment of us all, let's hope so.

GOLDEN GATE THEATRE

2,423 seats (reserved).
LOCATION AND BOX OFFICE
25 Taylor Street
(Golden Gate Avenue at Taylor and Market streets)
San Francisco, CA 94102.
BOX OFFICE TELEPHONE (415) 775-8800.
BUSINESS TELEPHONE (415) 673-6400.
PRODUCER James M. Nederlander.
RESIDENT PRODUCER
Carole J. Shorenstein.
GENERAL MANAGER H. Anthony Reilly III.
MANAGER Lisa DiGiacomo.
HANDICAPPED ACCESS There is a gentle slope from the sidewalk into the lobby and auditorium for wheelchair access. Restrooms equipped for the handicapped are on the main floor on the right-hand side of the foyer just before you enter the auditorium. Seats have been removed to allow placement of four wheelchairs in the side sections.

Architect G. Albert Lansburgh designed over fifty theatres. The Golden Gate in San Francisco was his twenty-first, and it was done for Martin Beck, a theatrical tycoon of the time. The Martin Beck, in New York City, was also built by Lansburgh for his boss. Other San Francisco

GOLDEN GATE THEATRE

landmarks by him are the Concordia Club on Van Ness and the Art Deco interior of the Clift Hotel's famed Redwood Room. The 1915 Pan-Pacific Exposition had several of his works as well. Lansburgh designed things to last through thick and thin. The Golden Gate Theatre has had plenty of both.

Opening night, March 26, 1922, saw top-hatted men and their formally gowned ladies waiting, in a line that went around the block, to see a program of "high class vaudeville" on stage and a Photoplay silent feature on the screen. James H. Cullen as "The Man from the West" was the main attraction, with Lillian St. Leon in an equestrian extrava-ganza titled "How Circus Riders Are Made." Animal acts were so popular that the Golden Gate had an animal room. It once housed Rin Tin Tin in the flesh—make that fur.

In 1928 the Keith-Albee-Orpheum Circuit merged with Joseph Kennedy's Radio Pictures, and RKO was born. That management guided the Golden Gate through the World War II years when this theatre was the only San Francisco house still doing stage shows. Vaudeville had died, and superstars took its place: headliners such as Frank Sinatra, Jack Benny, Carmen Miranda, Louis Armstrong, George Burns, and Gracie Allen (Burns once quipped, "Most people leave their hearts in San Francisco. I left my trunk at the Golden Gate")— and the list goes on and on. All of the important forties' big bands played the hall.

Howard Hughes bought RKO in 1948 and tried to end the live-show policy. San Francisco wouldn't have it, and Betty Hutton reopened the "stage and screen" format, which existed until 1954, longer than at almost any other theatre, outside of New York City, in America. Next were first-run movies, then Cinerama, then management by Walter Reade

Theatres, and, finally, darkness. By this time the lobby had taken on a tackiness almost unparalleled in movie-house history. The location at the lower tip of the Tenderloin didn't help. These were thin times.

A brief effort was made in the mid-1970s to refloat the foundered ship. A local group produced some of the most dreadful live shows I've seen in San Francisco. The ship sank a little deeper. It must be added that the Golden Gate, in its last throes, had been made into a "piggyback" house: The balcony became theatre No. 2, indignity heaped upon indignity.

All of the foregoing points up what a marvelous accomplishment Shoren-stein-Nederlander has achieved in restoring the Golden Gate back to its 1922 glory.

Reconstruction was hampered by the lack of original blueprints. Eventu-ally over one hundred of these were retrieved from garbage cans (where they were being used as liners) and stacks of debris. Molds were made from bits and pieces of the original ornamentation, and these were used to cast replacements for missing decorative details. A whole new set of plans evolved from the clues provided by the remaining badly damaged architecture. Photos pro-vided more valuable details. The lobby was gutted, false ceilings were removed, and walls were knocked down, and what rose from the dust was an exact duplicate of what Lansburgh had built in the first place.

Entering the Golden Gate from the corner of Taylor and Golden Gate you find yourself in the large, slightly sloping foyer of the theatre. The color scheme of sand-buff, ivory, browns, and gold begins here and is carried through the entire facility. A giant ornate column is the center focal point, supporting the elaborate, cathedral-like ceiling. Beyond this a

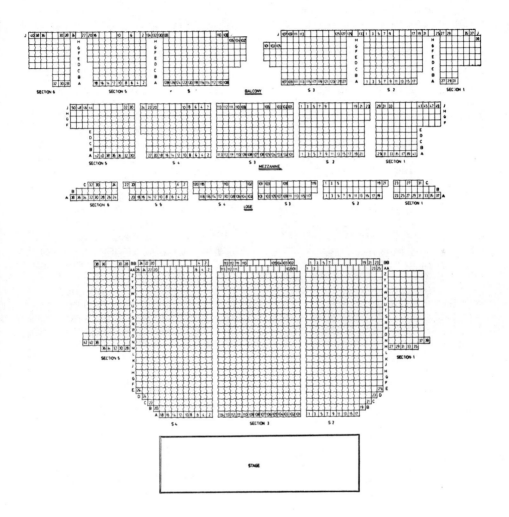

GOLDEN GATE THEATRE

majestic staircase leads to the upper lobby and balcony seating. The outer lobby floor is polished marble. The box offices are to the right as you enter.

The upper lobby is housed in a low-ceilinged hall with a balcony from which you can survey the lobby below. There is a long bar constructed of wood and brass. The overhead decor is a maze of highly detailed frames, floral designs and grillworks. The floor affords an opportunity to see an expanse of the latticework carpeting used throughout the theatre.

On the main floor, through a second set of arches, is the inner lobby, with a cocktail bar on the right and the entrance door to the orchestra floor. The men's restroom is to the left and downstairs, the women's to the right. The restroom for the handicapped is near the center of this area. Inside the auditorium the feeling is one of simple elegance, with the detailing of the trim blended tastefully into the overall decor. For so large a theatre, the Golden Gate immediately gives you a sense of coziness and intimacy. Even when you look at the soaring folds of the grand drape or back up at the sea of seats in the balcony, you feel that you're in a friendly room.

The acoustics of the Golden Gate Theatre are excellent. Many large, refurbished houses never conquer their audio problems but that seems to have been one of the chief considerations when this house was redone. Of course, if the actors are whisperers, even the best sound system won't help.

As do the other two Shorenstein-Nederlander houses, the Golden Gate plays touring Broadway shows. The theatre is too large for most straight plays, so it's safe to refer to this as an almost exclusively musical theatre. With its spacious dressing room areas and seating capacity, large-cast shows can either reach the break-even point or turn a profit here. The word has it that the greatest single night's box office take was at the Golden Gate on New Year's Eve 1981, when the revival of Richard Burton's *Camelot* grossed in excess of $80,000 for one performance.

The Broadway biggies don't come cheap. The cost of touring a show, plus inflated prices in all departments of production, has pushed the weekend orchestra-stall prices up to about twenty-five dollars each. If it's any comfort to your bank account, that's still about ten dollars less than a comparable seat in New York. The present economy could push local prices even higher. Lower-priced performances and locations are commonly sold out early. Equally common are total sell-outs of prime attractions. It's best to look at schedules and order tickets as quickly as you can make your plans; it saves disappointment.

The Golden Gate, as opposed to the restored Paramount in Oakland, has a decor of quiet grandeur, rather than sparkling opulence. The two houses give Bay Area and northern California theatregoers a unique opportunity to see, first-hand, excellent examples of differing concepts and philosophies of theatre architecture. I recommend that you see each one when the opportunity arises.

MASONIC AUDITORIUM

3,165 seats (usually reserved).
LOCATION AND BOX OFFICE
1111 California Street
San Francisco, CA 94108.
The box office at the auditorium operates only at time of presentation.
BOX OFFICE-BUSINESS TELEPHONE
(415) 776-4917.
OTHER TICKET OUTLETS All major agencies for most events.
GENERAL MANAGER Larry Stritenberger.
HANDICAPPED ACCESS Wheelchair access is through the garage level and then to the main floor level by elevator. There are no restrooms specially equipped for the handicapped. Wheelchairs are positioned on the main floor.

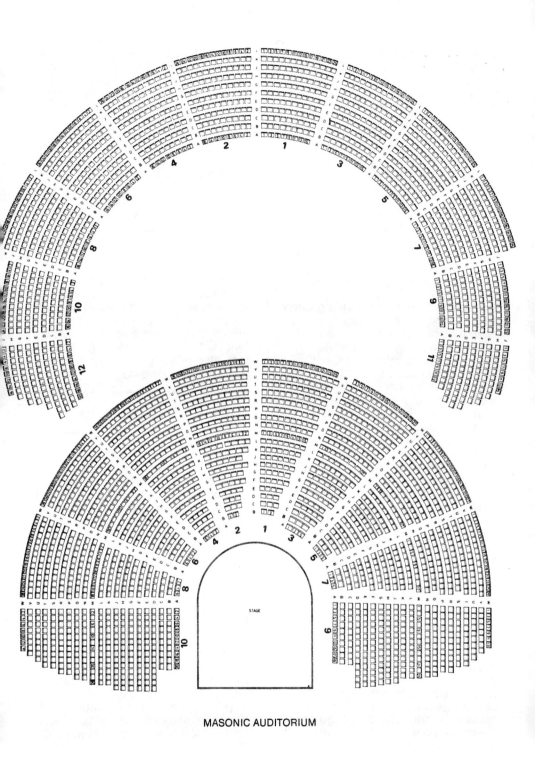

MASONIC AUDITORIUM

If you're from my generation or beyond, the phrase, "a Lucky Strike Extra," will have a pleasant meaning for you. In that spirit, I'm including a hall in this section that doesn't qualify as a theatre. But you might have occasion to attend it, so I'll give a quick "L.S. Extra" on the Masonic Auditorium. Besides, we had such a lovely seating chart done for it, it would be a shame not to use it.

Masonic Auditorium is the main rental facility in downtown San Francisco for concerts, flamenco companies, folkloric groups, travelogue film programs, and assorted variety shows presented on a one-time basis by political organizations, fraternal orders, and fundraising groups. A few of the more classical offerings have now defected to Louise M. Davies Symphony Hall (see San Francisco Performing Arts Center earlier in this section) but this is still the center for most independent local concerts or touring attractions.

Opened on St. Patrick's Day 1958, Masonic Auditorium is on the south side of California Street, on top of Nob Hill between Jones and Taylor streets. Directly across the street is Grace Cathedral, and a block east are the Fairmont and Mark Hopkins hotels. The imposing facade, with its tall, plain columns, is white Vermont marble with characteristic flowing black swirls. Spaciousness is the key to the outer lobby, dominated by a huge endo-mosaic mural. A semi-circular inner foyer leads to multiple entrance doors and stairways to the balcony and the lower-level restrooms. The stage is a simple thrust unit with no proscenium arch. The comfortable mohair theatre seats begin with a dark-brown section in the front of the house, then medium brown, and finally, light brown. The backstage hallway connects the dressing rooms with the stage area. There are no wings. The sound system is visible, with giant speaker screens mounted directly into the polished teak panels that stand forward of the brown drape covering the rear wall. A motion picture screen can be lowered from the ceiling behind this curtain, and the curtain can be drawn for showings of films. The rear wall is a continuation of the Vermont marble construction.

There is parking in the building (five floors of it), an additional public garage one block west on California, and another garage one block east. Ticket prices differ with each program and can range anywhere from $5 to $15.

On Nob Hill you can usually count on a strong wind coming up from the bay, so carry your brush or comb if you want to repair the damage after walking from one of the excellent restaurants in the area. (You may also need to repair your bank account after dinner.)

DISTRICT THEATRES

In the neighborhoods of San Francisco, there may be upwards of seventy-five little-theatre groups presenting plays, revues, musicals, mimes, and masques, or a combination of any of the above. Most of these bands of players don't appear again after the first presentation, and some just barely get past opening night before the realities of no money and no customers close them down forever. Seldom do these efforts take place in the downtown area. They may be in a hotel bar South of Market, or in a warehouse in an industrial area. Some theatrical facilities, such as Project Artaud's Studio Eremos performance space at 401 Alabama, and the Theatre Artaud at 450 Florida Street, have room for in-house work as well as rental space. Eremos (80 seats) and Artaud (200) are definitely not the settings for anything of a highly commercial nature, but provide inexpensive quarters for the development of experimental and unusual theatrical stagings (telephone [415] 552-3541 for information).

School auditoriums and storefronts break about even as choices for new theatre-company locations. There have been instances of garages and private mansions being used for presentations of theatricals. At least one former bakery (the Old Venetian Bakery Theatre, 2200 Powell Street) has tried to make a go of it near Fisherman's Wharf in the past couple of years. Parks and street corners provide unofficial, and sometimes official, theatrical production areas.

Many of the established district theatres rely heavily on grants and other funding for their existence. Much of the material presented is of limited interest and these theatres could not possibly make it on box office receipts alone. There are no theatres in the neighborhoods devoted to a diet of light comedy and old chestnuts such as you find in community theatres beyond the immediate San Francisco Bay Area. Children's theatre is sporadic, with one company having a sustained record of youth training and youth theatre. That's the San Francisco Attic Theatre at 2938 Washington (telephone [415] 929-0278).

In the following pages are listed the major theatres in the districts and the companies that occupy them.

EUREKA THEATRE

99 seats (reservations taken but not for specific seat locations).
LOCATION AND BOX OFFICE
2299 Market Street at Sixteenth Street

(Trinity Methodist Church basement) San Francisco, CA 94114.
BOX OFFICE TELEPHONE (415) 863-7133.
BUSINESS TELEPHONE (415) 863-5862.
BUSINESS MANAGER Debbie Crown.
ARTISTIC DIRECTOR Anthony Taccone.
ENSEMBLE DIRECTOR Richard E.T. White.
Equity waiver house.
HANDICAPPED ACCESS There is no access for wheelchairs. The theatre is located in a basement, down a steep set of stairs. The restrooms are small and located in a hallway with steps leading into it. The women's restroom has an additional level drop.

Unless you're a short actor, you have probably never even considered the fact that less-than-average-sized players have trouble getting parts. Well, it's true. In 1972, in the basement of the Trinity Methodist Church (in the Castro District), the Shorter Players were founded. Director Chris Silva, himself no Goliath, retained the company name for two years before changing it to the Eureka Theatre. In league with Robert Woodruff, he helped build a reputation and an audience for the theatre. By the mid-1970s the Eureka was the top community theatre in the city in the opinion of many critics.

The founders of the Eureka were dedicated to plays with social and political content, but, in their early days, they also mounted an admirable series of musicals. One of these, Rodgers and Hart's *Boys From Syracuse*, moved downtown to the Showcase Theatre and ran for better than half a year. Another Eureka play, *When You Comin' Back, Red Ryder?* became an Equity show and moved to the Little Fox Theatre (see North Beach section). Although it was financially unsuccessful, it is counted among the finest locally mounted shows of the decade.

Woodruff and Silva have since gone to New York, where they are making a considerable impact in theatre. Woodruff returns to the Bay Area annually as the guiding force of the Bay Area Playwrights' Festival. After a period of adjustment and reorganization, the Eureka blossomed out as the city's foremost presenter of contemporary British comedy and drama. More recently the emphasis has been on American classics, a smattering of new works, and West Coast premieres of contemporary American plays. Sam Shepard is a regular contributor to the Eureka repertory.

Grants have made it possible for this theatre to go from a nonprofessional status to a semiprofessional one. That means that the staff is paid and that the casts are given a stipend that provides them more with dignity than financial gain. Midnight productions and an experimental wing round out the activities at the Eureka.

The theatre has a small entrance lobby with a closet-sized box office on the left as you enter. Space is limited in this area, and many choose to sit on the stairway that leads upstairs to the church sanctuary. The restrooms and control booth are located off a hallway to the right, along with the company offices. The hall is down a couple of steps.

To enter the theatre, you must use the stairs at the end of the lobby. These take you into the basement, where the performance space can be whatever the play requirements demand. There is a small proscenium stage that may or may not be incorporated into the staging. Platforming and floor-level areas become part of the stage as needed. The seating platforms, elevated and movable, also change positions, depending on the play at hand. The chairs are the standard theatre type, aging but not uncomfortable.

Another distinguishing facet of the Eureka Theatre is that it employs more women as directors than other local theatres of a similar nature. Not that the others don't use female directors, it just isn't as regular an occurrence.

Parking is a problem, as it is all over San Francisco. You will have to fend for space on Market, Sixteenth Street, Noe, or Sanchez. All trolley and bus lines serving Market Street will let you off near the Eureka Theatre's door. Watch for the red brick church facade with the tall belltower. That's Trinity Methodist. The Eureka entrance is on the east side at the rear of the building.

There is no solid evidence that the Shorter Players ever discriminated against taller actors. As of now, the company at the Eureka Theatre is of assorted heights.

OPEN THEATER CAFE

75 seats (reservations recommended for space, not location).
LOCATION AND BOX OFFICE
441 Clement Street
San Francisco, CA 94118.
BOX OFFICE-BUSINESS TELEPHONE
(415) 386-3086.
MANAGING DIRECTOR Jack Anderson.
GENERAL MANAGER Yvonne Boggan.
HANDICAPPED ACCESS Even though this theatre is at street level, because of the cramped quarters wheelchair access is difficult. It is practically impossible to get to the restrooms (there is no special equipment) if you are confined to a wheelchair. If you can transfer to a regular seat, perhaps you'll find the experience worth the inconvenience.

In every large city there is a theatre space that has a flavor and a flare that set it apart from other operations and make it unique. In San Francisco,

OPEN THEATER CAFE

this place is the Open Theater Cafe. That's not a comment on the work that takes place there, for it varies in quality with the companies working the hall. But the theatre itself is worth a special trip.

Established in 1976 by Jack Anderson, a local high school theatre-department head and long-time entertainer in the Bay Area, it occupies a storefront building just east of Sixth Avenue on Clement Street. The street itself is about the last of the truly microcosmic neighborhoods that haven't been discovered by the tour buses. Look carefully for the small awning and the window displays that mark the theatre entrance.

Once inside, you'll confront a small ticket table, or the ducats might be dispensed from the corner of the bar. The front half of the space is all bar, with a row of tiny tables along the opposite walls. Stuck into available corners are such pieces of memorabilia as a wooden rocking horse and a perambulator. The upper portions of the walls are covered with photos and posters of the incredible number of shows and performers that have appeared here.

The standard bar ends and a more inventive one begins. The area that houses the food service is made up of bureaus and dressers (like your grandma's bedroom) snugly squeezed together. That arrangement turns a corner and halts just under an overhang that marks the beginning of the show room. During performances, a drape can be drawn here to cut off the bar sounds.

Inside is a tall room with a railed balcony on two sides and a windowed room (control booth-office-dressing rooms) on the Clement Street end. Lounge benches with leather padding cover one side at ground level, and the small tables continue to the slightly elevated stage platform. The rest of the place is filled with an assortment of unmatched tables and chairs that can be shifted around into any arrangement desired, depending on the type of show and the size of the audience. The stage ceiling is low since the playing area is tucked under the farthest end of the second story. Take the stairs to the right side and you'll find the men's restroom. The women's restroom is behind the stage (just walk across and make your debut), as is a small kitchen area.

By now you've probably surmised that you can eat at the Open Theater. It's true. There are crêpes, delicatessen plates, lasagne, sandwiches, and desserts available. Nothing fancy or heavy, but a nice light repast to accompany the entertainment course. For the eats you can spend anywhere from $1.50 to $6.00. The admission to the show will probably set you back less than $5.00, depending on the policy of the producer who is working the door the night you're there.

There's no real pattern as to what plays well as the Open Theater Cafe. Some small musical revues have run for over a year, others don't get past the second show on opening night. Plays such as *Moon Children* and *Indians* have made important contributions to the city's theatre scene at the Open, and bits of fluff such as *No Sex Please, We're British* have done little more than please lots of folks for several months. Interspersed with these standouts are the flops and fiascos that theatres are heir to.

Anderson produces and directs some of the presentations, other times he brings in guest directors, package shows, or entire companies that spend some time in residence. Considering the mortality rates of theatres that try to combine food with a smorgasbord of talent, the determination and resilience of this small-budget, small-facility house calls for admiration.

Parking is available on the streets

around the adjacent blocks, and, after 6:00 pm, there's free parking at the Lick Supermarket lot on Sixth, between Clement and Geary. There's an abundance of public transportation that drops you very close to the front door.

Speaking of a low-budget operation, there's usually little money to spend on advertising, so call and see who's filling the bill or treading the boards at the Open Theater Cafe. The room's almost never dark.

VICTORIA THEATRE

475 seats (generally unreserved).
LOCATION AND BOX OFFICE
2961 Sixteenth Street
San Francisco, CA 94103.
BOX OFFICE-BUSINESS TELEPHONE
(415) 863-7576.
MANAGING DIRECTOR Robert Correa.
ARTISTIC DIRECTOR Anita Correa.
HANDICAPPED ACCESS There is access from the street, through the lobby, and into the auditorium. Wheelchairs are placed in the front or the rear rows. There are no restroom facilities equipped for the handicapped.

Governor Brown's grandfather built this establishment in 1908. It was dubbed Brown's Opera House and featured high-class family variety shows until the twenties, when silent films and vaudeville (orchestra in the pit) shared the bill. In the 1930s and forties, vaudeville vanished, and the theatre became a neighborhood "grind" house: movies all day and into the night. Then, for a time, appropriate for its location in the Mission District, Spanish language films were featured. Next, it went from "grind" to "bump and grind" in the 1950s and sixties. Burlesque held sway, and where people once dressed up to see what was on stage, now people undressing on

stage was what people came to see. Finally, mercifully, in the mid-1970s, the house closed down.

It is interesting to follow the name changes all the way through from 1908 to the present: Brown's Opera House, the Sixteenth Street Theater, the Teatro de Victoria, the Follies Burlesque, and the Victoria Theatre.

Anita and Robert Correa took over the lease on this eyesore and refurbished it to its present state in 1979. It would have been an impossible task without help and funding from business organizations, friends, and grant foundations. What has emerged is a theatre that is available for all facets of the performing arts. Dance programs, ethnic cultural programs, musicals, comedies, dramas, touring folkloric groups—anything theatrical looking for a temporary home may wind up at the new Victoria.

The major part of the renovation of the theatre involved just getting it clean enough for human occupancy. The marquee was restored to its original condition. The box office under the marquee from the movie days was retained, the tile cleaned, and the exterior painted. Inside, the sloping lobby floor was carpeted and the refreshment stand refurbished. The red carpeting continues through the auditorium doors and down the aisles to the stage. The lobby walls are decorated with a "painted" wallpaper pattern in burgundy and brown. The walls of the auditorium and the proscenium arch carry through the same color scheme.

The theatre seats have moving backs to add to the patrons' comfort. The fabric on the seats is red, the metal and wood frames brown. The main color accent in the room is a gold lamé curtain on the stage. Dressing rooms are under the stage. The orchestra pit has been covered.

There is a balcony in the Victoria, and the total 475-seat capacity makes it the largest legitimate theatre in operation outside of the downtown area, with the exception of academic facilities. When Ionesco's *Rhinoceros* reopened the doors in 1979, it was the first live theatrical performance (as opposed to burlesque) in this durable house in 50 years.

The playhouse is just a few steps off Mission Street (east). Parking is on the street, and public transportation is handy. Muni bus lines Nos. 11, 14, 22, and 58 pass nearby, and the Sixteenth-Street BART station is at the corner.

It's an easy house to spot with its tall, vertical name sign. The Mission-style architecture, with its stucco and brick facade, blends nicely with the rejuvenation of the Mission District.

PRESENTATION THEATRE
THE LAMPLIGHTERS

---

498 seats (reserved).
LOCATION 2350 Turk Boulevard, San Francisco.
BOX OFFICE-BUSINESS ADDRESS
Lamplighters Production Center
68 Julian Avenue
San Francisco, CA 94103.
BOX OFFICE TELEPHONE (415) 752-7755.
BUSINESS TELEPHONE (415) 621-2112.
EXECUTIVE VICE PRESIDENT AND PRODUCER
Spencer Beman.
ARTISTIC ADMINISTRATOR-MUSICAL
DIRECTOR Gilbert Russak.
HANDICAPPED ACCESS There are stairs from the street to the foyer and additional stairs from the foyer to the theatre floor. There are no spaces for wheelchairs and no restroom facilities for the handicapped. The women's restroom is downstairs in the basement level.

I know, I said I wasn't going to cover academic theatres. Now, here I am writing a piece about a high school theatre. But I've got to do it; if I don't

I'll have to leave out one of San Francisco's finest theatre companies, the Lamplighters. They are the city's oldest continuous community-based nonprofessional theatre group. If you wish to be absolutely accurate, they are really semiprofessional. Certain key staff positions are paid, as are the members of the orchestra. The orchestra is on an amended pay schedule, courtesy of the American Federation of Musicians. The cast, when performing at the Presentation Theatre home base, is all volunteers. When they go on tour, as they often do to Vancouver, Kansas City, Pasadena, and Alaska, the performers are compensated. Many of the singers make a substantial portion of their income as vocalists in other mediums. The Lamplighters have also become regulars in the Stern Grove Summer Festival series (see Stern Grove section). The performers are incredibly loyal, and their longevity in principal and major supporting roles gives audiences a sense of the continuity of performance quality. Double casting is common.

The Presentation Theatre at Presentation High School was an inspired choice for the Lamplighters' showcase. For many years they were domiciled in the Harding Theatre on Divisidero, but the deterioration of the neighborhood made it unsafe at night, and the audiences began to desert the company, in spite of the fact that it had been doing superlative work since its inception in 1950.

The theatre is in an almost perfectly centralized area of San Francisco. This residential district is well lighted, and parking, though not ideal, is safe. When you enter the spotless facade you are aware that you have entered an institution that takes pride in the upkeep of its facilities. The outer foyer has a reception office, with an old-fashioned wood and glass entryway, that is used for the box office on performance nights and matinees. Go through the wooden doors in the foyer and you will find yourself in a typical high school corridor. Instead of hall monitors, there are well-dressed ushers to escort you to your seat. As you walk down the carpeted aisle, you should take note of the neoclassic flavor of the decor. A cinnamon-colored drape hangs on the proscenium. The room is done in browns, beiges, and ivory. Urns sit atop columns, and three muses, in bas relief, crown the center of the ornate arch. There is an impression of vaulted ceilings given by the alcoved and arched windows high in the side walls. These, too, are draped to match the stage curtain. The floors are wooden and in pristine condition. The seats are school-auditorium un-padded wood.

Above the main floor is a small balcony with fewer than one hundred seats. The projection-control booth occupies the middle section of this space. Looking down, you notice that there is no pit. The orchestra keeps its collective head as low as possible by using chairs with short-ened legs.

The Lamplighters are probably America's foremost practitioners of the art of Gilbert and Sullivan. Short of the D'Oyly Cart Opera company in England, you're not likely to see more spirited, colorful, or musically accurate practitioners of this highly specialized canon anywhere. They have been recognized with numerous awards and critical praise locally and nationally.

Though the staple of this theatre and this company is Gilbert and Sullivan, a tradition has been estab-lished of presenting a light opera by another composer during each sea-son. Lehar, Strauss, Menotti, Mozart, and Romberg are among those who have added a new dimension to San Francisco's only permanent resident musical theatre.

If you are driving to the Presenta-tion Theatre from almost anywhere, find your way to Geary Boulevard. From the Nineteenth Avenue end of town, turn east on Geary and travel to Masonic Avenue (staying to the right to avoid going into the tunnel and missing the turn). Turn right to Turk and right again. Within the first half block, on the right, you'll see the theatre. From downtown and Van Ness Avenue or Franklin Street, take Geary west and stay to the right to avoid the tunnel. Make a left onto Masonic and a right onto Turk and you're there. Make your Muni bus connections from all points to the No. 43, which will drop you at the corner of Turk and Masonic. The 43 crosses town from Chestnut and Scott to Mission and Geneva and back.

Top ticket prices at the Presentation for the Lamplighters are under ten dollars. The usual substantial dis-counts apply to senior citizens, stu-dents, and groups.

The name of the theatre? It has nothing to do with the fact that people present shows there: The school is staffed by the Sisters of the Presentation.

PRESENTATION THEATRE

SAN FRANCISCO REPERTORY THEATRE

80 seats (no reserved seat locations; call to verify space accommodations).
LOCATION AND BOX OFFICE
4147 Nineteenth Street
San Francisco, CA 94114.
BOX OFFICE-BUSINESS TELEPHONE
(415) 864-3305.
MANAGING DIRECTOR Lorraine DuRocher.
ARTISTIC DIRECTOR Michelle Truffaut.
Equity waiver house.
HANDICAPPED ACCESS It is necessary to negotiate two steps to get into the theatre. Wheelchair placement is possible in the auditorium on floor level. One restroom serves all and is large, but is not equipped for the handicapped.

Since 1976, when the San Francisco Rep first opened the doors to its storefront home, a great many physical changes have come about, all for the better. What was originally an ungainly, relatively uncomfortable, and somewhat shabby theatre plant has become a charming, well-thought-out performance space. It is still woefully lacking in seating capacity (an additional nineteen seats would do wonders financially), but, short of suspending chairs from the ceiling, eighty seems to be the practical limit.

The space now occupied by the San Francisco Repertory Theatre once provided food for the body as a bakery, and later served the soul as a Pentecostal Church. A steady growth of audience and reputation may make a larger facility necessary in the future, but for now the utilitarian structure at the corner of Nineteenth Street and Collingwood seems adequate.

A recent renovation gave the Rep Theatre a new box office to the immediate right as you enter the lobby. The lobby area itself seems larger, though it's not, because of the placement of the coffee bar on the far left and the addition of a gray carpet with red accents throughout, creating an illusion of more floor space. Pearl-gray walls lighten and open the room and hold production photo displays. The entrance to the small control booth is curtained, and that access is also from the box office area.

As you enter the auditorium, the single restroom is to your left. The right side of the oblong auditorium is devoted to a permanent thrust stage that has adjustable levels and can be altered in dimension and shape. To the right are three distinct elevated seating sections. The farthest one is to the side of the platform. Old-style padded theatre chairs are used for seating. The leg room isn't anything to cheer about, but, given a good show, you taller people will soon forget this minor limitation. Dressing rooms and the office and work space are upstairs in the rear of the building. Because of the steep incline of Collingwood, the door to the rear area doesn't require an outdoor stairway.

The shows presented by the Rep come closer to a standard commercial selection than those of most of the local community-based companies. Tennessee Williams, George Bernard Shaw, Arthur Miller, and Lillian Hellman are regulars. There are also new works from the London and New York stages (main-stem hits as well as off Broadway) and a smattering of new plays by unknown playwrights. An occasional midnight series on the weekend rounds out the varied and creative schedule.

The company isn't fixed, as the repertory label might imply. Open auditions are held, and guest directors sometimes spell artistic director Michelle Truffaut. Precasting, a highly intelligent practice where survival of a theatre is concerned, isn't unheard of here, or at any of these district theatres. A specific play may be selected because an actor who can handle the main role is available. Because of this policy, many of the productions at this theatre are of professional quality, even though economics make more than a token stipend impossible.

This is one of those theatres that instills more confidence the more you attend. To do so take the No. 8 Castro bus and it'll drop you at the door. Trolleys and other Market Street-traversing buses will drop you two blocks away at Market and Castro. There's a free school parking two blocks away. If you drive your car to a production at the S.F. Rep, you may have trouble finding a parking space in the residential areas surrounding the playhouse. You should have better luck a block away on Castro Street. There is also a school parking lot one block west (off Eighteenth) that has been made available to the theatre for free parking.

JULIAN THEATRE

100 to 175 (unreserved).
LOCATION AND BOX OFFICE
953 DeHaro Street
San Francisco, CA 94107.
BOX OFFICE TELEPHONE (415) 647-8098.
BUSINESS TELEPHONE (415) 647-5525.
OTHER TICKET OUTLET BASS.
GENERAL DIRECTOR Richard Reineccius.
HANDICAPPED ACCESS Ramping has been provided for entrance into the lobby from the main entrance. Wheelchairs are accommodated on floor level in the auditorium. The women's restroom is equipped for the handicapped of both sexes. New facilities in the future will provide fully equipped restrooms on the lower level of the building, accessible from sidewalk level at the side of the building.

Like so many politically oriented theatres founded in the 1960s, the Julian made its first (1965) home in a church. The parish hall of St. John the Evangelist Episcopal, at Fifteenth and Julian in the Mission District, was inadequate and too often unavailable, however, so founders Richard Reineccius, Brenda Berlin Reineccius, and Doug Giebel moved the operation, retaining the Julian name, to the Good Samaritan Center at 1292 Potrero. Production continued there for the next two years, with the emphasis on plays that commented strongly on the turbulent conflicts and changing mores and moralities of the time.

The present location, at the Potrero Hill Neighborhood Center, was occupied in July 1968, and the first play, a satire based on *Hamlet* and called *Yonder Stands Your Orphan with His Gun,* opened in the fall. The theatre operates from October to June. Often, touring companies, usually with California Arts Council grants, play the Julian when they're in San Francisco. New-playwrights' festivals are also a regular event. Premieres of new American works, along with first stagings of contemporary European plays in this country, are also prominent on the schedule.

The Potrero Hill Neighborhood House was designed by famed Bay Area architect Julia Morgan. It opened in 1922 with basically the same aims and purposes that it pursues today. Like the Julia Morgan Center for the Performing Arts in the East Bay (see Berkeley section), this building has gained official city landmark status. Wood is its primary material, with a broad front porch outside and heavy beams in the lobby and the theatre. The floors are hardwood, and a large stone fireplace holds the central focal position in the lobby. There are additional meeting rooms, a kitchen, class rooms, and so on, throughout the building, with a gymnasium on the lower level. Because the theatre is constructed on the crest of a hill, the top floor is at summit level and the full lower level where the hillside drops away.

The auditorium is extremely flexible in the movability of the seating platforms and the shape, size, and elevations of the stage platform. There is no proscenium arch, and the thrust concept is used with great imagination. The control booth is to the rear of the seating platforms, and the dressing rooms and the administrative office are on the street side of the house, to the right of the porch and main entrance.

This is a very casual theatre, and formality is carefully avoided. The seats aren't luxurious, the padding is light, and there are no decorative frills or plush intermission-area furnishings. Theatre is the main business of the Julian, and the finances and the effort are put into what the audience sees on the stage, not what surrounds it in the theatre.

This was an Equity waiver house, but that ended with the addition of seating that took its capacity well over the one hundred mark. Its union status is nebulous but the company is semiprofessional, with staff positions paid and some of the cast receiving a stipend. In addition to original works (Michael McClure is a favorite) and imports, Shakespeare is given a respectful mounting now and again. Musicals are rare.

Ticket prices are still around the six-dollar mark, with discounts available to groups, senior citizens, students, and military personnel. There are irregularly scheduled programs for children, with appropriate kiddie-sized admission scales.

If you use public transportation in San Francisco, Muni's No. 19 and No. 53 will drop you right at the door. The No. 35 will give you a two-block walk. Driving on Highway 101, take the Army Street exit, follow Army and turn right on Potrero, then follow Potrero to Twenty-third Street. Go east on Twenty-third, then north up the hill on DeHaro. The brown-shingled Julian Theatre is at the top of the hill. From anywhere else in town, go east on Sixteenth or Twenty-third streets to DeHaro, then up to the top of the hill.

BAYVIEW OPERA HOUSE

275 seats (unreserved).
LOCATION AND BOX OFFICE
4705 Third Street
San Francisco, CA 94124.
BOX OFFICE-BUSINESS TELEPHONE
(415) 824-0386.
EXECUTIVE DIRECTOR Jeanette Morris.
ARTISTIC DIRECTOR Danny Duncan.
HANDICAPPED ACCESS There is wheelchair access through the emergency exits. Though plans are in the works, at this writing the restrooms are not equipped for the handicapped or accessible to wheelchairs.

Because you have read this far, you will now be able to answer this question: What is the only San Francisco theatre facility, currently in use, that survived the 1906 earthquake and fire? It's the historical landmark located at Third Street and Newcomb Avenue: The lettering high above the double front door reads South San Francisco Opera House, 1888. That's what the Masons called the hall when they built it. The train from South of Market serviced the area, which was, those days, quite a distance from midtown.

Touring opera companies from around the West, and even a New York company or two, sang from the stage. Stars who played the opera house included David Belasco, Edward Mantell, Pawnee Bill (a rival of Buffalo Bill), and, of all people, Lydia

BAYVIEW OPERA HOUSE

Pinkham. As its use as a performance hall waned following World War I, it led a checkered career. It was at one time, for instance, a saddlery. The Masons used it as a meeting hall and rented it out to other fraternal orders for the same purpose.

Following World War II the opera house saw duty as a recreation center, a dance hall, and an economic-opportunities office. It had passed into private ownership, and it was from Arthur Viarques, in December 1971, that the city of San Francisco purchased the site for $150,000.

It would eventually cost nearly $3 million to reopen the historic doors to the public. It did so in November 1976 as part of the Neighborhood Arts Commission. It has continued to operate on a regular schedule since that date. The new name, of course, is the Bayview Opera House.

The theatre is located in a predominately black neighborhood in the Bayview-Hunters Point district. In its relatively short life as a community-oriented playhouse, it has done an admirable job of presenting theatre relevant to its immediate neighborhood. Even more impressive is the impact that the productions have had on the other areas of San Francisco, the northern San Francisco Peninsula, and the East Bay, primarily due to the efforts of the theatre's staff and to the brilliant work of artistic director-writer-choreographer Danny Duncan. His original musicals, including *Pinocchio Jones*, *Sister Girl*, and *Generations*, have showcased local black talent as no other theatre in San Francisco has.

The shows are ingeniously conceived and astutely and skillfully presented. Budgets are minimal, but energy is high. The companies are nonprofessional, often mostly teenagers. But Duncan and the material bring out the best in the performers, and the interracial audiences grow with each successive and success-ful production. The local press, slow to pick up on its impact at first, has recognized the theatre by giving it extended coverage and awards.

There is no permanent seating in the Bayview Opera House. Folding chairs are placed on the unraked, wooden floor. There is a balcony, but it is not approved for public seating; it is utilized for lighting and storage. The stage, as originally designed, was small and narrow. A large thrust apron has been added to give needed performance space. Dressing rooms are downstairs, under the stage.

The interior of the theatre is white, as is the outside. There's a brown fence around the perimeter, and the building trim is brown. The box office is located on the Third Street side, on a porch that runs most of the length of the building. If there is one problem with the facility, it is the acoustics. The auditorium is extremely "live," much of the bounce the result of the bare walls, the floor, and the metal chairs. This is a problem that is being addressed as funds become available.

Parking is on the street, as the Bayview Opera House has no parking lot of its own. Bus transportation is readily available, with the No. 44 bus dropping you a block away at Palou and Third. The No. 15 brings you directly to Third and Newcomb. From downtown San Francisco, by car, take Third Street all the way out. Coming from the East Bay, exit at Army Street, go east to Third, and turn right. From the south, take the Third Street exit off Highway 101. Marin and northern visitors cross the city on Gough, pick up the Central Freeway to James Lick-101, and exit at Army.

Because of the density of the population and the high unemployment rate in the Potrero-Hunters Point-Bayview districts, there is an extra amount of police attention paid to this area and you need have little fear in attending the theatre at night. Simply exercise the same alertness and care you would in any other urban district.

JAPAN CENTER THEATRE

1,200 seats (Las Vegas-style terraced seating; reserved or unreserved, depending on renting attraction's policy).
LOCATION AND BOX OFFICE
1881 Post Street at Fillmore
San Francisco, CA 94115.
BOX OFFICE TELEPHONE (415) 567-4820.
BUSINESS TELEPHONE (415) 346-3242.
MANAGING DIRECTOR Ron Kanzaki.
HANDICAPPED ACCESS There is a freight elevator from the Geary Boulevard street-level side for entrance to the theatre's main-floor level. There are also escalators at the main entrance on Post. The main auditorium is ramped for access to each seating level. The restrooms are equipped for the handicapped.

San Francisco's Japan Center occupies four blocks on the northern side of Geary Boulevard. The entire Japantown section is bounded by Sutter on the north and Geary on the south. The cross streets are Laguna, Buchanan, Webster and Fillmore streets. This area is mostly new construction (post 1965); the Japanese-inspired architecture provides housing and business centers for the Japanese-American community centered here. The central feature is the Peace Pagoda, the culminating point of a stone plaza devoted to pedestrian traffic, replacing a section of Buchanan Street between Sutter and Post streets. Next to the Pagoda, dedicated to eternal peace between the people of San Francisco and Japan, is an outdoor stage used for Japan Center promotions and festival presentations.

Across from the Japan Center at 1700 Post (at Buchanan) is the Kokusai Theatre, San Francisco's only Japanese movie theater. Here, along with the works of Akira Kurosawa, can be seen the films of lesser-known directors, and commercial products that may be playing concurrently in Tokyo or Nagasaki. In the Japan Center and along Post Street are some of the City's finest Japanese restaurants. The shopper can also browse through shops selling jewelry, clothing, art, and assorted souvenir items of both Japan and San Francisco.

At the eastern end of the center is the Miyako Hotel, as close to a hotel accommodation in Nippon as you'll find in the United States. Rooms can be had that offer sauna baths and sunken hot-water bathtubs for Oriental-style bathing. Shoji screens are everywhere.

At the other end of the Center, its tall stage house backed by Fillmore Street, is the Japan Center Theatre. When it was built in 1965 it was called the Kabuki Theatre, and that genre of entertainment was its sole function. Elaborate shows were mounted with Japanese casts, and the dinner-theatre arrangement of tables and chairs provided a unique setting for dining and Japanese theatre. The costs to producers and to the audience were prohibitively high, however, and the operation folded. Since then, the Kabuki has changed format and name. It is now a rental facility with no permanent production company of its own. The basic rental, sans lighting and sound equipment and union personnel to operate it, is about one thousand dollars per night.

Everything from touring stage musicals to children's theatre and drag-queen extravaganzas has graced the 48- by 132-foot main stage, with its 40-foot-diameter revolving turntable and elevating orchestra pit.

There are four levels of dressing rooms, all equipped with full bathroom facilities. To either side of the main stage are two smaller sub-stage units. They are all hung with Austrian drapes. Above the stage is a grid with batons to accommodate sixteen lines of hanging scenery. The lighting system has a five-scene preset capacity.

The decor in the theatre is a fusion of lavender and purple, with a black wall base and trim. The carpeting is in a mottled pattern of gold with purple accents, and the tables and chairs are white with purple seat pads and gold ornamentation. The carpets in the lobby are also gold and purple, but in a more formal pattern of purple squared frames encasing the traditional Japanese rosette pattern. The lobby walls are gold with purple trim. The south wall is mirrored and the east wall contains a fully equipped bar. There are chairs and cocktail tables scattered about the lobby space. Pieces of hanging art usually fill the area above the stairs and the escalators that bring you up to the lobby from the Post Street entrance. The box office is located just inside the large glass doors.

Prices for attractions at the Japan Center Theatre are as variable as the attractions themselves. Top dollar may be charged for a Japanese nightclub superstar, while an independent play may try to make ends meet with a ten-dollar tab. Each show must provide its own advertising and promotion, so, depending on the available budget, you may or may not see the current offering listed in the daily newspaper theatre pages. There is plenty of parking in the garages inside the Japan Center complex, making it unnecessary to leave the inner area from the time you park to the time you leave. This is one of the only places in San Francisco where you can park, eat, shop, and see a show all under one very long roof.

To find the Japan Center Theatre from all points simply find Geary Boulevard and travel east or west to Fillmore Street. Turn right on Post (where street parking is available) and enter the Center Garage. The presentation schedule is erratic but when something turns up that strikes your fancy, combine it with an extended visit to the entire Japantown area. You won't find anything quite like it without journeying another 7,000 miles to the west.

THE PRESIDIO PLAYHOUSE

180 seats (unreserved).
LOCATION Moraga and Montgomery Street, Presidio of San Francisco, San Francisco.
BOX OFFICE ADDRESS
Morale Support Activities
Presidio of San Francisco
San Francisco, CA 94129.
BOX OFFICE-BUSINESS TELEPHONE
(415) 561-3992.
MANAGING-ARTISTIC DIRECTOR
Donald Hess.
HANDICAPPED ACCESS There is ramped wheelchair access on the back side of the building and spaces for chairs on the unelevated floor level. There are no specially equipped restroom facilities. Some presentations are signed for the hearing impaired.

The Presidio Playhouse is as close to a true community-based, general-theatre-repertory, nonprofessional theatre as you're likely to find in the center of a large metropolitan city such as San Francisco. It's been going since 1967, first in a long, narrow, space-shy warehouse near the bay, and now in one of the best-equipped, most spacious performance spaces in town, on the wooded side of the Presidio, near the post movie theatre and the Officer's Club.

The theatre plays year-round, and the casting is open to the public, not just Army personnel. One nice part of this operation, from the theatre's point of view, is that it is a government-financed arts program. Allocations are always chancy, but this morale-building effort provides both recreation and diversion for the military and its dependents; it's not likely to be scuttled. For the public, a big plus is that you can see a full-scale show for $3.00 to $3.50. And on top of that plus, you can park on a lighted lot in a perfectly safe area, free of charge.

There are a large, cheery lobby and an even larger refreshment area for intermissions. The maroon theatre seats are mounted on a steeply elevated platform, and sight and sound are superb. You'll be impressed by the feeling of openness: a lack of being crowded, even when the auditorium is full. The "full" condition isn't rare, so call for curtain time and be early. Seating is first come, first served.

Many of the Presidio Playhouse's offerings are American standards that just don't get done anywhere else in town: *The Miracle Worker, Once upon a Mattress, The Andersonville Trial,* and so on. The way-out stuff is left to more avant-garde groups. That's not to say that there's never a *Marat/Sade* or a *Hot'l Baltimore* or a *Raisin in the Sun,* but there are also plenty of *South Pacifics, Fiddler on the Roofs* and *Mames.*

Since the reservoir of talent from which long-time director Don Hess can draw is so large, it's not surprising that the quality of the talent here is often high. What is surprising is the general technical quality of the productions. It is as good as, and often better, than that of many of the semiprofessional resident-theatre productions in San Francisco.

Finding the playhouse isn't too tough. Entering from the main gate at Lyon and Lombard, take a right curve at the lower end of Letterman Hospital where Presidio Drive becomes Lincoln. Follow Lincoln to the other side of the parade field, turn left on Montgomery, and end at the Presidio Playhouse. From the Twenty-fifth Avenue entrance, stay on Lincoln to Montgomery and turn right to the playhouse. The easiest way in is by the Arguello Boulevard entrance. There's a stop sign at the bottom of the hill. The Officer's Club is on the right, the post library on the left. Turn left for the theatre. If you get lost on the post, don't hesitate to stop a Military Police car for directions. If you violate the posted speed limits, these most courteous cops won't hesitate to stop you.

Public transportation is readily available on Muni bus lines 28, 43, and 45.

SIGMUND STERN GROVE

3,000 seats (benches; unreserved); 600 picnic area seats (reserved). LOCATION Nineteenth Avenue and Sloat Boulevard, San Francisco. MAILING ADDRESS Stern Grove Festival Association P.O. Box 3250 San Francisco, CA 94119. BUSINESS ADDRESS P.O. Box 44690 San Francisco, CA 94144. PICNIC TABLE RESERVATIONS (415) 558-4728 (Bernice Rodgers). BUSINESS TELEPHONE (415) 398-6551. EXECUTIVE SECRETARY James M. Friedman. CONCERT MANAGER Albert White. HANDICAPPED ACCESS Handicapped and aged audience members are provided with free shuttle bus service from the main entrance at Nineteenth and Sloat. One restroom for the handicapped is located backstage on level ground in dressing room No. 6.

Few cities in America can boast a wooded grove a few minutes from the heart of town where the citizenry can hear music, see plays, and bask in the summer sun, all for free. San Francisco's Sigmund Stern Grove is such a place—except that, every once in a while, the sun gets a bit overcast by a passing fog bank. But even that, in Stern Grove, is delightful.

Philanthropy has seldom benefited so many people of so many different walks of life so directly. In 1931, as a memorial to her husband, the late Sigmund Stern, Mrs. Stern (a long-time president of the San Francisco Park and Recreation Commission) donated the grove to the city and county of San Francisco. In 1938 she founded the Sigmund Stern Grove Festival Association. Over forty years later, the Association continues to produce the West's oldest seasonal arts event, the Midsummer Music Festival.

The amphitheatre is located at the bottom of a long, flat basin, surrounded by wooded hills on three sides. On the western side, the ravine continues level toward the Pacific. The foliage is thick and grandiose all around the open space that marks the stage and audience area. Eucalyptus, fir, and redwood trees soar into the sky, making the area almost undetectable from the air. Lush lawns surround the wooden benches that fill the space immediately in front of the large open stage. Behind the stage are low buildings housing the multiple dressing rooms. In recent years, the Association has equipped the Grove with one of the finest outdoor sound systems available. This ensures not only the volume of the sound, but the quality as well.

The sound is of ultimate importance since so many of the programs are purely musical. The San Francisco Opera, Symphony, Ballet, and many other local consortiums perform here for thousands of rapt listeners. Top names in jazz, pop, and Dixieland come from around the country and the world to take their turn at the Grove. Local radio and television personalities donate their time and talent as emcees, and corporations and individuals make yearly contributions to ensure that the free music in the Grove will continue. Local 6 of the American Federation of Musicians not only contributes financially from its Recording Performance Trust Fund, but also makes generous concessions in the area of rules, regulations, and pay scales. More money is added to the pot from the San Francisco Hotel Tax Fund. Finally, the audiences themselves are asked to stuff contributions into the glass jars that dot the park. A more cooperative community effort would be hard to imagine.

For those who wish to make a day of it, reservations can be made (see heading for details) for the picnic tables that occupy the raised knoll of ground directly behind the benches. These can be spoken for on the Monday before the concert you wish to attend, but call early or you'll probably miss out. If you do, bring the picnic anyhow, along with a blanket, and make your spread on the grass to the sides of the regular seating areas. The sight and sound are fine from ground level, and you have the advantage of being able to stretch out.

Dress at the Grove is whatever is comfortable for you, within the realm of good taste (even that is flexible). Expensive summer frocks mingle with bathing suits and cut-offs; polyester leisure suits sit beside patched and torn dungarees. The Stern Grove capacity is around 20,000, and on many occasions it has passed that figure by upwards of 5,000 more. It's one of the truly enjoyable summer things to do in San Francisco. It is also one of the few events that are dear to the natives and not dominated by the tourist trade.

The season begins in the second half of June and ends in late August. Performances are on Sundays only, and they begin remarkably close to on time, at 2:00 pm each week. If you are driving from anywhere, get to Nineteenth Avenue and watch for Sloat Boulevard. There's a large banner at the entrance of the Grove. Parking is on the street or in two limited-space parking lots at Wawona and Vale streets. If you're using the bus, Muni Nos. 10, 17, 18, and 28 all stop right at the corner. The M bus from West Portal stops close by, and, from Marin County, Golden Gate Transit No. 64 (out of Inverness) will drop you at the main entrance.

The concerts end no later than 4:00 pm, so since you're in the neighborhood anyway, you might want to go west on Sloat, before or after the concert, and visit the great gang of entertainers at the San Francisco Zoo.

FORT MASON CENTER

During the years of World War II, many Americans had their last look at their homeland for many years to come, or, in a tragic number of cases, forever, as their troop transport cast off from the embarcation piers at Fort Mason. Supplies, tanks, drums of fuel—they were all stacked here, waiting for transport to the South Pacific theatre of war.

Now a different kind of theatre is served by Fort Mason. In 1972 the U.S. Army turned the property over to the National Park Service. In 1975 that agency, through the management of the Golden Gate National Recreation Area, made space available to local and national cultural, arts, and environmentalist organizations. Today there are four operating playhouses in three of the major buildings, buildings that were once

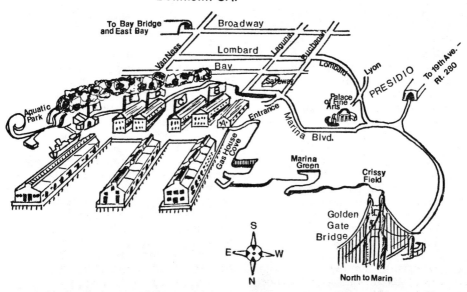

FORT MASON CENTER

warehouses and barracks: the Magic Theatre, with two playhouses in Building D; the People's Theatre in Building B; and the Actors' Ark Theatre in Building F.

I'll give you the directions to Fort Mason now; they apply to all the theatres discussed in the next few pages.

From the East Bay, once you've left the Bay Bridge, take the Broadway exit, follow it to Broadway and travel out Broadway through North Beach into Pacific Heights to Laguna Street. Turn right on Laguna and go to Marina Boulevard. You'll pass the side and front of a large Safeway market and intersect Buchanan Street. Turn right into the Fort Mason entrance. Muni bus lines 22, 30, 42, and 47 serve the Center.

MAGIC THEATRE

North theatre: 99 seats (unreserved); south theatre: 99 seats (unreserved).
LOCATION AND BOX OFFICE
Building D, Fort Mason Center
San Francisco, CA 94123.
BOX OFFICE TELEPHONE (415) 441-8822.
BUSINESS TELEPHONE (415) 441-8001.
OTHER TICKET OUTLETS San Francisco Ticket Agency and others.
GENERAL DIRECTOR John Lion.
ADMINISTRATIVE DIRECTOR Rossi Snipper.
Equity waiver houses.
HANDICAPPED ACCESS There is ramped access to the first floor of the building. Elevators to the third-floor theatres are available. The elevators also transport handicapped patrons to the first-floor men's room and the second-floor women's room.

The Magic Theatre is nationally recognized as the West Coast's prime source of works by new playwrights and by established writers who were new when the Magic gave them their first staging. Most prominent among the latter is Sam Shepard, whose *Buried Child,* a Pulitzer Prize winner, had its world premiere here, along with many other Shepard try-outs. Others who call the Magic their home away from New York are Michael McClure (also active at the Julian), Lanford Wilson, Israel Horowitz, Martin Epstein, and Adele Edling Shank.

The Magic started in Berkeley at the Steppenwolf Bar. The company's name is taken from a theatre in the Hesse novel that gave the bar its name. Crossing the bay in the early 1970s, the Magic built an indoor amphitheatre above Ye Rose and Thistle Pub at California and Polk streets. In this locale the superior work began to emerge that was to mark this troupe as San Francisco's best-known resident theatre. Another element that sets the Magic apart is a well-organized business and publicity arm that assures it of a flow of supportive financial grants and plenty of media coverage. The association of Dr. Martin Esslin (he named and defined the theatre of the absurd) as the theatre's dramaturge has added still more focus and prestige to the Magic.

The move to the bayside facilities at Fort Mason made the Magic Theatre the first organization to take advantage of the former Army-base buildings, offered at nominal rental and lease fees by the Golden Gate National Recreational Area of the National Parks Department. First creating a theatre on the south side of the third floor of Building D—a highly elevated, platformed seating area with a high stage platform—the company added the second ninety-nine—seater across the hall to the north. This theatre has a floor-level performance area surrounded by elevated seating on three sides. Both houses have lobby space and backstage dressing and workshop areas. The administrative offices are on the south side. Decor is limited to heavy fabric wall coverings to pad and soundproof the concrete walls. The lobbies display photos of current and past plays.

There's no way to discern any pattern of play scheduling. Musicals share the bill with contemporary comedies and drama and allegorical morality plays. Most of the offerings are new, but some works that have gained national or regional notoriety are presented.

Ticket prices are at the $6.00 to $7.50 level. Discounts are available to senior citizens and students. There's a lively subscription plan that also makes for savings.

THE PEOPLE'S THEATRE

99 seats.
LOCATION AND BOX OFFICE
Building B, Fort Mason Center
San Francisco, CA 94123.
BOX OFFICE TELEPHONE (415) 776-8999.
BUSINESS TELEPHONE (415) 885-2790.
EXECUTIVE DIRECTOR Susan Hoffman.
HANDICAPPED ACCESS There is a ramp on the east side of Building B for access to the first floor. From there, an elevator takes handicapped patrons to the third floor. Two restrooms are equipped for the handicapped. The men's room is on the same floor across from the theatre; the women's room is across the third floor tunnel in Building C.

Theatres dealing in the problems of urban living have generally been forced to perform on street corners, in storefronts, and in warehouses in unsafe urban areas. The spotlight that these performing groups try to throw on the flaws in our society often goes unseen because the public is afraid to brave the neighborhood where the play is being performed. That problem was solved somewhat with the establishment, in 1977, of the People's Theatre Coalition, a banding together of stage troupes who specialize in socio-political theatre pieces. The public is responding to their new theatre location.

The third-floor performance space now occupied by the People's Theatre was originally called the Marina Theatre. It's a basic performance space with folding chairs placed on a wooden elevated platform. Drapes separate the auditorium space from the refreshment-lobby area. The stage is flexible, with platform and playing areas determined by the need of each presentation. As funds become available, the lighting equipment is augmented, and the facility will undoubtedly have grown and changed even before this book reaches the stands.

What follows are thumbnail sketches of the organizations currently utilizing the People's Theatre. They are all members of the People's Theatre Coalition.

ASIAN AMERICAN
THEATRE COMPANY
An Asian-American troupe that focuses on the problems of retaining ethnic roots in modern American society. This group also has its own theatre facility and divides its performance schedule between the two houses. 95 seats (unreserved).
BOX OFFICE AND LOCATION
4344 California Street
San Francisco, CA 94118.
BOX OFFICE-BUSINESS TELEPHONE
(415) 752-8324.
HANDICAPPED ACCESS There is no access for the handicapped at the California Street theatre.

GAY THEATRE COLLECTIVE
Formerly the awarding-winning Gay Men's Theatre Collective. Lesbian performers have joined the ranks of this troupe, which presents theatre

about the gay life: its problems, victories, and rewards in the framework of a straight-dominated society.

HAIGHT ASHBURY THEATRE WORKSHOP
This company began in the Haight-Ashbury when that neighborhood was in the national consciousness. It provides a low-cost training center for politically oriented actors. The plays it produces are also presented in the neighborhoods and in public parks; the community is drawn into the entire process.

IT'S JUST A STAGE
An experimental women's theatre company that uses multimedia extensively. Other theatrical concepts employed are DeCroux mime, masks, and various forms of dance and stage movement.

LILITH
One of America's oldest and best-known women's theatre groups, their international tours have given them a world-wide reputation. Their original work, *Moonlighting,* gave them the attention that has continued to grow over the years. All of their plays are built from the contributions of the members of the collective.

MAKE-A-CIRCUS
A one-ring professional circus that takes its talents into the streets and parks. The emphasis is on self-confidence, discipline, and imagination. Members of the audience are encouraged to join in the performance and are taught rudimentary skills by the company members.

MOVING MEN THEATRE COMPANY
The development of a theatre piece takes time with the Moving Men, and when it is completed it runs for a longer time than is the case with most community-based productions. The play topics are derived from countercultural experiences.

SAN FRANCISCO MIME TROUPE
This company was born in 1959 and grew to prominence in the turbulent sixties. It is still the best-known political theatre ensemble in the country. Having realized that nothing conveys ideas better than the spoken word, the group is "mime" in name only. They are often out of the country or on the road in the United States.

TALE-SPINNERS
Theatre devoted to the telling of tales about the special circumstances and problems of aging characterizes the Tale-Spinners. The players are multigenerational and from many cultural and ethnic backgrounds. Much of their work is staged and presented in senior citizen centers.

THEATER UNLIMITED
A unique company combining able-bodied and developmentally disabled performers. Their works grow from improvisational theatre pieces based on the experiences of people with disabilities in the day-to-day world of the able-bodied.

TEATRO LATINO
This bilingual, nonprofessional company hopes to cast more light on Latino problems in the Bay Area through theatre and art. Much of its presentation format revolves around music, with political satire and protest adding strong undertones.

BAY AREA LABOR THEATRE
This collaboration of performers is drawn from both the theatre community and the labor force in the Bay Area. Their large and small productions represent modern living conditions in America.

In addition to the accommodations for the handicapped at the People's Theatre, many of the productions

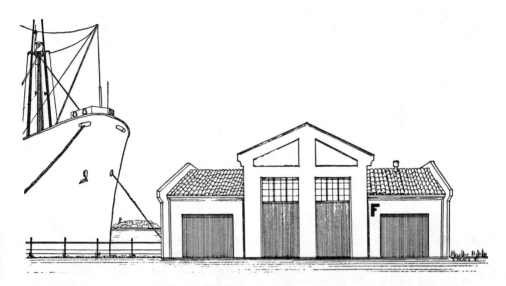

THE ACTOR'S ARK THEATRE

are also signed for the deaf.

Other frequent events at the People's Theatre are special programs, lectures, and seminars designed to address the social and political aims of the Coalition's membership. If there is one common bond beyond political philosophy and social commitment, it is the fact that so many of these groups tour locally, nationally, and internationally. Payment, even in the "professional" companies, is seldom up to accepted pay scales, and any remuneration is often little more than a token stipend.

There is no doubt that this type of theatre is outside the realm of pure entertainment and escapism. It is so by choice, and its role is one that has been important in the life of every country in the world that has allowed free expression and unbridled criticism of the government and the social structure.

THE ACTORS' ARK THEATRE

99 seats (unreserved).
LOCATION AND BOX OFFICE
Building F
Fort Mason Center
San Francisco, CA 94123.
BOX OFFICE-BUSINESS TELEPHONE
(415) 441-2453.
GENERAL MANAGER Matthew Holtz.
PRODUCING DIRECTOR Ugo Baldassari.
Equity waiver house.
HANDICAPPED ACCESS Entrance into the ground-level lobby is no problem through any one of three doors. Seats can be removed in the first row of the theatre for wheelchairs. All restroom facilities are in Building E, which is also at ground level.

It's a coincidence that the last of the old Liberty Ships, the arks that carried supplies to the beleaguered nations of the world in the years of World War II, is now berthed beside the latest theatre to join the Fort Mason Center, the Actors' Ark Theatre. It is housed in Building F, the smallest of the public buildings at Fort Mason and once the fire station for the Army post. Originally plans called for its conversion into a café. Fortunately, the plans were changed and Actors' Ark found a home.

This community-based theatre group had been a vagabond troupe for a decade before settling at Fort Mason. They were ensconced, on a temporary basis, at the Showcase Theatre, and they also set up shop for a season at the theatre at the University of San Francisco (Gill Theatre). This find-a-hall-and-use-it approach was confusing to the public; it was a new ballgame with each new production. The acquisition of a home should make things better for the Ark and its audience alike.

Because this building was a firehouse, it has two features essential to a good theatre plant: height, and open, unobstructed large rooms. By building high platforms and simple second stories, the facility has provided opportunities for inventive space design. The auditorium uses a thrust stage on an open floor space. The playing area is fronted by a steeply elevated amphitheatre with standard theatre seats and carpeted aisles. Additional seats are elevated in a shorter tier on the left side of the auditorium.

Taking the less convenient with the good, the building is without restrooms or heat. Large space heaters take the chill off the bayside structure, and the restrooms are a short walk across the parking area in the next building (E). The Actors' Ark Theatre has lobby and box office space through the northernmost door and a scene-shop storage area on the south side. There's a surprising amount of backstage room.

Tickets are around six dollars, and discounts are available to senior citizens, students, and groups. Plays are often works that are seldom produced, such as those that have fallen into the realm of literature rather than presentation. These are mixed with better-known attractions and recent arrivals from regional theatre festivals and the New York scene.

There's plenty of handy parking, and you can't miss the Actors' Ark Theatre if you follow the contour of the wall surrounding the Fort Mason Center. As you curve to the north you'll see the looming gray hull of the S.S. Jeremiah O'Brien (the Liberty Ship). You've found both arks.

NORTH BEACH

It didn't matter how bad the Barbary Coast was as long as there was at least one good guy trying to do what was right. Blackie Norton was that guy, and his Paradise Saloon at the corner of Pacific and Kearny . . . wait a minute! This sounds like a movie script. It is. Blackie Norton was Clark Gable's role in San Francisco. But the street corner's still there. It could be called the "gateway" to North Beach (some of which used to be the Barbary Coast). From there Columbus Avenue shoots off toward the bay, crossing one of the world's gaudiest streets, Broadway.

In June 1964 an exotic dancer let it all hang out at the Condor Club and "topless" was born. Five years later, off came the bottoms. Carol Doda began a whole new wave of entertainment in North Beach that spread to every city and town in most parts of America. Some communities stood for it, others didn't.

But for a few years, into the 1970s, legitimate theatre was not the big drawing card for San Francisco's Broadway.

Two houses did persevere and survive. One was on Broadway, the other almost directly behind it in the heart of the old Barbary Coast, on Pacific Street, not far from Blackie Norton's fictitious hall. Others have joined them, and, though topless and bottomless clubs still remain in business, live theatre is slowly gaining a foothold in North Beach, and in time this Broadway may be like the New York thoroughfare in more than name only.

To get to the North Beach district from the south and east, take the Broadway exit from the Bay Bridge or from Highway 101 north. That will put you at the foot of Broadway. The center of the area is three blocks straight ahead. From Marin County and north, take Highway 101 over the Golden Gate Bridge to Lombard Street, then right at Van Ness and left at Broadway. Through the tunnel and two long blocks later you're in the heart of it all, or at least in the chest region.

You may wish to eat either before or after the theatre. North Beach is famous for its Italian cuisine. For fun and a unique atmosphere, plus reasonable prices, large portions, good pasta and seconds, try the Old Spaghetti Factory on Green at Grant. For more formal dining, the food is good at Vanessi's on Broadway near Kearny. The prices are higher and the service more traditional than at the Spaghetti Factory (yes, it really was one prior to 1956). For sidewalk-café snacking and drinking, Enrico's is west on Broadway, next door to the world-famous female impersonation nightclub, Finocchio's. North on Columbus, on the west side of the street at 527, is the Golden Spike; you could encounter a line waiting here. For more elegance and higher prices, go further north on Columbus,

to Stockton and turn right. You'll be at the North Beach Restaurant's door. For a drink, a dinner, and some fine jazz musicians, continue north to Union, cross the street at the little triangular park across from Washington Square, and drop in at the Washington Square Bar and Grill. These are my favorite places, but you may drop into one of the many spots that look interesting and have a great meal; North Beach is full of that kind of adventure.

ON BROADWAY THEATRE

395 seats (reserved).
LOCATION AND BOX OFFICE
435 Broadway
San Francisco, CA 94133.
BOX OFFICE TELEPHONE (415) 398-0800.
BUSINESS TELEPHONE (415) 398-0802.
BAR OFFICE TELEPHONE (415) 421-2795.
OTHER TICKET OUTLETS Most major agencies, depending on producing company.
OWNER CONTACTS Keith Rockwell, John Guterres, Arthur Meyer, Bob Vincent.
HANDICAPPED ACCESS The theatre is located on the second floor and there is no elevator, making wheelchair access impossible. There are no restroom modifications for the handicapped.

There was a time when, if you wanted to see wrestling and boxing in North Beach, you'd climb the stairs to Garibaldi Hall at 435 Broadway. For a time after that, the same address was occupied by a Philippine social lodge. In January 1960, the auditorium began the new decade by starting a new life. It reopened, after extensive renovation, as the On Broadway Theatre. The opening show was *Under The Yum-Yum Tree,* and it was destined to run for 3-1/2 years. The On Broadway has a charm

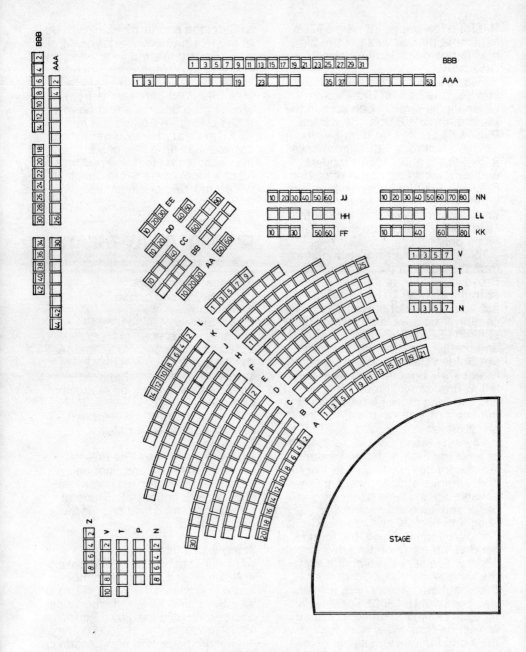

ON BROADWAY THEATRE

and an elegance that are partially derived from the decor and partially from the building itself. John Guterres, a partner in the ownership of the theatre, built the physical plant, as he would do later at the Little Fox and the Alcazar. The walls of the On Broadway, beginning at the base of the stairway that leads up from street level, are the traditional San Francisco red-flocked velour wallpaper. Old photos of bygone stage stars of the 1890s and turn-of-the-century theatre adorn the walls. The lobby itself has a floor-to-ceiling window looking out on midtown San Francisco. A large crystal chandelier dominates the ceiling.

There's a small service bar in the lobby, but, unless there is a special social function or a cast party going on, it's hardly ever used. The main bar, one of the first such services available in a modern-day San Francisco theatre, occupies a full room beyond the restrooms and the entrances to the auditorium. From this area, drinks are served by waitresses to patrons in the lobby and in the theatre as well.

Once inside the house you become aware of the high, steel-beamed hall and the balcony that rings the room, except in the far corner where a thrust stage has been nestled into the right angles formed by the walls. A deep-red Austrian-fall grand drape masks the fact that there is no proscenium arch. The lighting booth occupies a portion of the balcony to the right, and the balcony to the left has been masked with a wall to allow the actors to move from the stage to the dressing rooms unobserved.

There are three elevated boxes in the rear of the theatre and seats in the balcony above them. All of the seats are vintage theatre types, not overly padded but stable. Special racks have been fitted to the backs of the chairs to allow for the storage of drink glasses. Smoking is not permitted in the theatre, and drinks are not served during the performance.

The On Broadway is on the south side of Broadway between Kearny and Montgomery streets. There's an illuminated sign hanging over the sidewalk entrance. There's no outside box office, so you'll have to climb the stairs to purchase tickets. At night a series of upper-story window arches framed in chaser lights further identifies the spot. Downstairs is the popular new-wave music hall, the Mabuhay Gardens. Street parking is difficult, so use the lot next door or around the corner on Pacific; there's another next door to Finocchio's (America's most famous club featuring female impersonators).

Ticket prices vary with the shows and attractions, but they're usually a dollar either side of the ten-dollar mark; some touring shows go a bit higher.

If the name of this theatre is familiar to you, possibly it's because it was the 4-1/2-year home of Jon Hendricks' *Evolution of the Blues*.

LITTLE FOX THEATRE

286 seats (reserved).
LOCATION AND BOX OFFICE
533 Pacific Street
San Francisco, CA 94133.
BOX OFFICE TELEPHONE (415) 362-4430.
BUSINESS TELEPHONE (415) 788-7500.
OTHER TICKET OUTLETS Major agencies, depending on producing company.
OWNER CONTACT
Mary Alice Joyce
Sofia Properties
529 Pacific Street
San Francisco, CA 94133.
HANDICAPPED ACCESS The theatre is almost totally inaccessible to wheelchairs. There are steps up into the auditorium and elevated levels once inside. There are no restroom facilities for the handicapped.

In 1962 there were two small, inexpensive—oh, all right—shabby nightclubs sitting side by side at 533 Pacific. Owner Keith Rockwell heard that there was to be an auction of the fixtures from the demolished Fox Theater, a vaudeville-movie palace that had fallen to the wrecker's ball of progress. Thinking to have a look, Rockwell came home with $17,000 of fancy geegaws and gold-trimmed whatnots and found himself committed to building a first-class theatre. Out came the walls of the nightclubs and in went the Little Fox Theatre.

Today the Little Fox is one of the most attractive and comfortable of the small commercial houses in the city. Rockwell is no longer the owner; he sold the theatre to Frank Werber, who in turn sold it to Francis Coppola, the famed San Francisco filmmaker. The ownership may have changed again by the time you read this.

The elegant gold and white lobby features walls of French mirrors. They used to adorn the women's room at the old Fox. Those who remember that landmark claim that the restroom was larger than the entire Little Fox Theatre. The seats in the auditorium were the Fox's loge chairs, and the chandeliers once graced different areas of the fallen theatre. The stage trim and the sconces and ornamentation throughout are bits and pieces of a former glory, and all things considered, builder John Guterres made a plush mite from the mighty. The restrooms are small but clean, and there is a servicable refreshment area at the far end of the lobby. Unfortunately, there are almost no facilities for handicapped patrons.

The Little Fox has had some spectacularly successful runs on its small platform stage. Most famous was the international hit, *One Flew over the Cuckoo's Nest*. *You're a Good Man, Charlie Brown* had a respectable stay, as did the early winner, *The Fantasticks*. There have been many flops as well. One of the sadder instances of the latter was a fine staging of *When You Comin' Back, Red Ryder?* that couldn't hold out long enough for the audience to find it. This has been a problem with the Little Fox, which is hidden off the mainstream by just a block. Endurance and sufficient capital are prerequisites for success here, if history is to be heeded.

The ticket scale at the Little Fox is entirely up to the renting production company. It's safe to say, for the present at least, that the top is still under $15.00, usually about $12.50, with the bottom being in the $8.50 to $9.50 area. Parking can be a problem, though there is a lot directly across the street and another on Broadway next to the On Broadway Theatre. Some lucky people might find parking slots on the street within a six-block radius. To get to the Little Fox, follow the North Beach directions at the beginning of this section, turn down the hill toward the Transamerica pyramid, and drive one block to Pacific and then right to the theatre, which is midblock on the left. Welcome to the Barbary Coast. The building next door (to the west) used to be the Hippodrome Theatre in the good old days.

The show that opened the Little Fox? You shouldn't have asked. It was called *An Evening of British Rubbish*.

PHOENIX THEATRE

150 seats (reserved).
LOCATION AND BOX OFFICE
430 Broadway
San Francisco, CA 94133.
BOX OFFICE-BUSINESS TELEPHONE
(415) 397-3700.
OTHER TICKET OUTLETS All major agencies.

OWNERSHIP CONTACT Jim Freydberg, Roberta Bleiweiss (leaseholders). HOUSE MANAGER Mimi Sarkasian. HANDICAPPED ACCESS Because the lobby is at street level and there are no steps into the auditorium, wheelchair access is good. There are spaces for at least two chairs down front. The restrooms are not specially equipped, but access, though not ideal, is possible. Please inform the theatre of special needs when making reservations.

In the sixties 430 Broadway was a rock-and-roll night spot. For a brief time, in 1970–71, it was the showcase for a North Beach celebrity, Carol Doda. Then it went dark. No one walked the runway, and no spotlights bounced off the glitter particles in the ceilings and the walls. The mirror ball didn't revolve for the next five years. When the doors finally reopened, the mirror ball was one of the first things to disappear.

The Phoenix Theatre opened with ninety-nine seats set up in a cabaret arrangement. The runway was cut in half and an old Cole Porter show inaugurated the new Broadway showroom. *Out of This World* got a healthy run, under the direction of Donald McLean, but the economics of the street made the break-even mark tough to reach. For the next few months it appeared that the Phoenix, cursed by a series of one-night disasters, might go dark for another five years, or never reopen. McLean bounced back with a production of *Purlie* that won awards as the best musical of the year (1977) but, what with one thing and another, that show had a protracted run, the leaseholders lost the lease, and a new format was established. The house became the Phoenix Theatre of Magic. Many large cities have theatres devoted to legerdemain— why not San Francisco? There's no

answer to that question here, nor is there a magic theatre any longer. It went the way of the mirror ball, and what was left of the runway.

Next to arrive was a trio of midwesterners called the Asparagus Val-Cultural Society, and they made the Phoenix one of the most heavily trafficked theatres on the north side of Broadway since the long-running *Bullshot Crummond* played next door at the Hippodrome, a namesake of the Barbary Coast Hippodrome. (That house is no longer a theatre. There's more money to be had in a rock palace. Under the name of Stone, that's what the old Hippodrome has become.)

The cabaret setting is gone now in favor of elevated theatre seating. The hall is long and narrow, with a couple of posts, but they're no problem. The restrooms are through a hallway behind the stage. The dressing rooms, a big one and a two-person area, are back there as well. The lobby is raised on the right-hand side for a small cocktail area. The entire left side of the lobby is a bar. The license allows for beer, wine, and soft drinks. Because none of the beverages are allowed into the theatre, minors are welcome at the Phoenix.

The parking for the Phoenix is the same as for the other Broadway houses. Beware! Parking on the street itself during showtimes will almost always result in your car being towed away. Read the signs along the way. Some of the residential streets have time limits on how long you can tarry without a special parking sticker on your bumper. It's always safest to use one of the commercial lots.

Tickets for shows at the Phoenix Theatre vary in price with the individual productions, but the span is usually within two dollars on either side of the ten-dollar mark. More than likely a ten-dollar bill will get you a good seat in prime time.

CLUB FUGAZI

300 seats (cabaret arrangement; reserved).
LOCATION AND BOX OFFICE
678 Green Street
San Francisco, CA 94133.
BOX OFFICE TELEPHONE (415) 421-4222.
BUSINESS TELEPHONE (415) 421-4284.
OTHER TICKET OUTLETS All major agencies.
HOUSE MANAGEMENT Steve Silver Productions (same address as above).
HOUSE MANAGER Robert Pintozzi.
HANDICAPPED ACCESS Access is difficult to impractical. If the house is alerted when reservations are made, the manager and others will help carry a wheelchair up the front stairs. Once inside, the chair can be placed on limited space. Transfer to a regular seat is recommended. Restrooms are equipped for the handicapped.

In the strictest sense of the word, the Club Fugazi is not a theatre, but to omit it would be tantamount to omitting the name of Nob Hill from a list of San Francisco sights. You see, the Club Fugazi is, and has been since 1975, the home of the Steve Silver *Beach Blanket Babylon* series. First it was just *BBB,* then *BBB Goes Bananas,* then *BBB Goes to the Stars.* Who knows what's next? Whatever it is, *BBB* will be a San Francisco entertainment tradition for as long as Silver wishes to continue it.

The Fugazi itself was built in 1912 by a banker named John F. Fugazi. He put up $100,000 in gold to ensure that the Italian community would have an institution devoted to the propagation of education and philanthropy. As the years went by, Fugazi's bank disappeared and the hall, with its sedate, stable-looking portico, housed different functions. It was an Italian free school, a library,

the home of the Italian Benevolent Association, and, finally, a rental property handled in trust by the current ownership, the Italian Welfare Agency. Silver struck his deal with that organization, and the financial welfare has been spread around ever since. *BBB* in any and all of its manifestations is a runaway hit.

The show is a silly conglomeration of spectacular costumes, outlandish plots, and bizarre settings for some of America's most popular music. It's noise, dancing, music, and fun. Ticket demands make it advisable to order at least three weeks in advance. Around the holidays, any of them except, perhaps, Ground Hog Day, you'll need to be a first cousin of Cyril Magnin to get in if you haven't booked way ahead of time.

The interior of the Fugazi Hall is like a thousand other ethnic social halls across the nation. There's a wooden floor that is now covered, very closely, with small tables and individual chairs. In the balcony that fills the upper wall on either side there is additional seating at counterlike positions along the railing. The waiters and waitresses weave in and out throughout the performance and get to tables that seem impossible to reach except by block and tackle. The beverages served are beer, wine, and soft drinks. Because of this, minors are welcome at the Sunday matinees only (3:00 pm): No alcohol is served at that performance.

If you've come in from the north and you're on Columbus Avenue, watch for the Stockton intersection. Off Stockton, you can turn right onto Green, and just before you hit Powell you'll see the Club Fugazi on your right. There's a parking lot across the street, or turn onto Powell and go to the Powell Street Garage. Another choice is to go to Vallejo Street and turn right, and you'll find a large indoor garage next to the police station. Coming up Broadway from the bay end, turn right on Powell to Green and you're there. Street parking is possible but not probable unless you have the patience of Job.

The only thing that I can assure you of at the Club Fugazi and *Beach Blanket Babylon Doing Whatever It Is That It's Doing When You Get There* is that you'll see an audience enthusiasm that matches the mayhem on stage. You'll also witness a parade of the most fabulous hats this side of the Looking Glass.

Ticket prices: Depending on the night you choose, or the matinee, you'll pay $9, $10, or $11 per person. As with all such figures, these are subject to change. Verify prices when you call—well in advance.

CHI CHI THEATRE CLUB

140 seats (reserved).
LOCATION AND BOX OFFICE
140 Broadway
San Francisco, CA 94133.
BOX OFFICE TELEPHONE (415) 392-6213.
BUSINESS TELEPHONE (415) 392-6215.
OWNER-PRODUCER Miss Keiko.
HOUSE MANAGER Masa Neff.
HANDICAPPED ACCESS There is a low grade from the street level to the lounge. At that point aid may be required to negotiate two small steps down into the theatre. Wheelchairs can be positioned about halfway down the house in the unelevated section. Restrooms, though not specially equipped, are accessible. Note needs when calling for reservations.

Miss Keiko began her American career as an entertainer. Sally Rand had her fans, Gypsy Rose Lee her sophisticated nonstriptease; Miss Keiko was noted in Las Vegas and around the top clubs of the West for doing her exotic dancing "on point," toe shoes and all. In 1965 she decided it was time to own a club of her own. She purchased the 440 Club (across from the On Broadway), and the glamorous Japanese star became an entrepreneur.

The Chi Chi Theatre Club began with one foot in San Francisco and the other in Reno. The mini-showcase started its legit format with the Barry Ashton Revue from the northern Nevada hotel scene. As the years went by, the playbills became more and more musical-theatre oriented. The stage, though limited in floor space, is ideal for the small intimate revue that has characterized the Chi Chi's history. One of the long runs was an evening of Irving Berlin nostalgia. Satire and broad comedy are also at home in this combination cocktail lounge and theatre.

The large horseshoe bar is the first thing you'll see after you leave the closet-sized box office at the top of the entrance hallway. This area, along with the lounge walls, has become a gallery for the display of Miss Keiko's other artistic endeavor, painting. Also featured in this area are large photos of the owner as a performer.

The showroom is surrounded on both sides by high-backed leather lounges with small rectangular cocktail tables. This seating area is elevated about six inches above the main-floor level. About half of the main-floor table and chair arrangement in the center of the house is at floor level. Then, as you move back toward the rear of the house, there are elevations creating optimum sight lines in this long, narrow room. Leg space is at a premium but not unreasonably uncomfortable. There is an orchestra pit that can accommodate a half dozen musicians. Two dressing rooms, one large, one small, are backstage. Depending on the show, drinks may be served during the performance and smoking may be permitted.

Ticket prices at the Chi Chi are commensurate with other theatres in the area, and ten dollars for a good seat at a weekend performance is average.

The Chi Chi is a blend of legitimate theatre and Vegas glitter. But nowhere will you find a more gracious hostess or a more-involved theatre owner than Keiko Neff.

THE INTERSECTION THEATRE

99 seats (reserved).
LOCATION AND BOX OFFICE
756 Union Street
San Francisco, CA 94133.
BOX OFFICE TELEPHONE (415) 982-2356.
BUSINESS TELEPHONE (415) 397-6061.
EXECUTIVE DIRECTOR Jack Davis.
ARTISTIC DIRECTOR Edward Sisson.
Equity waiver house.
HANDICAPPED ACCESS Access is difficult to impractical. There are ten steps up to the auditorium. Once inside the auditorium, the seating is on stepped levels down to the floor. There are no restrooms equipped for the handicapped, and the regular restrooms are located at basement level.

The theatre facade is white stucco except for an area covered by a colorful mural. There are a tile roof and a large window with a cross worked into the glass. The building was a Methodist church from the 1940s until 1965, when it became the Intersection: a place where the arts intersect with the various cultures of the city. Set back from the street midway between Columbus Avenue and Powell Street, the facility has gone through various remodelings and transitions, and, today, though not completed or ideal, it is adequate and much used. It is still sponsored by the Methodists, but it is as

ecumenical an art center as you'll find anywhere.

On entering you are confronted with a wall of windows looking down into a spacious gallery. The ticket stand is immediately to your right. If you take the down stairway you'll pass the restroom entrances or move directly into the gallery-refreshment area. Take the up stairs to the right, make a left turn and you're in the auditorium. Inside you'll sit on dark-green padded seats that used to be in the Veterans Memorial (Herbst) Theatre before that hall was renovated. The space is plain and what is usually referred to as a "black-box theatre"—an auditorium and performance space with black walls or curtains. There is no regular proscenium stage.

The reader-board on the outside of the Intersection may announce the Traveling Jewish Theatre, a small interpretive dance company, a madcap new-wave musical, or a recreation of a nineteenth-century minstrel show. Whatever the attraction, the price of admission will be the lowest in the North Beach area. The scale seldom goes beyond $4 to $6. This does not necessarily reflect the quality of the work. The Intersection caters to small, limited-budget shows that wouldn't have a place to play if this converted church weren't open to them.

The schedule of events is varied and fast-paced. It is always best to call to find out what is on tap at any given time.

POSTSCRIPT

After taking such a concentrated look at the theatres of San Francisco, I feel that there are two problems that I need to bring to your attention.

The first, and most disturbing, is the fact that the theatres of the city and county of San Francisco have the poorest accommodations for the handicapped of all the northern California theatres that I've encountered. With the exception of newer and/or more commercial houses in the downtown area, any effort to make these accommodations is woefully absent. One or two district houses and the Fort Mason Center have made meaningful moves toward correcting the problems of access. The others, almost without exception, have the attitude that "we do the best we can." From the point of view of the handicapped who might like to attend these theatres, it isn't good enough. Perhaps some strong grant applications for these specific improvements are in order. The situation is even more distressing when you realize that some of the prime offenders are those whose format is to present plays dealing with social problems and the dilemmas of those with special needs.

Second, the price of theatre admissions: Most of the community-based houses are still under the ten-dollar mark, but that is climbing each year. The commercial prices are almost out of sight. This is a situation that isn't apt to change in the foreseeable future. Therefore, any move toward ticket-price reductions is devoutly to be wished. There is an organization at work with just that goal in mind. It's called Performing Arts Services (PAS). In the past (BPT: Before Proposition 13), PAS provided a voucher system for limited income people that gave substantial savings to ticket buyers at most of the nonprofit theatres in the Bay Area. In some instances, the voucher was accepted as payment in full at the box office. Because it was not a self-supported program, the cuts brought on by Prop 13 ended that marvelous plan for the time being.

Performing Arts Services, determined as it is to keep the arts ship from sinking, is hard at work on another project. In New York City, nestled in Times Square near the statue of George M. Cohan, is a tent. It is the location of the operation of TKTS. This isn't an abbreviation for anything; it means "tickets." Better than that, it means half-priced tickets! About noon of any performance day you can go to that Manhattan mecca for moderation in monetary managing and, based on availability, get tickets to the biggest hits on Broadway at one-half the regular cost. This shouldn't be confused with "twofers," which give you two tickets for the price of one and usually can be purchased anytime a show is on its last legs.

Why, you may ask, are you telling me this? Well, if all goes well, a service built on the lines of TKTS will soon be available to San Francisco Bay Area theatregoers. Consideration is being given to a spot in Union Square, where, as in Gotham, you'll be able to purchase half-priced tickets to dozens of commercial and nonprofit theatre presentations on the day of performance.

An attendant benefit to this plan is that, with the profits derived from the operation, and with the continued cooperation of the theatres, the PAS voucher system can be restored. So that you can keep abreast of developments, here are the particulars on this much-needed theatre support unit:

Performing Arts Services
Larry Campbell, Executive Director
1182 Market Street
Suite 311
San Francisco, CA 94102
Telephone: (415) 552-3505

Marin County

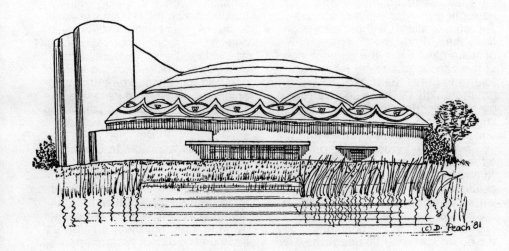

MARIN VETERANS' MEMORIAL AUDITORIUM, SAN RAFAEL

People who live in Marin County have been nonsupportive of live theatre for many years. The growth of playhouse groups was hampered by this inattention, and the quality of the plays presented was, for many years, lower than in the surrounding counties of the San Francisco Bay Area. But the theatres didn't expire from this neglect. While the general public devoted itself to other pursuits, Marin theatre devoted itself to survival—and it has survived. Many of the troupes have only a community center or a school gym to work out of, but work they do. The Marin public has ended its policy of neglect.

There seems to be a distinct movement afoot to amalgamate, consolidate, and inundate California's most talked about residential county into one of the state's most active and fastest growing theatre communities. It is hoped that this expansion will be matched with a growth in the number of performance facilities available to Marin thespians.

The College of Marin in Kentfield (take the Sir Francis Drake exit west off Highway 101) has a nicely appointed, well-equipped theatre with 604 seats. In addition to its own collegiate productions, the Department of Arts and Lectures presents comedy and musical programs and lectures by well-known actors. The box office number is (415) 485-9385 for theatre presentations, and (415) 485-9480 for the Arts and Lectures series information.

MILL VALLEY CENTER FOR THE PERFORMING ARTS

99 seats (unreserved).
LOCATION 267 Buena Vista Avenue, Mill Valley.
BOX OFFICE-BUSINESS ADDRESS
22 Miller Avenue
Mill Valley, CA 94941.
BOX OFFICE TELEPHONE (415) 383-7074.
BUSINESS TELEPHONE (415) 388-5200.
MANAGING DIRECTOR-PRODUCER
Sali Lieberman.
ARTISTIC DIRECTOR Will Marchetti and guest directors.
HANDICAPPED ACCESS There is ready entrance to the theatre from the upper parking lot next to the facility. Once inside the auditorium, chairs can be removed to make space for wheelchairs on the floor level. The restrooms nearest the concession stand are large enough for wheelchair entrance.

For my money this is the most consistently excellent theatre company in Marin. It's been at it since 1965 and has emerged as one of the better resident groups in the Bay Area (again, my opinion, although critical observations from many quarters are in agreement). The auditorium, a flexible space rented from the Park and Recreation Department of the city of Mill Valley, can be re-arranged to suit the needs of the play. In this way the stage becomes part of the audience, so that a wall with a large walk-in stone fireplace can be the focal point of the set for Arthur Miller's *The Crucible,* for example.

The acting company is made up of both professional and nonprofessional actors. The same is true of the production and directorial staffs. The blend seems to be balanced sufficiently to result in presentations that, while not always even in individual performances, have an overall ensemble proficiency.

The theatre plant is a redwood structure originally meant to be a golf clubhouse. Set on the side of a hill, with dense foliage surrounding it, it is typical of the rustic charm of Marin. The seating, on padded folding chairs, is elevated. There is a long lobby that runs the length of the auditorium, separated from it by draped doorways. The dressing rooms are behind the stage, along with the restrooms. At the opposite end of the building are a hallway with a snack bar, more restrooms, and a large open room that serves as an auxiliary lounge area. For large cast shows, this room doubles as an assembly area for the acting company.

From Highway 101 take the East Blithedale exit from the north, or the Tiburon-Belvedere exit from the south, and head west on East Blithedale to Carmelita. Carmelita ends at Buena Vista, which is where you make a left and follow the incline up to the theatre, which will be on your left. If the upper lot is full, there is additional parking on the road level.

Ticket prices are around the five-dollar mark. Performances generally take place Thursday, Friday, and Saturday.

ROSS VALLEY PLAYERS

250 seats (unreserved).
LOCATION Sir Francis Drake Boulevard at Lagunitas, Ross (on the grounds of the Marin Art and Garden Center).
BOX OFFICE-BUSINESS ADDRESS
P.O. Box 626
Ross, CA 94957.
BOX OFFICE TELEPHONE (415) 459-9937.
DIRECTOR A guest is hired for each production.

HANDICAPPED ACCESS It is difficult to get to the theatre from the front parking lot off Drake Boulevard in a wheelchair. The entrance for the handicapped is beyond the main entrance and up Laurel Grove Drive to a lot level with the theatre. Here you can enter through the cast entrance into the auditorium. There are no facilities for the handicapped in the restrooms. Call ahead to make entrance arrangements.

The Ross Valley Players may be the Bay Area's oldest community-theatre group. It started in 1930 as an offshoot of the St. John's Church couples' club. Photo records show the embryonic company performing out-of-doors on the William Kent Estate (now the Kent Woodlands), and there's evidence of production tenancy at the old Ross Community House. Since 1945, however, home for the Ross Valley Players has been the barn at the rear of the Marin Art and Garden Center. This property, too, had been a private estate, but the house has long since burned to the ground and only the auxiliary buldings remain. The beautifully landscaped area is maintained by a volunteer committee that creates and sells decorations to provide for the upkeep of this garden and park.

Variety is the key to the Ross Valley Players' play schedule. The directors are paid for their services, but the casts are purely community theatre-oriented, with volunteers filling all of the necessary production slots. Many of the leading performers in Marin County, along with visiting artists from around the Bay Area, participate in the productions, which range from classic drama to contemporary comedy—from Molierian farce to American musical comedy. The configuration of the stage, low in front and high in the rear, makes inventive set design a must. Ross excels in this area and is also very creditable in costuming.

Ticket pricing for this picturesque barn theatre is usually at the five-dollar level. Musicals can run a dollar more. The seating is elevated, and there is a charming lobby leading to a small deck for intermission chatting. Inside the auditorium proper is a large snack bar that serves coffee, juices, and homemade baked goods.

From north or south take Highway 101 to the Kentfield-San Anselmo turnoff. Follow Sir Francis Drake Boulevard through Greenbrae and Kentfield to Ross. Just beyond the Ross Community Hospital, turn right into the parking lot at the entry to the brick-walled Marin Art and Garden Center.

MARIN COMMUNITY PLAYHOUSE

245 seats (generally unreserved; depends on producing organization).
LOCATION AND BOX OFFICE
27 Kensington Road
San Anselmo, CA 94960.
BOX OFFICE TELEPHONE (415) 456-8555.
BUSINESS TELEPHONE (415) 459-5511.
EXECUTIVE DIRECTOR Ron Krempetz.
GENERAL MANAGER Coralie J. Susser.
HANDICAPPED ACCESS There are a parking facility behind the theatre and a ramp to the theatre for wheelchairs. Restroom facility improvements are under way and should be completed in early 1982. There are spaces in the front rows for wheelchairs, and adjacent theatre seats for those accompanying handicapped patrons.

For a long time the story was that the Marin Community Playhouse, located on the grounds of the San Francisco Theological Seminary (Presbyterian) in San Anselmo, was a century-old milk barn. It has now come to light that the milk barn was elsewhere on the estate and that this building is actually a gymnasium that was built about 1917. Does this mean that we shouldn't refer to the playhouse as "the barn" anymore? Au contraire! Because of the rustic, almost New Englandish, architecture, complete with wood shingles, there really isn't a term that better describes the feeling conveyed by this Marin County landmark.

Beginning as a gym, with occasional use as a public meeting hall, the structure moved into the realm of the arts in the 1960s. It was then that the Festival Theatre performances began the trend that culminated in the current fulltime activities of the center.

As the 1970s came in, more play dates and more diversified programs made the demand for a community performance space greater and greater. The College of Marin used the building as an auxiliary theatre for special summer seminars and festivals. It was still the responsibility of the seminary to maintain the property, but the ancient electrical wiring and the plumbing gave way to age and the "barn" was closed to public use until it could be brought up to safety codes.

Because a lot of people realized that this type of reasonably accessible theatre facility was essential to the artistic life of Marin, funds were raised, services and materials donated, and grants obtained so that, in 1980, the rejuvenated Marin Community Playhouse reopened under the administration of a nonprofit coalition. It has since become one of the area's most-used performance facilities. Rental bookings are sometimes made a year in advance.

Once inside the theatre, after crossing a large front porch area, you enter the lobby. The administrative office is to the right, and the box office, a simple stand, on the left. Refreshments are served in that area as well, and the entrance to the restrooms is to the extreme left. Straight ahead is the auditorium. The performance area may or may not be elevated and occupies about two thirds of the left front of the house as you enter. To the right, as well as in front of you, are the steeply platformed arena-styled seating sections. The seats are the standard theatre type.

The stage has no proscenium arch and no drape. The lighting instruments are visible at the beamed ceiling level. The limited dressing room space is to the rear and above the main seating area. Plans call for an expansion of the dressing rooms, with new restroom facilities for the performers.

What's meant by a "reasonable rental fee" for the playhouse? Here's the schedule: $55 per performance; $165 per week; and $550 per month. Rental of the lighting equipment could add a maximum of $60 to the weekly tab, and the sound system, $15 to $20 for a like period. If you're in for several days you'll need to share the utilities costs, and there may be an insurance premium. Of course, there are your own production costs, but those also apply in halls where you would pay over $500 a night to rent four walls with no power for lights.

Before you put together a year-long season and head for San Anselmo with your check, be advised that no one can rent the Marin Community Playhouse for more than two months at a clip, including rehearsal time. But even with that restriction, there aren't many Bay Area locations that can match the facility or the price.

If you're going to see an event at the theatre, or if you'd like to participate as a member of the coalition, or if you'd like to be a tenant, here's how to get there: From Highway 101 north or south, take the Sir Francis Drake Boulevard exit. You'll pass the

College of Marin and travel the wooded road through Ross. Just after entering San Anselmo, look for Bolinas Avenue and signs directing you to the San Francisco Theological Seminary. You'll pass the sign for the institution at an old turreted stone church. The next street is Kensington Road. Turn right on Kensington and follow it for a short distance to the Playhouse sign on the left. If you are handicapped, pass Kensington and take Waverly Road up behind the theatre for parking and ramp access.

From San Rafael or the coast, get to the center of San Anselmo and turn east on Sir Francis Drake. You'll see the Seminary sign at Bolinas Avenue. Follow the above directions. Golden Gate Transit buses Nos. 20, 23, 27, and 47 will bring you to the San Anselmo bus hub, and you will have a half dozen blocks to walk. The No. 20 will drop you near Bolinas Avenue, making the jaunt a couple of blocks shorter. The tree-lined street with its stately old houses makes walking or riding to the Marin Community Playhouse a pleasure.

Admission prices are set by each individual show or program, but the cost per ticket is always well under $10 and usually nearer to $5.

MARIN VETERANS' MEMORIAL AUDITORIUM

2,092 seats (reserved for most events).
LOCATION AND BOX OFFICE
Marin Center
San Rafael, CA 94903.
BOX OFFICE TELEPHONE (415) 472-3500.
BUSINESS TELEPHONE (415) 499-6396.
OTHER TICKET OUTLETS Most major Bay Area ticket agencies.
GENERAL MANAGER James Farley.
EVENTS COORDINATOR Gwen Graham.

HANDICAPPED ACCESS There is total wheelchair accessibility, with positioning for chairs on main floor. There are restroom facilities for the handicapped.

Though it is adjacent to the Frank Lloyd Wright–designed Marin Center, the master of twentieth-century American architecture didn't design this theatre. His concepts, however, were closely copied, so that all facilities in the center have a common visual effect.

The auditorium is actually two rooms. The rear half is elevated on steel scaffolding, and a folding wall can cut the performance hall in half. The decor is ultramodern and less than warm, and renovation and a general brightening would add greatly to this somewhat worn facility. The lobby offers little other than a way to get from one side of the building to the other. Rock concerts held here in the past were financially successful but took a heavy toll on the physical well-being of the theatre. It must be noted that the Marin Center and the Veteran's Memorial management are making a positive effort to upgrade the plant and the programing. The technical facilities are good, and, with careful sound engineering during performances, the acoustics are acceptable.

Many of the county's drama, musical comedy, light opera, opera, and orchestral companies avail themselves of this accessible complex. For smaller productions, the Showcase Theatre, just east of the Veterans' Memorial, is ideal.

Highway 101 is the access artery again. From the north, exit at Freitas Parkway. Coming from the south, make the turn at the North San Pedro Road exit. From both directions, once you have left the freeway there are ample signs to lead you to the Marin Center and the almost unlimited parking facilities.

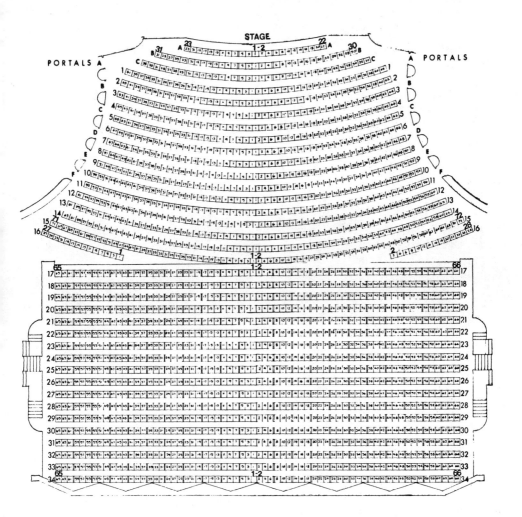

MARIN VETERANS' MEMORIAL AUDITORIUM

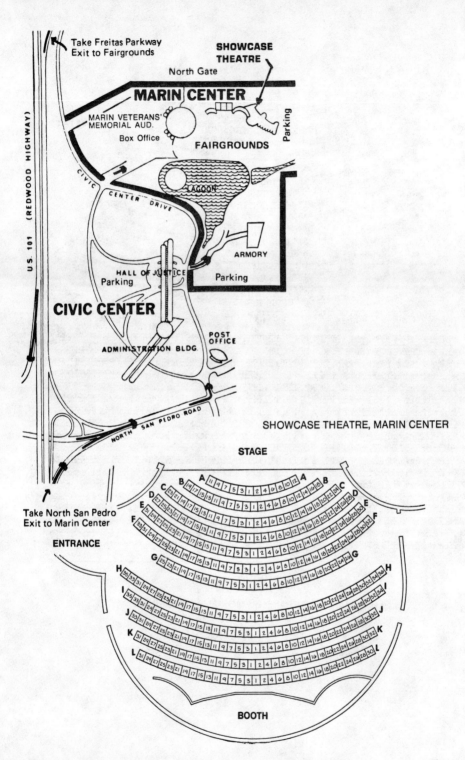

SHOWCASE THEATRE, MARIN CENTER

SHOWCASE THEATRE

340 seats (most events unreserved seating).
LOCATION The Exhibit Center on the Marin Center grounds, east of the Marin Veterans' Memorial Auditorium, San Rafael.
BOX OFFICE Same as for Marin Veterans' Memorial Auditorium, above.
HANDICAPPED ACCESS The parking lot close by the Showcase Theatre has marked parking spots for the handicapped. There is wheelchair access to the lobby and auditorium, and two wheelchair spaces in aisle positions on two lower rows. Restrooms have facilities for the handicapped.

This house has the warmth and comfort that the bigger house lacks. But it's give and take. In return for the auditorium pluses the stage takes on some minus aspects. Limited wing space and a small orchestra pit, as well as a much tighter playing area, restrict the scope of shows that can be done here. It is, however, an ideal situation for smaller, less elaborate productions.

MOUNT TAMALPAIS AMPHITHEATRE

5,000 seats (earth and stone terraces).
LOCATION AND BOX OFFICE Near the summit of Mount Tamalpais, above Mill Valley (box office open at time of performance).
BUSINESS ADDRESS
Mountain Play Association
Box 1201
Ross, CA 94957.
BUSINESS TELEPHONE (415) 388-2871.
OTHER TICKET OUTLETS Most Bay Area agencies.
PRODUCER Marilyn Smith.

ARTISTIC DIRECTOR Guests each season.
HANDICAPPED ACCESS This area has a hard-packed path for wheelchairs, specially equipped restrooms for the handicapped, and reserved parking areas for vans.

There have been theatrical productions high up on Mount Tamalpais since 1913. With a spectacular view of Marin County, the East Bay, and San Francisco in the distance, this is as near to a Greek amphitheatre as you're going to get in northern California. It's rough-hewn from rock, and you'll want to take cushions to sit on. A few gnarled trees punctuate the multiple levels that look down on the earthen stage. There are spring-fed drinking pipes at the upper extremities of the semicircle. The sun beats down but is often tempered by a cooling summer breeze. A hat and sunglasses are always in style—and wise.

Plays include great pageants and mighty battles by Shakespeare, and melodies, floating to the valley below, by Irving Berlin or Richard Rodgers. High schools graduate their seniors from this lofty perch, and hikers rest their feet and listen to the birds when no players dominate the scene.

There are special shuttle bus pickup points around Mill Valley that make it unnecessary to make the drive up the mountain. If you decide to drive your own car to the Mountain Amphitheatre, here's how to get there—and be ready for a brisk walk if you park at one of the more distant parking lots. From north or south on Highway 101, take the Stinson Beach-Muir Woods exit. Drive west to Tam Junction and turn left. From there the signs will lead you to Mount Tam and the Mountain Theatre.

Sonoma County

CINNABAR THEATER

The county directly north of Marin isn't noted for its theatrical events, unless you count Petaluma's nationally famous arm-wrestling contest as show business. There are also plenty of opportunities to watch wine being pressed and, what is even more entertaining, to savor the finished product. It should be noted that several of the major Sonoma County wineries present outdoor concerts and plays in July and August.

The most famous exports from the region, other than spirits and bubbly, are poultry and apples. The Russian River is a popular summer resort area, and the lodges there feature top northern California and national nightclub stars. There are also country music concerts, jazz festivals, and rodeos to fill the glorious summer days on the river.

The coastal portion of the county is rich in scenic splendor done many years ago by the greatest designer of them all. But anything resembling a permanent theatre facility is as rare as snow in Santa Rosa.

Speaking of Santa Rosa, it's there that Sonoma's theatre development seems to be centered. In addition to the performance spaces listed here, there is an ambitious program of summer musicals and plays presented at the Santa Rosa Junior College under the auspices of the Santa Rosa Summer Repertory Theatre (call [707] 527-4342 for the box office and [707] 527-4328 for business calls). The Luther Burbank Auditorium isn't included in this edition due to the fact that it is undergoing a major renovation program that will completely redo the theatre inside and out. That should be completed in about a year and a half (mid-1982). The Burbank is the home of the Summer Rep.

CINNABAR THEATER

80 seats (unreserved).
LOCATION AND BOX OFFICE
3333 Petaluma Boulevard North
Petaluma, CA 94952.

BOX OFFICE-BUSINESS TELEPHONE (707) 763-8920.
MANAGING DIRECTOR Marvin Klebe.
ARTISTIC DIRECTORS Marvin Klebe (Cinnabar Opera Company), Ann Woodhead (Ann Woodhead Dance Company).
HANDICAPPED ACCESS There are positions for wheelchair placement at the sides of the theatre, and the restrooms are equipped for the handicapped.

Have you wondered whatever happened to the little red schoolhouse? Well, in Petaluma it's been freshly painted cinnabar (very bright Chinese) red and turned into a miniature opera house. This schoolhouse was constructed around the turn of the century. No longer in demand as an academic entity, it now entertains its visitors with song and dance.

Two groups use Cinnabar. The Cinnabar Opera Company presents the likes of *Don Giovanni* (with a small statue), *Tales of Hoffman,* and *The Beggar's Opera.* Ann Woodhead leads her troupe of modern dancers in programs when Mozart and others are in rehearsal. Tickets are $3 to $5.

There's no lobby, but paintings and engravings are prominently displayed on the auditorium walls. The theatre seats are movable on the raked floor, while the stage area is floor level. As always, the seats carry on the cinnabar-red motif with black trim. The exterior trim, by the way, is white. The floors are wooden and the walls are brown. Anyone knows that schoolhouses don't have marquees, so a small handpainted sign in the front yard suffices.

On Highway 101, from north or south, take the Penngrove exit and travel west for about a mile. You can't miss the cinnabar-red Cinnabar Theater.

SANTA ROSA PLAYERS COMMUNITY THEATRE

250 seats (reserved).
LOCATION AND BOX OFFICE
709 Davis Street
Santa Rosa, CA 95405.
BOX OFFICE-BUSINESS TELEPHONE (707) 544-STAR (7827).
DIRECTOR Changes with each production.
HANDICAPPED ACCESS Accommodations have been made for wheelchair access, and there are specially equipped restroom facilities.

God helps those who help themselves, and the same can usually be said for civil administrations, where the arts are concerned. In Santa Rosa, self-help is paying off. In a county (Sonoma) that had almost no viable theatre facilities for performing arts groups, the artists of Santa Rosa have started things rolling.

In a school building that was new in 1922, there is now a theatre for public use. With the Sonoma County Arts Council administrating, and the performers pitching in to help, the theatre is active and growing. The two-story Spanish-flavored tile-roofed plaster facade still needs work, and the lobby is a bit drab, but tickets can be purchased. The choice of presentations is broad. For under $5 ($3 for seniors) you can see Woody Allen's handiwork one month and Gilbert and Sullivan's the next. The fall might feature flappers and the spring an English king or two. The season runs September to June.

The city of Santa Rosa has shown its appreciation to the Players by awarding the theatre a Cultural Achievement citation. The community is responding with ever-increasing crowds in the auditorium. That room has a gently raked stage that can be converted to a thrust apron. Gilding accents the restored molding that frames the arch. The seats are well-padded traditional theatre seats in red, against wall-to-wall carpeting of gold. The lobby contains both the concession stand and the box office.

A second theatre is in the offing. Again, the performers are the prime movers. The Dohn Theatre in the Community Center, run by the Department of Parks and Recreation, is under renovation. People connected with groups such as the Dancers' Workshop and the Actors' Theatre for Children are housed there, and they are putting box office receipts from their productions back into the facility. It's hard for everyone to believe that the area might have two working theatres—but it's true.

To find the Santa Rosa Players Community Theatre, take the Downtown Santa Rosa exit off Highway 101. You'll travel through an urban renewal project. Turn left on Third Street, then right on Wilson to Ninth. Go around the block, backtrack to Eighth and Davis, and you've found the theatre.

THE MARQUEE THEATRE

180 seats (caberet seating; reserved).
LOCATION AND BOX OFFICE
15 Third Street
Santa Rosa, CA 95401.
BOX OFFICE TELEPHONE (707) 545-1906.
BUSINESS TELEPHONE (707) 526-6616.
EXECUTIVE-ARTISTIC DIRECTOR Larry Nau.
HANDICAPPED ACCESS Access for handicapped couldn't be better. The facilities are so good that the theatre has been awarded a special citation by the Handicapped Society of Santa Rosa.

So far we've visited theatres that are city, county, and state historical landmarks. The Marquee Theatre is smack-dab in the midst of Santa Rosa's Old Railroad Square, a national historical landmark. This is another of several theatres that feature melodramas and olios. This one differs in that it's a professional troupe of players. It also has another characteristic that I hadn't run into before: It's not really a dinner theatre, as we know them, for served from the bar are hot dogs, popcorn, beer, tea, soft drinks, and desserts. The shows are the standard villian, hero, damsel-in-distress melodramas. There are vaudeville olios after the play. If the performers look familiar, they probably ushered you to your seat when you first arrived.

The brick facade of the Marquee Theatre was erected in 1800. The marquee of the Marquee was hung 179 years later. There's a redwood deck in front of the building, bordered with a white Victorian-style railing. Once in the front door, having purchased your ticket at the box office located under the marquee, you're in a small hallway rather than the usual lobby. This leads right into the auditorium, with its cabaret seating. The tables have Tiffany-style lamps, and there's sawdust on the floor. There's no front curtain but there are roll-drop olios. And, of course, there are the traditional old-fashioned footlights across the front of the elevated stage.

The walls are natural brick. The decor is limited to a hand-tinted display of photo blowups of the greats of the stage and screen: Lotta Crabtree, Buster Keaton, Lola Montez, the Dolly Sisters, and the Cohans. It's all very cozy and extremely family oriented. There's no reason not to take the whole tribe.

Take the Downtown Santa Rosa exit if you're arriving by Highway 101. That'll put you on Third Street. Coming in from the east (from the Valley of the Moon direction) get to the center of town and Third Street. Off the freeway, Railroad Square is just two blocks. The Marquee Theatre is on the right-hand side.

ARMSTRONG GROVE AMPHITHEATRE

1,200 seats (outdoor amphitheatre; unreserved).

LOCATION Armstrong Woods and Watson roads, Guerneville.

BOX OFFICE ADDRESS (for Arts Foundation–sponsored events only)
Russian River Creative Arts Foundation Guerneville, CA 95446.

PROGRAM INFORMATION TELEPHONE (707) 887-7720.

ADMINISTRATED BY California State Parks and Recreation Department.

INFORMATION ON RENTAL
Park Ranger Station
Armstrong Woods
Telephone: (707) 869-2015.

HANDICAPPED ACCESS There are relatively hard-packed paths for access to the amphitheatre grove. Wheelchairs can be placed forward of the first row or at the outside edges of rows. Restrooms are at ground level and are accessible.

This is one of the most beautiful outdoor facilities in northern California. Just minutes from the center of Guerneville on the Russian River, the Armstrong Grove Amphitheatre was opened in 1936. It has been used in the past for pageants, Shakespeare, weddings, reunions, and songfests. If it weren't for certain restrictions on the use permit, it might be one of the most-used outdoor facilities in the area. Imagine the Russian River Country Music Festival or the Russian River Jazz Festival among the towering, majestic, thousand-year-old redwoods.

You can imagine it but you won't see it or hear it unless it happens in the daytime. Armstrong Grove has no electricity. That eliminates most modern music, with its amplification devices. Despite these limitations it's hard to envision a more beautiful setting for an afternoon's diversion of theatre, dance, or classical music.

To get to the Guerneville-Armstrong Grove Amphitheatre area, take Highway 101 from the north or south and exit at the River Road sign, which also reads Russian River Resort Area. After about sixteen miles you will enter the town, and at the first and only stop sign you will be at Armstrong Woods Road. Turn right, and in about five miles you'll be parked in the Watson Road lot. There's a shuttle service to the grove if you're at one of the Creative Arts Foundation's events. If you're coming in from Highway 1, turn east on Highway 116 and left at the Guerneville stop sign. For information on the activities of the River Players, contact the Arts Foundation or pick up a copy of the *Russian River News* or the *Paper.*

(A trivia note: Many years ago the Guerneville area had a troupe of melodrama players who went by the name of the Stump Town Players. A young actress who worked for them for a spell was—Carol Burnett.)

RIVER PLAYERS
For the past several years Guerneville's resident theatre troupe has been working in local lodge halls and at the local movie house gone live, the River Theatre. It also appears in the above-described Armstrong Grove and at resorts, restaurants and most any other space large enough to emote in, from Rio Nido to Jenner-by-the-Sea. Given the resort atmosphere of the Russian River and the River Players' growth over the years, I wouldn't be surprised to see this nonprofessional organization stabilize in a permanent home and provide the rustic setting with a strong, regularly scheduled entertainment season.

East Bay-Contra Costa

PARAMOUNT THEATRE OF THE ARTS, OAKLAND

Once upon a time Gertrude Stein uttered what became a famous (or infamous, if you live there) line about Oakland: "There is no there, there." That may well have been true in Gertrude's time, but it certainly isn't true in the East Bay today where theatre is concerned. Professional, semiprofessional, and nonprofessional companies are growing from Oakland and Alameda to Hayward and San Leandro. Contra Costa County is extremely active. Facilities range from old walnut factories to brand new playhouses to outdoor amphitheatres. Yes, Gertrude, there really is a there, there.

In downtown Oakland, you may have occasion to visit the Oakland Auditorium Theatre at 10 Tenth Street. The ticket information numbers are (415) 451-9986 and (415) 273-3186. These numbers may also be used to gain theatre rental information. The house seats 2,002 patrons. Major agencies also handle tickets.

Because there are so many non-academic theatre presentations on the University of California campus at Berkeley, I'm going to include the necessary information you'll need to attend those performances. Zellerbach Auditorium has a capacity of 2,074 seats. The Theatre at Zellerbach is the more intimate house with just 563 seats. Ticket information for these theatres can be obtained through either the CAL Box Office (telephone [415] 642-9988) or the ASUC Box Office (telephone [415] 642-3125). Both box offices are located in the same place on the main floor of the Student Union Building.

Also on the UC Berkeley campus are the Wheeler Auditorium and the Greek Theatre. Wheeler has 779 seats. The Greek Theatre is an outdoor amphitheatre and has 8,500 seats. It is used primarily as a musical concert stage. Both of these theatres are handled by the box offices noted above.

Another theatre facility, owned and operated by the city of Berkeley until Proposition 13 made that impractical, is now controlled by the Actors' Ensemble. The much-used facility is located at Shattuck and Berryman Street in Live Oak Park, hence the name, the Live Oak Theatre. The box office number is (415) 841-5580. For rental information call (415) 526-5760.

Hayward has two college theatre facilities. Chabot College Community Auditorium at 2555 Hesperian Boulevard (zip code 94545) has 1,500 seats. Ticket information numbers are (415) 786-6800 and (415) 786-6647. The University Theatre of Cal State Hayward is located at 25800 Carlos Bee Boulevard (zip code 94542). There are 486 seats and you can have as many of them as you like by calling the box office at (415) 881-3261.

It is safe to assume in all of the above situations that the box office at the theatre is open about one hour before the performance. Since policies fluctuate so often it is always the safest practice to call for information well in advance of visiting the theatre.

Though not technically a legitimate theatre, you may want to attend a show at the Concord Pavilion. That's out on Kirker Pass Road off Highway 4, close into Pittsburg. There are 3,555 seats under the big open-air roof and an additional area for 4,500 out on the sloping lawns. The box office telephone number is (415) 798-3311. The general manager, should you ever need to contact him, is John Toffoli, Jr., and the varied programs are booked by the Shorenstein-Nederlander Organization of San Francisco and New York (see the Curran, Orpheum, and Golden Gate theatres under San Francisco Downtown Theatres).

ALTARENA PLAYHOUSE
ALAMEDA LITTLE THEATRE

177 seats (arena style; nonreserved by location, but advance reservation of a seat is recommended).
LOCATION AND BOX OFFICE
1409 High Street
Alameda, CA 94501.
BOX OFFICE TELEPHONE (415) 523-1553.
BUSINESS TELEPHONE (415) 865-2476.
MANAGING-ARTISTIC DIRECTOR Dick Shore.
HANDICAPPED ACCESS There is one level entrance from the street to the front row of the theatre. The theatre has one wheelchair location only, in the front row of Section B. Restrooms are very difficult for handicapped use.

The Alameda Little Theatre takes great pride in being called "the Granddaddy of Bay Area community theatres." Such pride is admirable, but the facts are a bit shaky. There is no doubt that the Altarena-based troupe is the oldest regularly scheduled little theatre in the East Bay. But in the Bay Area as a whole, the Ross Players (see Marin County) seem to have them beaten by a few years. Alameda raised its first curtain in 1938, Ross Valley in 1930. But if the question is one of continuity, Alameda has had only one break in the chain of company history. They, like many theatres, stopped operations from 1942 until 1946 during World War II.

Auditions for ALT productions are open to the public. There's no pay for the five shows that each bask in the light of the Kleigs for an average of eight weekends. The emphasis is on light, commercial plays and one musical a season. The policy pays off with good houses and crowds rushing in to see *Charley's Aunt, Enter Laughing,* and revivals such as Jerome Kern's *Very Good, Eddie.* They've been in their cozy arena-

theatre location for the past twenty-four years. Before that they spent eight years at the Hideaway Playhouse at Neptune Beach. The present situation is cramped for the acting company, with virtually no off-stage-back-stage space available.

Amazingly enough for a Bay Area theatre, the tickets to Alameda Little Theatre presentations are still under $5.00, usually $3.50 general and $2.00 for seniors and students. The special discounts don't apply to Saturday nights. There are group rates for all performances.

From either the Nimitz (Highway 17) or the MacArthur (Highway 580) Freeway, turn off at the High Street exit. Head toward Alameda (signs will direct you) and over the High Street Bridge. Past the second stoplight after the bridge, between Santa Clara and Central avenues, you'll see the Altarena, home of the Alameda Little Theatre. If they're not the granddaddy they're at least the great-uncle of the Bay Area's legions of community players.

PARAMOUNT
THEATRE OF THE ARTS

2,998 seats (reserved).
LOCATION AND BOX OFFICE
2025 Broadway
Oakland, CA 94612.
BOX OFFICE TELEPHONE (415) 465-6400.
BUSINESS OFFICE TELEPHONE (415) 893-2300.
OTHER TICKET OUTLETS All major agencies.
GENERAL MANAGER Peter J. Botto.
HANDICAPPED ACCESS All restroom facilities have been adapted in renovation, and there are ample wheelchair positions behind the last rows on the right and left sides of the main orchestra floor.

If you're performing on the stage of the Paramount Theatre in Oakland, you'd better be doing something worth watching. If you're not, you'll lose the audience very fast, because there's too much else to look at in this monument to Art Deco and Moderne architecture. There is literally not an inch of unadorned space in the building's public areas. In what is perhaps the most faithfully reconstructed movie palace in the country, authenticity is the watchword and "breathtaking, spectacular, amazing" are words that fall trippingly from the tongue when you first enter the incredibly high-ceilinged lobby with its elaborate grillwork and backlighting. The opulence of gold is everywhere.

Each new room, foyer, stairway, and hall is pervaded with the glamour of early Hollywood. History's fabled palaces become dim memories when you're faced with this unabashed splendor of gilded plaster and cloth of gold. Even the restrooms are elegant, almost to the point of decadence.

There's no way to drink in all of the joys of the auditorium from a seat anywhere in the house. For that you must stand on stage and look out at the sea of crimson and burnished gold. Unless you've done that in the old, long-gone Roxy Theater or the world-famous Radio City Music Hall in New York, this may be your only such experience in an American Taj Mahal dedicated to Hollywood's golden age.

Paramount-Publix, a part of that great dream factory to the south called Paramount Studios, began building showcases for its silver-screen epics in 1925. The first was in Times Square, the very same Paramount where Frank Sinatra would drive the bobby-socksers of the forties into squeals of ecstasy two decades later. It has since fallen to the wrecker's ball. Publix ended its building spree in Oakland. After a period of years in the 1950s and 1960s, when it was nip and tuck with the demolition crews, the grand old ornament closed down in 1971. Even Mickey Mouse, Donald Duck, and Bugs Bunny had given up on its ever being a jewel in the crown of entertainment again. It appeared that the Paramount was dark forever. Not so!

When the Oakland Symphony Association explored the possibility of building a new performance hall from scratch, the price tag was in the millions. In 1973, after careful studies of the feasibility of its restoration and the quality of its acoustics, the Paramount was purchased from the National General Corporation for $1 million. The renovation cost another million. On September 22, 1973, the Paramount "played again."

Noted San Francisco architect Timothy L. Pflueger is the man whose mind conceived the grandeur of the Paramount. Other commercial works of his that survive are the Top of the Mark at San Francisco's Mark Hopkins Hotel on Nob Hill, and the giant office tower at 450 Sutter Street. The culmination of his art was this theatre. (His other area theater is the Castro in San Francisco.)

In 1975 the city of Oakland took title to the Paramount, and it is now administrated by a nonprofit corporation, Paramount Theatre of the Arts. Besides being the permanent home of the Oakland Symphony and the Oakland Ballet, it plays host to privately produced film festivals, touring Broadway shows, rock star concerts, jazz and classical presentations, and business conclaves. It has even starred in a movie—well, played a supporting part anyway—*The Candidate,* with Robert Redford. The Paramount has been designated a city, state, and national landmark.

If you'd like to rent this magnificent setting for your event for one day (sixteen hours) with a minimum of

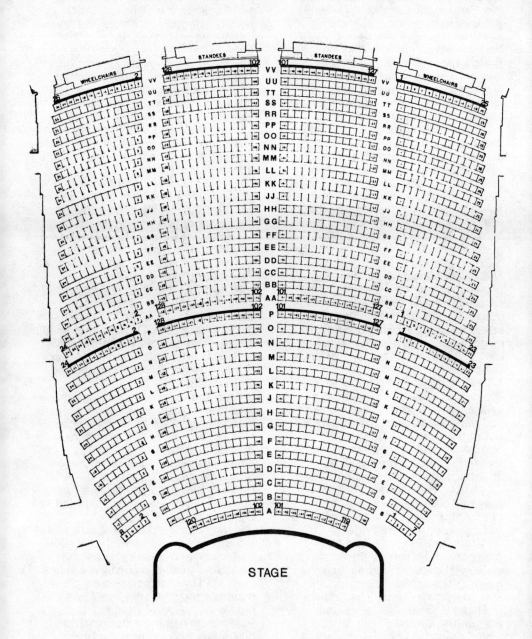

STAGE

PARAMOUNT THEATRE OF THE ARTS

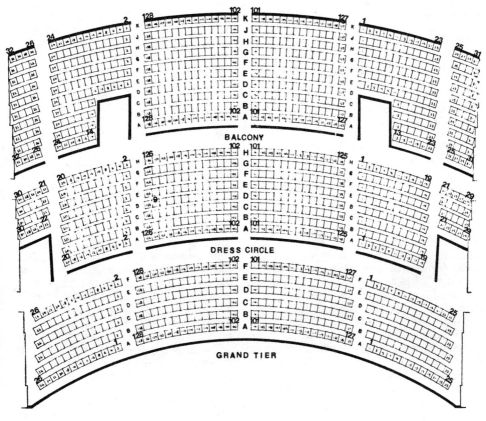

BALCONY

DRESS CIRCLE

GRAND TIER

PARAMOUNT THEATRE OF THE ARTS

equipment and no staff, stagehands, musicians, or such, figure something around one hundred dollars an hour. That's just a rough number to use for fun. If you really want to book the house, call the business number for complete details.

The Paramount Theatre is located at Broadway and Twentieth Street in midtown Oakland. From the MacArthur Freeway (580) take the Broadway exit west. From the Nimitz Freeway (17) take the Broadway exit east. There are parking garages in the area and street parking in the evening hours.

Ticket prices for events at the Paramount are at the discretion of the promoters and producers. Most are in the $10 to $20 range, but that's only a ballpark estimate. Ticket information and programing publicity are easily available in the local Bay Area press, or you can call the box office.

It's hard to believe that there won't be something in the Paramount's varied annual schedule that will appeal to you. Make your selection and then luxuriate in the glow of yesteryear. With any luck at all, you'll be serenaded by the rebuilt Wurlitzer theater organ that emerges from the depths of the orchestra pit as though by wizardry.

WOODMINSTER AMPHITHEATRE

1,500 seats (reserved).
LOCATION AND BOX OFFICE
3300 Joaquin Miller Road
Oakland, CA 94602.
BOX OFFICE-BUSINESS TELEPHONE
(415) 531-9597.
OTHER TICKET OUTLETS All major
agencies.
MANAGING-ARTISTIC DIRECTOR
H. James Schlader.
HANDICAPPED ACCESS The parking lots
are difficult because they are rough
and unpaved, so wheelchairs may
have some problems, though not in-
surmountable ones. The restrooms
are modified for handicapped use.
The only spots for placement of
wheelchairs are at the top of the
amphitheatre bowl, as the entire
theatre is stepped. Because of these
conditions, it is the policy of the
management to allow wheelchair-
confined patrons in at no charge
when accompanied by another ticket
purchaser.

The environs of the Woodminster
Amphitheatre in Joaquin Miller Park
have some of the most impressive
views of the San Francisco Bay Area
of any elevation in Oakland. It took a
WPA project two years to complete
this concrete structure (1937–39)
and it was another two years before
it was officially dedicated to the
California Writers' Association and
opened to the public. Nine months
later its entertainment career was
drastically curtailed by events at
Pearl Harbor. The postwar years saw
it in sporadic use until 1967, when
the present producers of the Woodminster Summer Musicals (the Producers Associates) took over operation of the facility.

The park and amphitheatre are
owned and operated by the city of

Oakland and a committee hired by
the Oakland Department of Parks
and Recreation. The park is named
after the famous East Bay writer and
poet, Joaquin Miller, and a replica of
his cottage can be seen on the
lower slopes of the area near the
roadway.

Heavy foliage and tall trees dominate
the surroundings at Woodminster.
The seating area consists of wooden
benches with backs. There's no built-
in cushioning, so it is highly recommended that you bring along pillows
to sit on. An additional aid to a
summer evening outing here is a
blanket, quilt, or sleeping bag; there's
often a nip in the air and the fog
rolling in from the bay can chill you
to the bone. Refreshments available
include good warming things such
as coffee and popcorn. Sight lines
are fine from every point of the
theatre, and, with the use of micro-
phones, there's no problem in hearing.

The present scheduling of summer
musicals employs a small number of
Actor's Equity principals and sometimes a star. The balance of the
casts is local nonprofessionals. There
is also full orchestral accompaniment.
The material utilized goes from light
opera to light fluff from the twenties
to shows fresh off the Great White
Way. There are three presentations
in the period from July to early
September.

Tickets, depending on location,
are from $4 to $7. Take 50¢ off for
children and senior citizens. For a
bit less than $10 to $17, you can
buy the three-show season all at
once.

If you're attuned to landmarks,
watch for one of the best in the
Oakland hills, the gleaming white-
walled, gold-roofed Mormon Temple
(largest outside of Salt Lake City) at
Lincoln near the Warren Freeway. If
you're coming from the flatlands off
Highway 5 (MacArthur Freeway) take
the Fruitvale exit and head east, up
the hill. Signs will lead you. From the

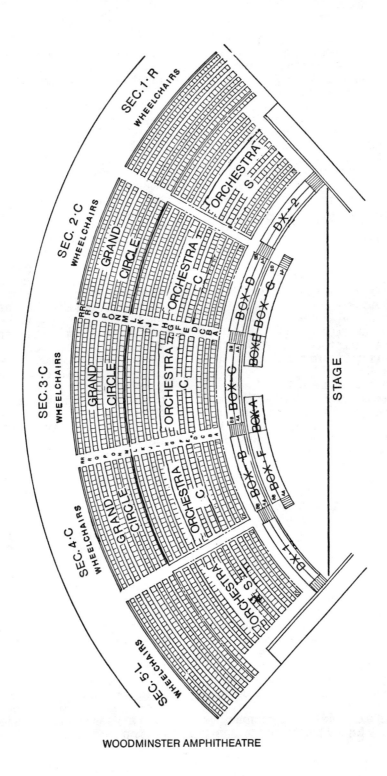

WOODMINSTER AMPHITHEATRE

Warren Freeway, take the Lincoln-Joaquin Miller off-ramp (at the Mormon Temple) and travel upward for one mile to the entrance to the park. A large sign at the entry announces the season's shows. If you'd like to enjoy a picnic dinner prior to curtain time, make reservations for the picnic facilities (free of charge) when you call to reserve your theatre seats.

BERKELEY REPERTORY THEATRE

401 seats (reserved).
LOCATION AND BOX OFFICE
2025 Addison Avenue
Berkeley, CA 94704.
BOX OFFICE TELEPHONE (415) 845-4700.
BUSINESS TELEPHONE (415) 841-6108.
OTHER TICKET OUTLETS Emporium-Capwell.
GENERAL MANAGER Mitzi K. Sales.
PRODUCING DIRECTOR Michael W. Leibert.
HANDICAPPED ACCESS The latest in facilities and considerations for the handicapped, including special Sennheiser sound amplifiers for the hearing impaired.

Of all of the theatres in northern California (academic excluded), I have seen none to compare with the new Berkeley Repertory Theatre on Addison Street just off Shattuck in downtown Berkeley. Theatre architect Gene Angell, an artist and craftsman whose skill in the theatre is well known, has created a functional facility that not only meets the needs of the productions, but also addresses the comfort and well-being of the audience. It is seldom that a theatre plant outside of the financial abilities of the academic world is as complete as the Berkeley Rep.

This is a professional company, the only Equity theatre in the San Francisco Bay Area except for the American Conservatory Theatre at San Francisco's Geary Theatre. The plays presented are from the classical to the contemporary, with only musicals excluded from the production schedule. Founded in 1968, the Berkeley Rep built its audience and its fine reputation at an ever-more-limiting small theatre on College Avenue. In 1975 it became evident to all concerned that either the old house would have to have its walls knocked out and its ceiling raised, or that serious consideration would have to be given to finding a new location and building a plant designed to fill the needs of the company. Enter Angell, the acquisition of the Addison Street site, the massive fundraising, and the grand opening of the new house on September 20, 1980. As they say, the rest is history, but, of course, none of it was easy. It was, however, an example of a concerted effort in a common cause that bore fruit in an amazingly short span of time.

The clean brick front of the Berkeley Repertory Theatre is broken only by the gold letters of the theatre's name, and the windows of the box office on the ground level and the administrative offices on the second floor. Four colorful vertical banners catch the passing breezes. The lobby is open and airy, with a skylight piercing through the second floor, bringing the outside to the center of the lobby. There's a wooden refreshment stand, a wall area devoted to recognition of patrons and benefactors, and a picture wall with the acting company's photographs and names. At the far end are the restrooms and, beyond that, the set and costume shops. There's also a space that contains a small (sixty seats) performance area for readings and rehearsals. Glass doors lead out onto a pleasant courtyard for intermission relaxation. Stairs lead upward

BERKELEY REPERTORY THEATRE

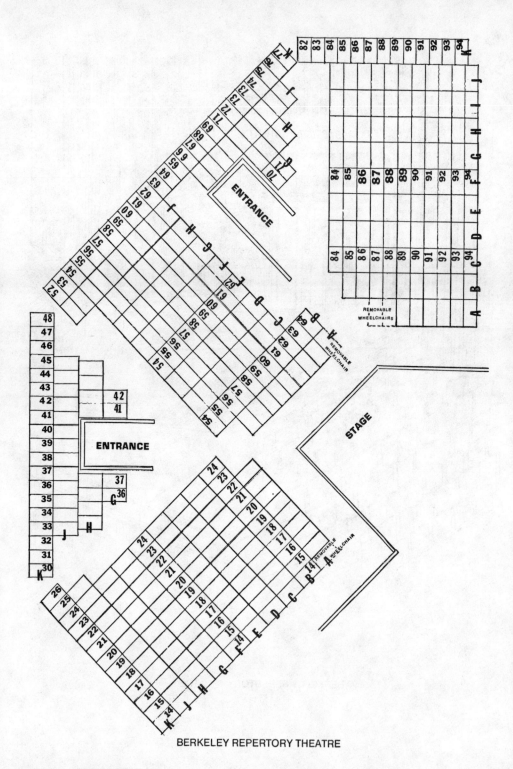

BERKELEY REPERTORY THEATRE

from there to the green room.

The auditorium has a feeling of simple richness. It's named for Mark Taper, whose financial generosity is also honored by Los Angeles's Mark Taper Forum. The carpeting is a blue, and the modernistic theatre seats are burgundy with black metal frames. They are mounted on a steep, platformed elevation. The rear row is only eleven rows from the stage. The stage is an open thrust platform with good backstage space, and entrances from the rear of the house through the audience, a common staging practice.

The price range for tickets is scaled from a modest $4.50 for previews to a top of $12.50 for opening nights. The prices charged are reasonable, indeed, for the quality of the productions.

Parking is nearby, in a large city-operated garage. Driving from most anywhere in the Bay Area, take Highway 80 to the University Avenue exit, travel toward the hills to Shattuck, turn right for one block, then right again. If you are in Oakland, San Francisco, or Berkeley, there is an abundance of choices in public transportation. The stops for both BART and AC Transit are a short walk from the Berkeley Rep front door.

For a rewarding theatrical experience on several levels, make a point of attending this excellent playhouse.

BERKELEY STAGE COMPANY

99 seats (unreserved, but seat assignments usually made at door).
LOCATION AND BOX OFFICE
1111 Addison Street
Berkeley, CA 94702.
BOX OFFICE-BUSINESS TELEPHONE
(415) 548-4728.
OTHER TICKET OUTLET UC Berkeley Box Office, (415) 642-4013.
MANAGING DIRECTOR Susan E. Daly.

ARTISTIC DIRECTOR Angela Paton.
Equity waiver house.
HANDICAPPED ACCESS The theatre is accessible to wheelchairs. The women's restroom can accommodate a wheelchair but the men's room cannot. Handicapped patrons are requested to call ahead to make arrangements.

The Berkeley Stage Company theatre is located just a few steps off San Pablo Avenue. The facility started life as an automobile maintenance garage, but since 1974 it's been a playhouse. This is another case of putting effort into what's presented on stage rather than on the theatre plant. The director of the productions, Angela Paton, is equally well known for her work as an actress, with a fine artistic reputation not only on the West Coast, but on Broadway as well.

The lobby contains a small box office, a refreshment stand, one small bench, and little else. The concrete floor has been left exposed. The stairway to the control booth and a single administrative office is next to the door into the auditorium.

Once into the performance space, there can be no permanent description of the arrangement. The seating elevations can be, and are often, moved about to suit the mood and the needs of the play. Obviously, the stage platform is a traveler as well. If the stage is removed, the performance takes place at floor level and around and about the audience. The seats are old standard theatre types. The walls are cement block (unadorned), and open beams are visible at ceiling height. Dressing room space is limited, as are set-building facilities, although large complex sets are not an issue at BSC.

Most of the plays presented are new works, mostly nonmusical, but an occasional revue or play-with-music slips in. Interesting productions of classics such as *The Great God Brown* are also mounted. Prices are

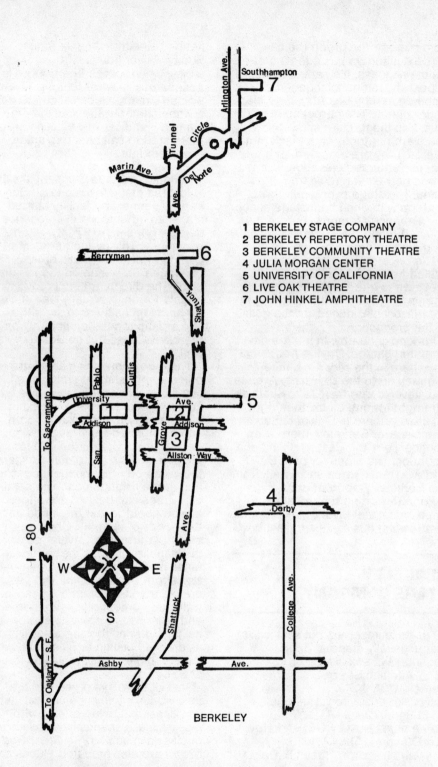

1 BERKELEY STAGE COMPANY
2 BERKELEY REPERTORY THEATRE
3 BERKELEY COMMUNITY THEATRE
4 JULIA MORGAN CENTER
5 UNIVERSITY OF CALIFORNIA
6 LIVE OAK THEATRE
7 JOHN HINKEL AMPHITHEATRE

BERKELEY

below $10, with a sampling being $7 for Friday and Saturday, $6 for Thursday and Sunday, and $5 for a preview.

The simplest directions bring you in from most areas on Highway 80. Exit at University Avenue. Go one block past San Pablo to Curtis, turn right on Curtis, go the block to Addison, turn right again, and near the end of that block, on the right-hand side, is the gray, blue, and wine facade of the Berkeley Stage Company.

JULIA MORGAN
CENTER FOR THE ARTS

350 seats (reserved admission but not specific seat location; second performance space features movable seating and the number is flexible).
LOCATION AND BOX OFFICE
2640 College Avenue
Berkeley, CA 94704.
BOX OFFICE TELEPHONE (415) 548-7234.
BUSINESS TELEPHONE (415) 548-2687.
MANAGING DIRECTOR John Maynard.
ARTISTIC DIRECTOR Leigh Lightfoot (additional directing credits accompany the outside shows that play in this facility).
HANDICAPPED ACCESS There is total access for the handicapped and one restroom fully equipped for handicapped men and women.

If you recognize the name Julia Morgan, you're absolutely right: This is the same architect who designed the Julian Theatre in San Francisco. As is the Julian, this wooden structure is a historical landmark. The first section, an assembly room-ballroom, was completed in 1908. In 1915 the building was finished as St. John's Presbyterian Church. It functioned as that institution until it was sold in 1973. In 1979 it was reopened as the Julia Morgan Center for the Arts.

The outside is Douglas fir and redwood. Beautifully finished wood continues into the interior. Because of the hazard of fire, absolutely no smoking is allowed anywhere in the building. The ceilings complete the architectural theme with open beams. The main performance space floor, as are all the other floors, is exposed hardwood. The main stage is in what was the church auditorium. Appropriately, seating is in pews. The thrust stage measures 32 by 24 feet. There's minimal masking and rear stage space. The old ballroom is the second performance area. It's a 40- by 60-foot open room. The chairs and elevations can be moved about, and the floor is the stage. Because of the Morgan's great talent for maximum space usability, the upper floor contains a grand array of small rooms for storage, offices, and so on.

The variety of attractions at the Julia Morgan covers the spectrum of drama, music, and dance. Ethnic and folkloric groups share the hall with mimes, dancers, and California Arts Council touring programs. Jazz concerts and locally produced new works are as common as lectures on any subject imaginable.

Ticket prices are geared to individual events, and sometimes additional ticket outlets are engaged, but that is rare. A ten-dollar top is as high as you're likely to pay, and it'll probably be half that, or less.

These directions depart from those for the other Berkeley playhouses. If you're taking Highway 80 from either direction, you will exit on Ashby Avenue this time. Follow Ashby to College Avenue and turn left to Derby. You'll recognize the old church facade. If you're using East Bay public transportation, AC Transit's Nos. 51 and 58 will let you off right in front of the Julia Morgan Center for the Arts door.

BERKELEY COMMUNITY THEATRE

3,491 seats (reserved or general admission; policy depends upon the presenting company's decision).
LOCATION AND BOX OFFICE
1930 Allston Way at Grove Street
Berkeley, CA 94704.
MAILING ADDRESS
2246 Milvia Street
Berkeley, CA 94704.
BOX OFFICE TELEPHONE (415) 845-2308.
BUSINESS TELEPHONE (415) 644-6863.
MANAGING DIRECTOR Judson Owens.
HANDICAPPED ACCESS There are no restroom facilities equipped for handicapped use. Wheelchairs can be placed in the rear of the auditorium or on the side aisles.

This is Berkeley's public theatre facility. It is also the largest theatre in the Bay Area. Begun as a WPA project, it bears its cement-designed look, with limited bows to the Art Deco movement. Almost every conceivable type of entertainment attraction has played this enormous hall since it opened in 1950. Because of its capacity and its availability to a large number of people, the Berkeley Community Theatre is a favorite of international dance and ballet companies such as the Royal Ballet.

Built on a two-floor plan, the bulk of the theatre seats are on the raked main floor. The two-leveled balcony is well back in the auditorium and very high. The stage is massive, with a large orchestra pit and an ample backstage and dressing room area. Because it was inspired more by a need to provide employment than by artistic demands, the theatre seems rather cold, and the pink walls with green seats and carpets in the aisle don't raise the temperature a great deal. It is, however, a very functional house and the work-horse of northern California public theatres. Events come and go with amazing rapidity.

Once again, get to Highway 80 for the quickest way into central Berkeley. (By now you may have memorized these directions.) Take the University Avenue cutoff and drive to Grove Street (about a mile and a half). Turn right on Grove and travel three blocks to Allston. Left on Allston Way will bring you to the Berkeley Community Theatre about midblock. It's on the campus of Berkeley High School.

Ticket prices are set by the individual event producers so the range can go from $4 to $25. Usually it's under half of that.

JOHN HINKEL PARK AMPHITHEATRE BERKELEY SHAKESPEARE FESTIVAL

400 seats (outdoor facility; unreserved).
LOCATION John Hinkel Park, Arlington and Southhampton, Berkeley.
BOX OFFICE ADDRESS
Berkeley Shakespeare Festival
P.O. Box 969
Berkeley, CA 94704
BOX OFFICE-BUSINESS TELEPHONE
(415) 548-3422.
OTHER TICKET OUTLETS UC box office and BASS.
MANAGING DIRECTOR Bernard Taper.
BUSINESS MANAGER Carol Zimmerman.
ARTISTIC DIRECTOR Varys with each production.
HANDICAPPED ACCESS Handicapped persons can drive directly to the amphitheatre and park close to the main stage area. Wheelchairs are accommodated forward of the first seating riser. Special restroom facilities are rented for this outdoor location.

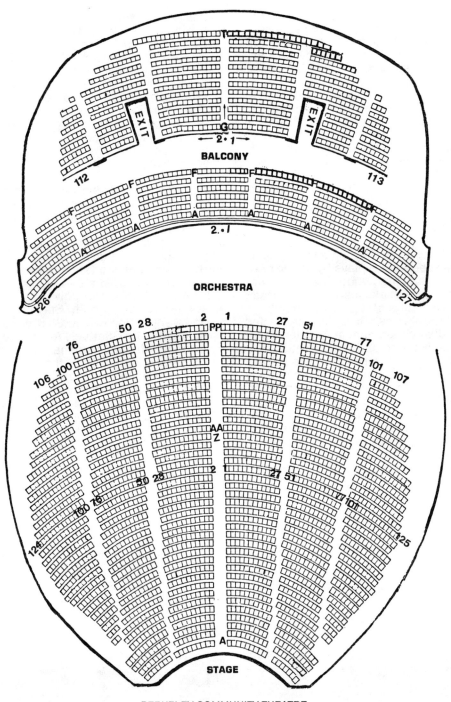

BERKELEY COMMUNITY THEATRE

The John Hinkel Park Amphitheatre is another of the WPA projects set up by the Roosevelt administration in the late 1930s. Here the building materials are not cement but stone. Each tier of seating levels has its own stonemasonry wall. The amphitheatre is one of the smaller facilities of its type in northern California, but it is this aspect, plus the tree-lined grounds and surrounding hills, that makes Hinkel an extremely pleasant and intimate outdoor amphitheatre. Parking isn't ideal—it's all streetside in a residential area—but the overall joys of the evenings make the slight inconvenience more than worth the effort.

Since 1974, July through September has seen three plays by the Bard of Avon mounted under the stars. The Berkeley Shakespeare festival has grown, through travail and many financial woes, into a highly respected, well-attended annual tradition. It is a California nonprofit corporation, a professional company whose strength lies in its concern for all the production values. Director, designers, actors, technicians, and support and administrative personnel are all selected for their excellence in their fields, and this concerted effort brings about a surprisingly good locally produced season of classic drama.

Please note that once in a while a play that's not by Will is also presented, such as *The Duchess of Malfi*.

Ticket prices hover right around the ten-dollar mark, with variations a dollar above or below, based on the evening preferred and other considerations. Since the seats are not reserved, the earlier you get there, the better the choice. I find it a great spot to go with a picnic dinner, some wine, and even the kids. Because the ground is hard, bring cushions, pillows, blankets, what have you. An ideal padding is provided by either an air mattress or the cushions from patio furniture.

AC Transit (East Bay) public buses bring you almost into the park. That's one transportation option. If you're driving from areas served by Highway 80, take the University Avenue exit at Berkeley. Stay on University all the way to Shattuck. Make a left on Shattuck. At a curve to the left this will become Shattuck Place for a block or two, then Henry. Just before the tunnel, make a right onto Del Norte. Arlington intersects at the traffic circle, and there you'll see a sign for the park. Follow the arrow up the split-level road to Southhampton and turn right into the park.

HAYWARD AREA RECREATION DISTRICT LITTLE THEATRE

250 seats (reserved).
LOCATION AND BOX OFFICE
22311 North Third Street
Hayward, CA 94541.
BOX OFFICE-BUSINESS TELEPHONE
(415) 881-6777.
MANAGING DIRECTOR Nancy McCullough.
ARTISTIC DIRECTOR Differs with each production.
HANDICAPPED ACCESS The theatre has complete wheelchair access, spaces behind the last row for wheelchair placement, and total restroom facilities.

This facility is operated by the Hayward Area Recreation District (HARD). Built in 1978, it's one of the newest theatres for public use in the East Bay. It is also one of the most attractively designed and technically well equipped—the sort of dream theatre that you'd like to own in the middle of some major city's theatre district so that you could retire in a year or two from the rental revenues.
From the outside this theatre has the characteristics of a pagoda,

HAYWARD AREA RECREATION DISTRICT LITTLE THEATRE

sharing a Japanese garden setting with a senior center. Wood is the primary structural material.

As you enter the small lobby you're greeted with photographs of past productions mounted on cork display boards. Brown remains the dominant color, but the decor moves away from the Japanese to a more modern style. Inside the intimate auditorium, multicolored theatre seats on a raked floor contrast with gray walls. A rich green front curtain closes off the thrust stage rising above a small orchestra pit. Comfort is the key to the room.

If you're a theatre buff or a performer, here's something to make you drool a bit: a backstage tour of the Little Theatre facilities. There are ample dressing rooms for male and female cast members, all with modern illuminated mirrors, restrooms, and showers. There are equipped shops for prop, costume, and set construction. There's a separate rehearsal hall. Technically, the lighting is first-rate, and the control booth features all of the latest computerized lighting control equipment. And, remember, this is a community theatre, not a professional playhouse.

Though the Japanese Gardens are closed at night, matinee patrons can have the run of them at intermission. For evening performance breaks there is a wooded area nearby. Shows produced vary from comedies and dramas to locally produced musicals. Prices are usually under five dollars, with further price breaks for senior citizens and juniors. There is ample parking in the lot located at Third and Crescent, next to the theatre.

Take the Nimitz Freeway to A Street East and follow it to Ruby Street. Turn left on Ruby to Crescent, then left on Crescent to Third and you've arrived.

TOWN HALL THEATRE DRAMATEURS

200 seats (unreserved).
LOCATION AND BOX OFFICE
Moraga Road and School Street
Lafayette, CA 94549.
BOX OFFICE-BUSINESS TELEPHONE
(415) 283-2040.
BUSINESS MAILING ADDRESS
Dramateurs
P.O. Box 216
Orinda, CA 94563.
MANAGING AND ARTISTIC DIRECTORS
Volunteer positions that change periodically.
HANDICAPPED ACCESS Because of the antique architecture and character of the building, there are practically no considerations for the handicapped, especially the wheelchair confined.

If it looks to you as if the two-story brown-shingled barnlike structure at Moraga Road and School Street should be in a rural community in the Midwest rather than in Lafayette, California, join the crowd. If you also think that it's probably the town hall, you'd only be a few dozen years wrong. When it was erected in 1913, that's exactly what it was. Now the "barn" is a county historical landmark and, since 1953, the theatrical home of the Dramateurs.

A complete range of dramatic and musical works is presented. *As You Like It* makes way for *Arsenic and Old Lace*. Another season might set *The Fantasticks* back-to-back with *The Fifth of July*. Individual directors propose projects, and each mounting has its own staff and cast. The players are nonprofessionals who get the parts through open auditions.

Once inside the small foyer of the Town Hall Theatre, you'll be looking in on a larger lobby with a black-

TOWN HALL THEATRE

and-white–squared floor. The walls, what you can see of them, are white and gold, but mostly they're covered with photo displays of past productions. The rest of the first floor contains the restrooms, a green room (where the patrons are encouraged to meet the cast after the show), and dressing rooms for the actors. There is also limited costume storage space. Speaking of limited storage space, that's the reason you sit on a throne or a Victorian settee in the lobby at intermission. It's the only place the group has to store its furniture props (necessity is the third cousin of . . . or whatever that saying is).

Once you're up the stairs that take you to the right side of the hall, follow the red carpeting to a seat either on the lower main floor or on the elevated rear section. Most of the theatre seats match, with a red and brown color scheme, but from place to place an old trouper has

expired and a maverick nonmatcher has come in as the understudy. The stage is elevated, with a proscenium arch and stage curtain. There's almost no wing space, stage right, but stage left offers more room for exits and entrances.

Ticket prices are still under five dollars, usually around $4.50. Add 50¢ for musicals, or subtract $1 if you're a senior citizen or a child under twelve.

Lafayette is one of those charming towns that are built along one main street, in this case Mt. Diablo Boulevard. The Town Hall Theatre and the Dramateurs' productions are about four blocks from the main thoroughfare. Coming off Highway 24 from the west (Oakland, Berkeley, San Francisco) take the Oakhill exit and turn left on Mt. Diablo. From the east on 24 (Concord, Walnut Creek) turn off on the Central Lafayette exit and turn right on Mt. Diablo. After two blocks you'll see Moraga Road.

You can only turn one way there or you'll be in someone's store. Four blocks down you'll see the elementary school that gave School Street its name. Park. You've arrived.

If you're hungry when you visit Lafayette, one of my favorite stops there is Petar's, located on that very same Mt. Diablo Boulevard you've just heard so much about.

CIVIC ARTS THEATRE

449 seats (reserved).
LOCATION AND BOX OFFICE
1641 Locust Street
Walnut Creek, CA 94596.
BOX OFFICE TELEPHONE (415) 943-5862.
BUSINESS TELEPHONE (415) 943-5866.
MANAGING DIRECTOR Scott Dennison.
ARTISTIC DIRECTOR Each working group has its own.
HANDICAPPED ACCESS There is practically no access for the handicapped. The entrance to the theatre and the theatre itself are a series of steps and levels. There are no facilities for the handicapped in the restrooms.

There may be bigger and newer theatres in the San Francisco Bay Area but I know of none that are in more constant use nor any that have the Sold Out sign hanging at the box office more often. Housed in a converted walnut storage and processing warehouse, the Walnut Creek Civic Arts Theatre has been one of the most successful city-owned and -operated artist centers in northern California for more than a decade because of careful administration. Equally important has been the consistently high quality of the local theatre groups that utilize the limited-stage facility (limited wing and backstage space and no fly-loft) and the audiences that regularly fill the seats. Musicals, as in most locations, are the biggest draw, but straight plays do well also. One-nighters and concerts are common.

The Civic Arts Theatre is almost completely surrounded by parking lots. You'll probably never walk more than a block regardless of the size of the crowd. Once inside the clean, white-plaster, oak-floored lobby you'll be facing the box office and the auditorium entrance. As noted above, the stairs and the steep elevation of the theatre make wheelchair access virtually impossible and entry by the very elderly and the handicapped difficult at best.

The auditorium seating is comfortable, with good sight lines and unamplified sound. Heavy rain on the roof can create the illusion of a snare drum school, but that is a rare happening. There's a good-sized orchestra pit for the big instrumental accompaniment that is typical of the musicals done here. Most shows run from fifteen to twenty weekend performances.

Immediate plans call for the construction of a new theatre complex for Walnut Creek. All of the deficiencies of this make-do house will be corrected, and access for the handicapped will be assured.

You may want to arrive a bit early for the show or visit the building during the day. Reason? There is an extensive art gallery and gift shop just off the lobby featuring the works of local artists and craftspersons. Also, look at the lobby floor carefully, and see if you can detect the marks of scales once used for weighing walnuts in this historic building. If you want to use public transportation to get there, the Walnut Creek Bart Station is only three blocks away.

From Highway 680, turn off at the Ignacio Valley Road exit and travel toward downtown (east). At North California Boulevard, turn right. In three blocks you're at Locust Street. Turn left for parking and you're there.

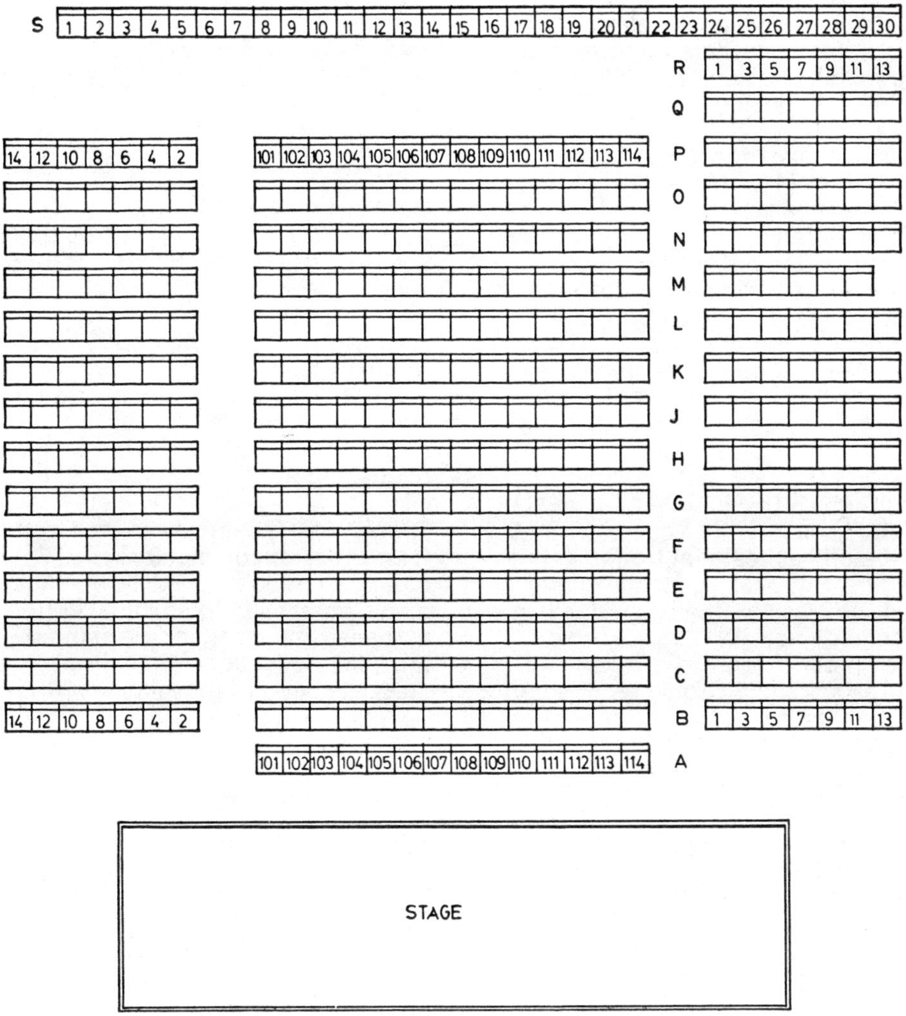

CIVIC ARTS THEATRE

The primary users of the Civic Arts Theatre are:

DIABLO LIGHT OPERA COMPANY (DLOC)
The oldest of the Contra Costa-based musical theatre companies, DLOC presents two major shows a year. Usually these are modern musical comedies, but this organization isn't afraid to tackle an operetta or two. Large casts are obtained through open auditions. Producers, officers, and directors change with elections and individual shows.
CONTACT Greta Eagan
TELEPHONES (415) 837-5255 and (415) 930-6375

CONTRA COSTA MUSICAL THEATRE (CCMT)
An off-shoot of the original DLOC group, the two groups interchange staff members and casts while main-

taining separate administrations and nonprofit corporate structures. Casting here is also open to the public. Some staff positions, as with DLOC, are paid.

MANAGING DIRECTOR Clay Englar
TELEPHONE (415) 687-0321
MAILING ADDRESS
 1601 Broadway
Concord, CA 94520
 The above address is a costume storage facility. A large and well-kept collection of every conceivable type of costume is available for individual or ensemble rental by schools and other musical comedy-producing organizations.

CIVIC ARTS REPERTORY COMPANY
A city-sponsored rep company that is the official resident troupe in this theatre. Specializing mostly in drama and the classics, they also throw in a comedy now and then for spice. They present four plays a year. All correspondence should be directed to the theatre.
PRODUCER Jay Hornbacher
TELEPHONE (415) 943-5865

WILLOWS THEATRE

198 seats (reserved).
LOCATION AND BOX OFFICE
1975 Diamond Boulevard
Concord, CA 94520.
BOX OFFICE TELEPHONE (415) 798-6525.
BUSINESS TELEPHONE (415) 671-3065.
THEATRE PROGRAMS SUPERVISOR
James L. Jester.
ARTISTIC DIRECTOR Newly appointed for each production.
HANDICAPPED ACCESS The theatre has complete wheelchair access and restroom facilities equipped for the handicapped.

The Willows Theatre joined the Contra Costa theatre community in 1977. Ideally situated in the Willows Shopping Center with acres of parking and easy access from all around the area, its productions are geared to musical comedy presentations. There

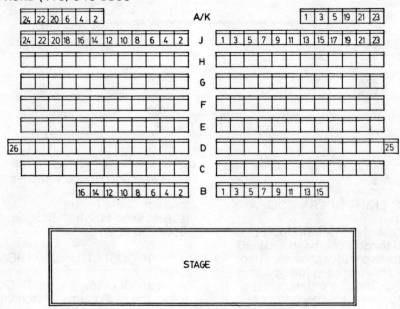

WILLOWS THEATRE, CONCORD

are also a children's performing arts program and a special series of family-type films on the weekends. Other forms of entertainment and arts representation include the Contra Costa Ballet and the Amici Musica.

The Willows Shopping Center is not a covered mall. Rather, brick pathways lead from store to store and to the rustic natural-wood entry to the theatre. The box office is outside, and, as you enter the lobby, you'll notice that the wood decor continues in with you. Posters of past shows are the primary wall hangings. The lobby is sparse in furniture, and intermission refreshments are served outside among the pleasant setting of trees and greenery.

Rust carpeting and dark-orange-cushioned theatre seats set the color scheme in the auditorium. There are no stage draperies, and the lighting instruments are visible, with no effort made to mask them. There's no orchestra pit, so the front row is close to the stage. The incline of the theatre floor and the small size of the room make sight lines and acoustics very good.

There's a subscription series available, with appropriate savings on the already modest price scale of $7 and $6. The regular season runs October through June. Though this is a modern facility, there is still a comfortable, homey feeling about the place.

Take the Willow Pass exit from Highway 680 and go east one block to Diamond Boulevard. At Diamond turn left, and in a block you're at the shopping center entrance. Follow the perimeter road to the freeway side of the center; there's the Willows.

Both this theatre and the Parkside Playhouse are operated by the city of Concord's Leisure Services Department (a modern innovation in government). That office, if you want rental information, is located at 1950 Parkside Drive, Concord, CA 94519.

PARKSIDE PLAYHOUSE

89 seats (unreserved).
LOCATION AND BOX OFFICE
2750 Parkside Circle
Concord, CA 94519.
BOX OFFICE-BUSINESS TELEPHONE
(415) 671-3065.
SUPERVISOR James L. Jester.
ARTISTIC DIRECTOR Varies with each presenting group.
HANDICAPPED ACCESS The playhouse is fully wheelchair accessible, with a restroom equipped for the handicapped.

This is your basic performance space: very small and certainly not fancy. Only the tiniest of musicals are performed, and an occasional revue. The rest of the independently produced shows are light, small-cast comedies. The nondescript, simple exterior is boxlike and of a nononsense functional design. The theatre lobby is shared by the show room and an art gallery where local artists display their works.

Inside the modest auditorium the floor is raked, and the seats are of the type you might remember from your high school days—if your alma mater was as old as mine—colorful red foam padding, not heavily cushioned. The aisle carpets are green and the walls basic white.

The Parkside Playhouse is in Baldwin Park. Take the Willow Pass exit from either Highway 680 or 24 and go east to Parkside Drive. Turn left; after three blocks, the street deadends in the park.

If you have a little show you've always wanted to stage or if you want to sing for a small group of your friends, this might be just the opportunity for you. Rental rates are a lot better than at Carnegie Hall.

Stockton

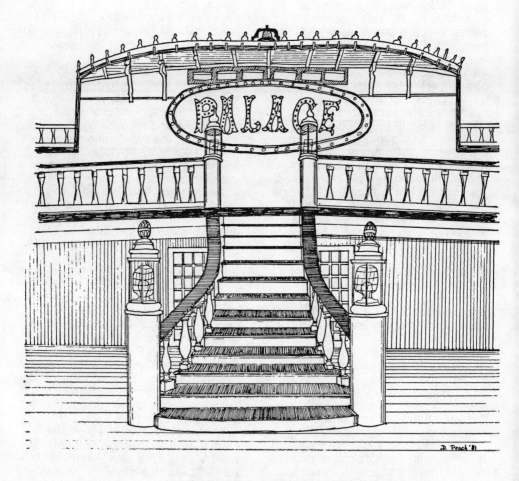

PALACE SHOWBOAT DINNER THEATRE

PALACE SHOWBOAT DINNER THEATRE

280 seats (reserved).
LOCATION AND BOX OFFICE
10464 North Highway 99
Stockton, CA 95212.
BOX OFFICE-BUSINESS TELEPHONE
(209) 931-0274.
MANAGING DIRECTOR Goldie Pollard.
ARTISTIC DIRECTOR Gregory Pollard.
HANDICAPPED ACCESS There are ramps for wheelchairs, and removable seats for wheelchair placement. Restrooms are totally equipped for the handicapped.

Edna Ferber was so impressed by showboats that she wrote a bestselling novel about one: *The Cotton Blossom*. Jerome Kern and Oscar Hammerstein II were caught up in the mystique and further immortalized these floating showplaces with a musical based on the Ferber plot and called *Show Boat*. Midwesterners like me may have even been aboard the real thing on the Ohio, Missouri, or Mississippi rivers; a few still remain. And now you can go to Stockton and board the Palace Showboat Dinner Theatre. It's only fair to warn you that, like all good theatrical presentations, this showboat is an illusion.

The Pollard family, the owners and producers, started to build this landlocked replica over fifteen years ago. The main section of it began in the San Joaquin Delta, not as a ship, but as a cannery building on an island. The Pollards were told they could have it if they'd move it. They did, piece by piece. Once reassembled on its present plot of ground, renovation began.

Today, the Palace Showboat Dinner Theatre can do everything but sail away. It's got a forward- and an aft-deck superstructure, a side-mounted paddle wheel, and a smoke stack.

Inside it's got a theatre-restaurant that presents melodrama and vaudeville every weekend, except for major holidays, all year long. And, if you choose, you can have a dinner of chicken or prawns right there at your theatre-seat location: Each two-person set-up has its own cocktail table.

If thirst strikes you at any time throughout the evening, there's a bar that specializes in strawberry daiquiris and also serves beer, wine, and assorted soft drinks. The decor is rough and rowdy, but all in good fun. On the upper level of the lobby you might spot the red light where the madam plies her trade. If you want to divert your eyes, check out the old–beer can collection or the steer horns or the antique bicycles and baby buggies.

Back in the auditorium you'll be seated in theatre seats from an old San Francisco theatre. The drapes and wallpaper are decidedly red. Hanging from the ceiling are fire buckets. The stage curves around the front of the house, and there's a runway and an orchestra pit. Chaser lights dash around every inch of the oak proscenium arch. All in all, it's a pretty racy spot.

The chicken dinner sells for $10.50 for a quarter of the bird and $11.50 for a half. Prawns are $13.50. The tab includes dinner, show, tax, tip, and a nonalcoholic beverage. If you want to just catch the show it's $6.00 for adults and $4.50 for kids.

If you're going to Stockton by way of Highway 580, turn north on Highway 5 to 8-Mile Road. Head east on 8-Mile Road until you cross over Highway 99. Once over 99, make a right-hand turn on the frontage road on the east side of 99. In a quarter-of-a-mile's hop you'll be looking up at the pilot house of the Palace Showboat Dinner Theatre. Don't feel you have to rush. Each show plays for six months, and the boat won't leave without you.

STOCKTON CIVIC THEATRE

310 seats (reserved).
LOCATION AND BOX OFFICE
2312 Rose Marie Lane
Stockton, CA 95207.
BOX OFFICE TELEPHONE (209) 463-6813.
BUSINESS TELEPHONE (209) 463-5765.
BUSINESS MANAGER Clyde Nielsen.
ARTISTIC DIRECTOR Varies with each
presentation.
HANDICAPPED ACCESS Every area of
the building has been designed for
access to the handicapped.

This is the newest theatrical facility
in this book. As a matter of fact, the
book and the theatre are scheduled
to open within weeks of each other.
Primary use of the new Stockton
Civic Theatre is by the Stockton
Community Theatre. This well-established, nonprofessional troupe of
players works year-round. The schedule includes five nonmusicals and
one musical comedy a year. These
shows run for four weekends, with
one additional Thursday and a Sunday matinee. The summer months
are filled with a children's theatre
production staged by children for
children (with an adult staff). The
average ticket price for straight plays
and comedies is $7.00, with $2.00
off for students (eighteen years old
and under) and senior citizens. Musicals are $1.50 more expensive in
each category. If you want to save

$1.00 a ducat across the board,
attend the Thursday evening performance or the Sunday matinee.
The Civic Theatre is the latest
addition to the Venezian Bridges
Recreational Complex in North
Stockton. The modern architecture
of the rest of the development is
carried through the theatre. The
gray-painted wooden building is on
a man-made lake, and the area is
landscaped and is punctuated by
swimming pools, tennis courts, and
other leisure-time features. The
theatre is easily distinguished from
the other facades by its large marquee.
Look sharp and you can see it from
March Lane.
The lobby carries nature indoors
with an aggregate rough-finished
floor that is broken up by area rugs.
The auditorium takes on a "tweedy"
complexion, with seats upholstered
in brown and black, and carpeting
that continues the theme. The curtained proscenium arch frames a
fully equipped stage. There are ample
attractive dressing rooms and workshop areas.
Take the March Lane exit off
Highway 5 and go east on March
Lane for two blocks. That's where
you'll encounter the Hilton Hotel. It's
at the corner of Venezia Boulevard,
where you turn right. In two short
blocks the street will deadend and
you'll be at the Stockton Civic Theatre.
If you're not, they didn't get it
finished for this edition of Front Row
Center. Call ahead.

Sacramento

OLD EAGLE THEATRE

The state capital of California seems to have more active theatres than any other such political center I've heard of, including Washington, D.C. Keeping all the bad actors in the halls of government seems to be about as much as most such cities can handle.

Seats of government always have an abundance of saloons and nightclubs. The reason is obvious: Most of our elected representatives live under the stress and strain of public and media scrutiny, fearful that some harmless impropriety will be blown into a major shenanigan by some overzealous snoop. But that's no explanation for the number of playhouses in this city.

Rather than try to find an answer to the riddle of the prominence of legitimate theatre in Sacramento, let's just give credit where credit is due and congratulate our capital for having so much that can be called "legit" so close to the statehouse dome.

EAGLET THEATRE ELEANOR McCLATCHY PERFORMING ARTS CENTER

300 seats (reserved).
LOCATION AND BOX OFFICE
1419 H Street
Sacramento, CA 95814.
BOX OFFICE TELEPHONE (916) 441-6991.
BUSINESS TELEPHONE (916) 446-7501.
ADMINISTRATIVE SECRETARY Genevieve Aalgaard.
ARTISTIC DIRECTOR Guest directors for each production.
HANDICAPPED ACCESS There is a private entrance for wheelchairs. Call ahead to assure that the entrance is attended. There are no special restroom facilities for the handicapped.

The Eleanor McClatchy Performing Arts Center, formerly the Sacramento Civic Theatre, performs an eight-month season (September through May) in its Eaglet Theatre. No newcomers to the scene, the group was incorporated in 1942 and built the theatre in 1949. Play selection attempts to provide a balance between comedy and drama. Most plays are from American playwrights, and many are family oriented: Something old, something new, some things borrowed, but not much blue. There is, by the way, a children's wing connected with the operation. Casts are local nonprofessionals.

The box office entrance, across Fifteenth Street from the Mansion Inn on H Street, opens onto a spacious outdoor courtyard. A pleasant blend of redwood and tile accents the typically California architecture, and the comfortable auditorium with its fan-shaped arrangement has excellent sight lines with a gently raked floor.

Tickets are reasonable at five dollars per person, and season subscriptions are available.

The theatre building takes up the entire block at H and Fifteenth streets. Coming north on Highway 80, take the Fifteenth Street exit; from the south on Highway 5 take the H Street exit, and, from the north traveling south into Sacramento take the G Street exit. In all cases, once you're off the freeway, head for the center of town.

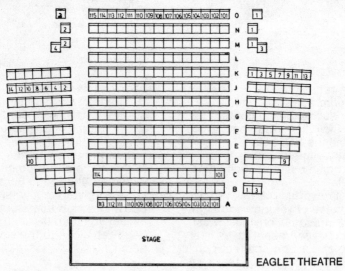

EAGLET THEATRE

BACCHUS THEATRE PLAYHOUSE

110 seats (unreserved).
LOCATION AND BOX OFFICE
1025 Second Street
Sacramento, CA 95814.
BOX OFFICE-BUSINESS TELEPHONE
(916) 446-6542.
PRODUCER-CO-OWNER Dez Larson.
MANAGING DIRECTOR-CO-OWNER
Victor Larson.
ARTISTIC DIRECTORS Karen Defoe, Dan
Defoe.
HANDICAPPED ACCESS There is no
wheelchair access. The theatre is
located on the second floor, with no
elevator service.

Once you negotiate the steep stairway leading to the second story of
this restored brick building in Old
Sacramento, you'll find yourself in a
long, narrow lobby with showbills on
the walls, a miniature box office, and
a small concession stand. Once
inside the auditorium, the elevated
seating area and the shallow stage
give the impression of an old-time
music hall.
   The Bacchus specializes in a pot-
pourri of light entertainment, much
of it original. Comedy is emphasized
by the nonprofessional company.
Children's shows are presented, as
are improvisational offerings. Encour-
aging new writers is one of the aims
of this house, which has been in
year-round operation since 1971;
scripts are welcomed for consideration and should be accompanied
with a stamped, self-addressed en-
velope to ensure return.
   Again, all freeways have signs
directing traffic from all directions to
the Old Sacramento State Park.
Ticket prices are under five dollars
for adults and about half that for
kids' shows.

SACRAMENTO EXPERIMENTAL THEATER

75 seats (unreserved).
LOCATION AND BOX OFFICE
2130 L Street
Sacramento, CA 95816.
BOX OFFICE TELEPHONE None; tickets
sold at the door on performance
nights.
BUSINESS TELEPHONE (916) 391-1662.
MANAGING DIRECTOR Michael S. Boyd.
ARTISTIC DIRECTORS Boyd, Leonard
Simon, and Shirley O'Key.
HANDICAPPED ACCESS The theatre wel-
comes the handicapped, but it must
be noted that there are angular
stairs leading down to a narrow
aisle, making wheelchair access very
iffy. There are no restroom facilities
for the handicapped.

One of the newer (1978) and more
adventurous fledgling theatres in
Sacramento is the Experimental.
Working on limited budgets, with
rudimentary facilities, only previously
unstaged works are performed. The
schedule also offers from time to
time the films of new moviemakers
from in and around the state capital.
Housed in a large Victorian structure
that also hosts a music conservatory
on the upper floors, the Experimental
Theatre group plays in the half-
basement. It's a nonprofessional
company.
   For under five dollars you can
witness the birth of new play, musical,
or film, or listen to a still-unknown
poet read his or her own works. The
theatre accepts new scripts on a
regular basis and looks for traditional
as well as experimental work.
   Once you reach downtown Sacramento by any of the numerous
routes, find your way to Twenty-
second and L streets. Not knowing
for sure what will be on the stage is
part of the adventure.

CHAUTAUQUA PLAYHOUSE

138 seats (unreserved).
LOCATION AND BOX OFFICE
1731 Twenty-fifth Street
Sacramento, CA 95816.
BOX OFFICE-BUSINESS TELEPHONE
(916) 451-9604.
PRODUCERS Rodger A. Hoopman,
Charles F. Slater.
GENERAL MANAGER Bill Wahl.
HANDICAPPED ACCESS There is wheelchair access, with a ramped entry and accommodations for four or five chairs in the auditorium. The restrooms are wheelchair accessible but are not specially equipped for the handicapped.

Since 1976 the Chautauqua Playhouse (a venerable old sawdust-trail tent-show name) has kept one eye on the public's taste and the other on the audience's comfort. Producing recently released Broadway and off-Broadway comedies and dramas, with a very strong children's theatre performing on Saturday afternoons, this community playhouse is firmly established on the Sacramento theatrical scene.

Located at Twenty-fifth and R streets, the playhouse is in an older section of downtown Sacramento where substantial private homes blend with an occasional warehouse. One of the latter has been converted into a comfortable, unpretentious theatre site by the Chautauqua operation. A single door leads into a nicely appointed lobby with a refreshment stand and restrooms. Once inside the auditorium, regular theatre seats on a gradually raked floor look down onto a wide, shallow stage with a low but unrestricting ceiling.

Take any downtown freeway exit. All streets are numerical north to south and alphabetical east to west. Once again, a ticket purchased with a five-dollar bill will give you change.

OLD EAGLE THEATRE

175 seats (unreserved).
LOCATION AND BOX OFFICE
925 The Embarcadero
Sacramento, CA 95814.
BOX OFFICE-BUSINESS TELEPHONE
(916) 446-6761.
MANAGING-ARTISTIC DIRECTOR
Robert Irvin.
HANDICAPPED ACCESS The main entrance and the auditorium are accessible to wheelchairs. The restrooms, however, as is so often the case in old buildings, are downstairs.

It's conceivable that the sudden move to the rich ore fields that closed California's First Theatre in Monterey led to the original opening of the Old Eagle Theatre in Old Sacramento in 1849. The present structure, rebuilt in 1975 as part of the Old Sacramento Embarcadero State Park project, now has a levee to keep it from the woes of the early days. Back then the river would rise and flood the theatre, often trapping the patrons until they could be rescued in rowboats.

Today, seated on benches (with backs) as in the past, audiences see modern plays and musicals rather than the melodramas that might be expected in such a house. The season, like many in the Sacramento area, runs from September to June, taking a break when the heat of the summer makes indoor, non-air-conditioned entertainment an untenable enterprise.

Tickets are scaled at six dollars and under, and a call ahead is advisable for curtain time and seat availability. From all freeways you'll see signs directing you to Old Sacramento. The Historic Park complex, with crafts shops, restaurants, boutiques, and art galleries, is situated between I and J streets and makes for a fine all-day visit finished off with a play at the Old Eagle.

SACRAMENTO COMMUNITY CENTER THEATRE

2,436 seats (reserved).
LOCATION Community-Convention Center, Sacramento.
BOX OFFICE ADDRESS
Community Center Box Office
L Street between Thirteenth and Fourteenth streets
Sacramento, CA 95814.
BOX OFFICE TELEPHONE (916) 449-5181.
BUSINESS TELEPHONE (916) 449-5291.

OTHER TICKET OUTLETS Major ticket agencies and all Sacramento Savings and Loan branches.
GENERAL MANAGER Sam J. Burns.
ASSISTANT MANAGER Leonard Zerilli.
HANDICAPPED ACCESS Every possible consideration has been given to the handicapped and aged. The theatre has wheelchair access, the restrooms are fully equipped, and there are passenger elevators to all floors.

In June 1974 the big touring musicals, concerts, singing stars, and dramas found a new home in the center of Sacramento. The Community-Convention Center in midtown Sacramento (between J and L streets and Thirteenth and Fourteenth streets) opened the Community Theatre. It's part of a convention complex that includes the theatre, an exhibition

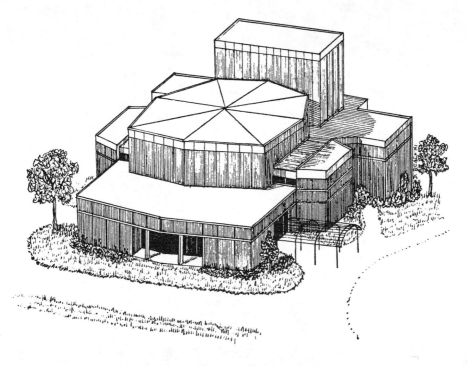

SACRAMENTO COMMUNITY CENTER THEATRE

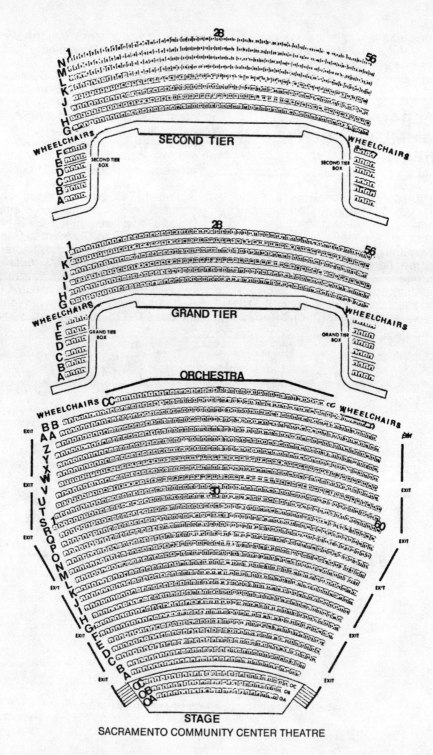

SACRAMENTO COMMUNITY CENTER THEATRE

hall, an activities building, and the venerable old Memorial Auditorium. The latter is seldom used for legitimate theatre, except for the 295-seat Little Theatre. Built 1926, this massive hall is better suited to sports events and circuses, and is just a block from the main center.

The striking lobby area contains large box office facilities and is dominated by floor-to-ceiling windows looking out on the State Capitol and the malls and gardens that surround the area. To the right is the central staircase leading to the theatre proper. Paintings grace the dark-gray walls, along with an enormous metal etching. The rugs are a rich burgundy. The specially designed starburst lighting again accents metal.

The burgundy color continues into the auditorium as the predominant color of the seating fabric. It's Continental seating (no center aisle, wide spacing row to row), with two grand rear balconies, and boxes that seem to fly out into the hall, suspended in space.

The stage and backstage facilities are the latest in theatrical technology, with a fifty-four–line fly-grip for suspending drops and sets. There are a full orchestra pit, a large green room, and an elevator designed to transport costume trunks and personal effects to the dressing rooms. A tunnel links the basement (under the double-leveled lobbies) to the orchestra pit and stage area. There's also a full-service bar in the first lobby.

Ticket prices vary from show to show. Some have gone as high as $25 (closed-circuit boxing), but the general top is usually around $18 and the bottom about $10 below that.

There's no problem finding downtown Sacramento from any of the surrounding freeways. From Highway 50, take the Sixteenth Street exit; from Highway 80, L Street gets you there. Off Highway 5 the exit is J

Street. There is almost limitless parking for all of the Community-Convention Center facilities.

STAGEDOOR COMEDY PLAYHOUSE

220 seats (reserved).
LOCATION One Sacramento Inn Plaza, Sacramento.
BOX OFFICE ADDRESS 1820 Professional Drive, Sacramento, CA 95825.
BOX OFFICE TELEPHONE (916) 927-0942.
BUSINESS TELEPHONE (916) 485-1011.
MANAGING DIRECTOR Laura Darzell Grisham.
ARTISTIC DIRECTOR Jerry Grisham.
HANDICAPPED ACCESS There are double doors for wheelchair access, with ground-level seating availability for wheelchairs. The restrooms are accessible to wheelchairs but are not specially equipped for the handicapped.

Since 1973 this facility has been a tribute to Neil Simon and other comedy writers. Except in the month of July and a couple of weeks in August, you can reserve tickets for a semiprofessional cast romp for laughter's sake most any weekend (Friday and Saturday) of the year.

Prior to 1973 this facility was called the Jayrob Theatre. Throughout the sixties it, too, featured comedy. Actually, only the name and the ownership have changed. The format, strong and very commercial, hasn't been tampered with. The homey lobby could be a neighborhood cocktail lounge. Beer and wine are served, along with soft drinks and coffee. The beverages may be taken into the auditorium, where you'll find small tables between every two seats to accommodate glasses.

Though they are not conventional theatre seats, the chairs are comfortable, and any location in the three sections has a good sight line to the stage. This optical and aural advantage is increased with elevated seating.

On the days that the theatre is unused (in theatrical parlance, "dark"), the hall can be rented for seminars, meetings, weddings, bar mitzvahs, and so on. Neil Simon would like that.

To reach the Stagedoor Comedy Playhouse, travel northeast on Highway 80 to the Arden Way exit. You'll see the Sacramento Inn as you exit, and that's what you want to head for; the playhouse is around behind it.

SACRAMENTO MUSIC CIRCUS

2,545 seats (reserved).
LOCATION AND BOX OFFICE
1419 H Street
Sacramento, CA 95814.
BOX OFFICE TELEPHONE (916) 441-3163.
BUSINESS TELEPHONE (916) 446-5880.
OTHER TICKET OUTLETS All Sacramento Savings and Loan Branches.
PRODUCERS Lewis and Young Productions.
GENERAL MANAGER Richard Lewis.
ARTISTIC DIRECTORS AND CHOREOGRAPHERS Vary with the season and with specific attractions and shows.
HANDICAPPED ACCESS There's no problem getting into the theatre, and spaces are set aside for wheelchairs. Restroom facilities are also accessible.

There's a line from a Sheldon Harnick lyric that says, "Winter is gloves and Homburg, winter is cold cement,/ summer is Sigmund Romberg in a music tent." Years ago that was an accurate observation throughout the eastern half of the United States. Then music tents spread into Texas, and finally California joined the fad. Huge, colorful tents appeared in major municipalities to house musical comedies and operettas about the same time that circuses were abandoning the big tops in favor of public auditoriums. For about a decade the smell of canvas mingled with the smell of greasepaint. Of course, California, being fancier than most other places, left tents pretty quickly for large, permanent, air-conditioned arena theatres with giant revolving stages, such as the Anaheim Music Circus and San Carlos's Circle Star. Alas, the tent fad faded fast. As of this summer there are four summer musical tents in America, and only one of them is west of the Mississippi: the Sacramento Music Circus. (Harking back to the Harnick lyric, it's seldom these days that we hear Romberg anywhere, whether in musical tents or roofed playhouses, more's the pity. But with opera houses reaching ever further into general audiences for support, it won't surprise me if we are soon hearing Romberg, Friml, Herbert, and even Richard Rodgers in the major opera houses around the land.)

If the names of producers Lewis and Young sound familiar to San Francisco–area readers, they should. Many years back, the Garden Court of the Palace Hotel rang with the strains of shows such as *Guys and Dolls* under their aegis. They began the summer Sacramento operation in 1951, and it's been going strong ever since.

The Music Circus policy is to present Broadway musicals with professional casts and stars in the leads. The usual season runs late June through Labor Day. Recent seasons have also included engagements by superstars of the pop-music world, and television personalities presented outside of the Broadway show format. That saves you taking that drive to Reno or Tahoe in the summer heat.

Seating in a theatre-in-the-round has both advantages and disadvantages. Sight and sound are usually good; in the case of this show tent, for example, you are never more than twenty-one rows from the stage. A drawback is that you may be staring at some performer's back at some point during the evening. This distraction is usually solved by a competent director, and you'll never even notice it. If the mikes are working well, it won't matter where the singer is facing. If they're not, well—there's always the concession stand. Here's another plus: The stars enter and exit, and sometimes even sing, in the aisles, maybe right next to your chair. The chairs, by the way, are designed somewhat like directors' chairs, with canvas seats.

Tickets are reasonable for the size of the shows and the name value of the stars. Top price for a tuner is $10.95, with a dollar less if you pick a Monday night. The big star specials get up around $17.00, but Monday is again cheaper than the rest of the week. Music Circus, unlike most theatres, doesn't have a "dark" night. It plays seven evenings a week. Mail orders are accepted, and there is a savings by purchasing a season ticket.

The big tent is just a hop, skip, and a jump from the Convention-Community Center. To get to the Fifteenth and H Street location, use the same instructions I gave you for the Sacramento Community Theatre one section back.

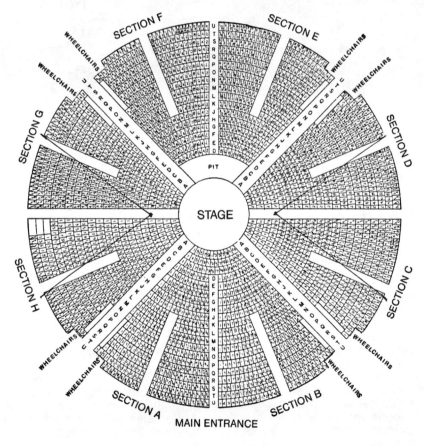

SACRAMENTO MUSIC CIRCUS

Theatres to the North

THE OLD OPERA HOUSE, AUBURN

When gold was discovered in 1848, not only did hopeful miners head north to the Sierra and its environs, but all manner of support troops as well: merchants, preachers, dance hall girls, blacksmiths, and ladies of ill repute. Also in the entourage were actors and entertainers, musicians and circus performers. Men far from home and family had needs to be filled, and there were people who made more money filling those needs than the men made in the gold fields.

Among the phenomena of the times were the child actors, including the "fairie princesses" such as little Lotta Crabtree and petite Lola Montez. Fame came to them later as adult enchantresses, but they began in the saloons and dance halls of the boomtowns. Even Helen Hayes would one day perform as an impish waif in this setting. The form native to the northern California wildlands was called melodrama: tales of the never-ending struggle between good and evil. Subtlety was an unheard-of ingredient of the form; it was a time when emotions were close to the surface and the audience was at least as vocal as the performers.

I'm sure that everyone by now has heard the famous story of the world's most convincing actor. In one of the Gold Rush camps a traveling company of Shakespeareans was presenting *Othello*. So dastardly was the actor playing Iago and so vicious his machinations that a miner in the front row stood up, drew his revolver, and shot the culprit dead. That's immediate critical reaction for you.

Melodrama still continues as one of the most popular theatrical attractions in theatres to the north. Each summer, weekend players from the San Francisco Peninsula travel to Dry Town to entertain the locals and the tourists with the genre (the Clay Pipers). In Fort Bragg, the Footlighters have a theatre of their own devoted to the "mellerdramer"—(707) 964-3806.

As you read this section you'll also come across theatres doing more traditional productions, and groups that perform works they create from scratch (Ukiah Players; [707] 462-9226). At the Pacific Art Center in Arcata you might choose the evening's entertainment from O'Neill or George M. Cohan—(707) 822-0828.

As you can see, theatre came to stay in the north of California, even when the gold and the miners had moved on to brighter prospects. There's still gold and actors in them thar hills. I can't swear to some of the other original migrant types.

GASLIGHT THEATRE

170 seats (reserved).
LOCATION AND BOX OFFICE
720 Sutter Street
Folsom, CA 95630.
BOX OFFICE TELEPHONE (916) 985-2093.
BUSINESS TELEPHONE (916) 456-5807.
PRODUCERS AND CODIRECTORS
Lawrence J. Korosec and
Virginia Lee Korosec.
MUSICAL DIRECTOR-PRODUCTION MANAGER
Kenneth J. Kligerman.
HANDICAPPED ACCESS Theatre and rest-room facilities are totally accessible.

It occurs to me that melodramatic theatre is alive and well in northern California. If you'll recall, I've already covered four other Gold Rush–inspired, nostalgia-oriented playhouses: in Monterey (California's First Theatre), Campbell (the Gaslighter Theatre), Stockton (the Palace Showboat Dinner Theatre), and Santa Rosa (the Marquee Theatre). We now move north

of Sacramento to Historic Old Folsom, a three-block restoration of Gold Rush–era buildings and shops. It's a commercial venture that's had great success, the theatre as well as the rest of the business district, since 1962.

The Gaslight Theatre is operated by a production team called the Old Town Troupers. Remember that name, because it's the same group that presents the shows at the Old Opera House Dinner Theatre twenty-five miles to the north in Auburn. The following description of the melo-drama and olio programs applies to both theatres.

Each show runs for six months. The Auburn show is always new, not a rework of the Folsom attraction. No material is repeated house-to-house within a two-year span. The melodramas are either authentic scripts from before the turn of the century or adaptations thereof. During set changes, solo acts work in front of the roll drop. After the play, there is a full session of olio entertainment (that's vaudeville before it went big-time on the Orpheum Circuit). As is customary in these kinds of presen-tations, the melodrama audience is encouraged to boo the baddy and cheer the hero. They are not en-couraged to try to date the ingenue. Booing and hissing are also dis-couraged when the olios are on, unless they absolutely deserve it.

The Gaslight Theatre is located in the Sutter Club Saloon, Card Room and Restaurant (green room). It began doing melodramas under other man-agement in 1962. The present pro-duction company took over in 1979.

The theatre has a stage with dressing rooms off to one side. There's walk-space between the back wall and the cyclorama wall. Roll drops make set changes possible. The decor is, as in almost every Gold Rush–inspired room in California, red with much gold trim. Oh, to own a red-flocked–wallpaper factory in California! The main floor is filled with small round cocktail tables and seating is on padded folding chairs. Beverages are served. The back three rows are elevated and the chairs there are plusher and more padded. The tables are long rather than round. If you enjoy the feeling of the Old West, this is your glass of sarsaparilla.

It's a snap to find the Gaslight Theatre. If your journey takes you on Highway 50, take the Folsom exit and signs will direct you to Historic Sutter Street. From Highway 80 take the Greenback Lane exit east into Folsom.

THE OLD OPERA HOUSE DINNER THEATRE

120 seats (reserved).
LOCATION AND BOX OFFICE
111 Sacramento Street
Auburn, CA 95603.
BOX OFFICE-BUSINESS TELEPHONE
(916) 885-7708.
MANAGING DIRECTOR Sandy Knox.
ARTISTIC DIRECTOR Larry Korosek.
MUSICAL DIRECTOR Ken Kligerman.
HANDICAPPED ACCESS This theatre has total access and fully equipped rest-room facilities. The dining tables are at the proper height for easy dining by those in wheelchairs.

This is the theatre that I told you about above. The Old Town Troupers of Folsom produce the melodramas and olios here. Neither the material nor the casts are the same, but the shows are identical in style to those at Folsom's Gaslight Theatre.

Gold Rush Plaza is everything MGM ever told you a Gold Rush town was like, which is no coincidence: An MGM set designer did this whole tourist-oriented shopping center. The building that houses the reconstructed opera house was actually built in the latter half of the nineteenth century. As you enter the complex, note the glassblower's shop, a metalsmith crafting metal sculpture, a candy store, an ice cream emporium, a real estate office, and the original Jelly Belly's Restaurant.

You know what the decor will be the moment you enter the plaza through the double doors beneath the huge painting of a Forty-niner panning for gold. The glass in the windows is etched, and the walls and ceilings sport gaslights and large old portraits. At the end of the red-dominated hall is another set of double doors. The box office is just across from the restaurant, next to the realtor's office. Beyond the doors is the theatre, an exact replica of an 1850-vintage opera house. The stage has an ornate gold frame around the proscenium. The drapes are rich-red velvet and the walls—you guessed it—are flocked red-and-gold wallpaper. This isn't a constant, however, because the old natural brick wall is allowed to share the space. The color continues in the rugs and the tablecloths. There are period pieces among the furnishings, and antique mirrors on the walls. The overall effect is to make you expect Alice Faye to emerge at any minute and sing a jilted soubrette's lament.

I mentioned tablecloths, and this is, indeed, a dinner theatre. The repast is served buffet style. The entrées differ from week to week, but the food is always home cooking with fresh-baked rolls, and fresh fruits and vegetables are served. The desserts are scrumptious. There's a beer and wine bar that serves specialties such as the Villian and the Hero (a strawberry-wine daiquiri), a Sluice Box Special (a salty dog concocted with white wine), the Miner's Dilemma (Ready? A wine bloody Mary), and a Dirty Sally Phizz (a wine sunrise cocktail). I confess that I haven't sampled any of the above but those who have tell me that they aren't half bad. Some don't even miss the hard stuff.

What's the tariff for all of the foregoing? Dinner and show combos are $13. The show alone is $6. It's essential that you call in advance for reservations. If you want a private party or you need a fun setting for a fundraiser, both this house and its sister, Gaslight Theatre in Folsom, are available.

Actually all of Auburn is a historical site. You may want to come early and spend the day in the town and in the surrounding areas. You'll find it hard to believe that the opera house itself didn't open until 1970. Ain't MGM grand?

Leave Highway 80 at the Auburn-Maple Street exit. That'll bring you to the heart of town. From Maple make a right on Lincoln Way, then a right on Sacramento Street. Gold Rush Plaza's on the right, and the theatre is at the rear of the plaza.

SUTTER BUTTES REGIONAL THEATRE

233 seats (reserved).
LOCATION AND BOX OFFICE
629 G Street
Marysville, CA 95901.
BOX OFFICE-BUSINESS TELEPHONE
(916) 742-2533.
MANAGING DIRECTORS Gilbert Reade, Robert L. Hoberg.
ARTISTIC DIRECTOR Gilbert Reade.
HANDICAPPED ACCESS There are positions for wheelchairs adjacent to the fourth row on the main floor. Restrooms are completely equipped for the handicapped.

Marysville is a town that takes you by surprise. The caliber of the Victorian architecture around the area is unrivaled by any of the places famous for these queenly domiciles. There's one, near a small picturesque park

SUTTER BUTTES REGIONAL THEATRE, MARYSVILLE

across the street from the Sutter Buttes Regional Theatre, that'll knock your eye out. After you've finished oohing and aahing, head for the golden-tan walls with dark-brown trim and the welcoming awning that mark the entrance to the Sutter Buttes Regional Theatre.

In 1912 the building was part of Marysville High School. The doors first opened to enthusiastic young athletes: This was the school gymnasium and it remained so for decades. Finally, as happens to so many aging structures that aren't needed any longer, it was marked for demolition. There were those, lead by Gilbert Reade, who felt that it could be put to better use than as another pile of rubble. In 1975 it opened to its new life, the Sutter Buttes Regional Theatre.

What has evolved over the intervening years is a six-play series, with a special production added for good measure each season. It's mostly a lighthearted house, with more comedy and farce being offered than heavy drama. The musicals staged are of the small-cast variety.

Gyms are notorious for bad acoustics, what with all those bare walls and hard floors. That's been modified in this instance by the use of burlap and natural-colored wooden batons in the auditorium and the same arrangement in the lobby, except that in the foyer the wood trim is dark. The primary color throughout is rust, with that warm shade incorporated in the conventional theatre seats. The seating arrangement is Continental.

The playing area is open and flexible. If desired, a proscenium arch can be added, as can an additional thrust section. The brown and tan carpeting that covers the L-shaped lobby floor extends on into the theatre. On the lobby walls are the artistic endeavors of local painters and craftspeople. Photos of produc-tions past and present fill assorted bulletin boards.

Marysville is forty-five miles north of Sacramento. If you make it to the Denny's Restaurant, you've only got three blocks to go to the theatre. I'm assured by natives that you can't get lost in Marysville. Once you find the box office, the most they'll charge you is $5.50 each for musicals and $1.00 less for plays.

THE AMERICAN VICTORIAN MUSEUM THEATRE
THE FOOTHILL THEATRE COMPANY

200 seats (subscription seats reserved).
LOCATION 325 Spring Street, Nevada City.
BOX OFFICE ADDRESS
The Company
123 Nivens Lane
Nevada City, CA 95959.
BOX OFFICE TELEPHONE (916) 265-5804.
BUSINESS TELEPHONE (916) 265-9320.
MANAGING-ARTISTIC DIRECTOR
Diane Fetterly.
HANDICAPPED ACCESS There is parking for the handicapped in the lot to the rear of the theatre, with wheelchair access into the building and to the main-floor chair locations. The restrooms permit wheelchair access but there is no special equipment for the handicapped.

Highway 49 from Auburn doesn't take on major motorway dimensions until just outside Grass Valley. From there it broadens out and stays that way until it gets where it's going: Nevada City. When I was growing up in Pennsylvania we would refer to a town affectionately as "a wide spot in the road." We never had the road get wide for it miles in advance.

The Company, as the Foothill Theatre Company is called, was started in 1977, but the building that houses the playhouse dates from before the turn of the century. Originally an old mining foundry, it's now the American Victorian Museum. The stone-walled, tin-roofed edifice is one block from Nevada City's main street, Broad Street. In it are an archive of Victorian memorabilia, a book bindery, a community radio station, a stained-glass manufacturer, and a beautiful old-fashioned dining room.

The auditorium has no fixed seating, making it possible to stage productions with flexibility. It's especially conducive to new works, which are done frequently. High up in the left wall is an organ loft, pipes and all. This has figured in productions such as an original mounting of J.R.R. Tolkien's *The Hobbit*. The plays presented are representative of world theatre, with Hellman sharing the bill with Stoppard and Shakespeare. All of the work is volunteer in this enthusiastic, well-bespoken theatre. The casts are local nonprofessionals.

The regularly scheduled season runs from March through December. Best seats are sold for about $5.50, and children under twelve can get in for $3.00. Season subscriptions are available.

There are a couple of ways to get to this scenic foothill location. From the south follow Highway 80 to Auburn and Highway 49 into Nevada City. From the north the roads aren't quite so developed, but you can be adventurous and take Highway 20 off 80 at Cisco, or 174 out of Colfax to Grass Valley and north to Nevada City, the American Victorian Museum Theatre, and the Foothill Theatre Company.

HELEN SCHOENI THEATRE MENDOCINO PERFORMING ARTS COMPANY

81 seats (reservations recommended).
LOCATION Little Lake and Kasten streets, Mendocino.
BOX OFFICE
Zacha's Bay Window Gallery
P.O. Box 7
560 Main Street
Mendocino, CA 95460.
BUSINESS ADDRESS
P.O. Box 800
Mendocino, CA 95460.
BOX OFFICE TELEPHONE (707) 937-4477.
MANAGING DIRECTOR Bob Cohen.
ARTISTIC DIRECTORS Ben Benoit, Sandra Hawthorne, Ramelle Irish, Don Murray, Sue Winn.
HANDICAPPED ACCESS There is a ramp leading to the main entrance of the theatre, and a seat can be removed from the front row to accommodate a wheelchair. Seats are made available on the main floor rather than in the elevated section. Wheelchair access to the restrooms is extremely difficult due to the small sizes of the rooms.

HELEN SCHOENI THEATRE, MENDOCINO

Rough, weathered redwood is the motif of the Helen Schoeni Theatre. It shares the block with the galleries and studios of the Mendocino Art Center. Just about the only thing that's permanent in the lobby is the huge redwood bar that serves as a refreshment stand for soft drinks, juices, and coffee. Though called the "gold room," the decor changes from show to show to reflect the subject or mood of the current stage presentation. In the auditorium, originally intended as a children's theatre, there are nine rows of standard theatre chairs elevated to give maximum sight lines to the floor-level playing area.

Since 1976, the months from March through November have been the prime performance times for the Mendocino Performing Arts Company. The seasons have expanded from some 36 performances a year to a schedule currently approaching 125 showings a season. Reading the list of playwrights gives one the impression that this is a producing group leaning toward more intellectual stage fare than like-sized companies elsewhere. But then, Mendocino is an artistic community. And for all of the Tom Stoppard, Kurt Vonnegut, Jr., Harold Pinter offerings there is also a G. B. Shaw, a Neil Simon, a Woody Allen, or a Noel Coward. Balancing off these are newer names in theatre, such as Michael Cristofer (*The Shadow Box*), David Mamet (*American Buffalo*), and Lanford Wilson (*The Rimers of Eldrich*). Now and then there are a musical and a Tennessee Williams.

Future plans call for a theatre enlargement program and an expanded subscription roster. The initiation of a Stage 2 session in the winter off-season for new plays and playwrights will put an emphasis on nontraditional and experimental works.

There are various ways to get to Highway 1 on the coast from Cloverdale to the south (Highway 128) or from Willits and Highway 101 to the north. If you're out for the whole scenic drive you can take Highway 1 all the way from the Marin coast to Eureka. As you reach Mendocino, watch for the Little Lake Road turnoff. Take it to the jog at Lansing, then continue on with it to Kasten. You're there. Enjoy, not only the theatre but the entire town.

P.S. If you're in Mendocino during the summer, check Crown Hall at Ukiah and Osborne streets. You'll find the Gloriana Opera Company there doing musicals. Usually it's Gilbert and Sullivan, but lately they've expanded their repertoire. Call (707) 937-5205 for information and tickets. Crown Hall (circa 1904) is the local public auditorium. It belongs to the Volunteer Fire Department and, if it were in the eastern part of America, would probably have been a Grange Hall. Here, it's a part-time playhouse.

THE OLD VILLAGE PLAYHOUSE FERNDALE REPERTORY THEATRE

267 seats (reserved)
LOCATION 447 Main Street, Ferndale.
BUSINESS ADDRESS
P.O. Box 892
Ferndale, CA 95536.
BOX OFFICE-BUSINESS TELEPHONE
(707) 725-2378.

MANAGING-ARTISTIC DIRECTOR
Charles Morrison.
HANDICAPPED ACCESS The playhouse is ramped from the street to the auditorium. Wheelchairs will not fit into the men's restroom. Some signed performances are given for hearing-impaired patrons.

The Old Village Playhouse (the original sign is still there) is a state historical landmark. The fact is, so is the whole town of Ferndale. If you thought San Francisco has great Victorian homes and architecture, wait until you see Ferndale's. The town was settled in the 1850s by the Danish, and outside of Solvang in southern California, also a Danish contribution, you would have to go some distance to match this kind of vintage charm.

Ferndale (population 1,400) specializes in the sorts of things you'd drive a goodly distance for: antiques, art galleries, jewelry, leather crafts, redwood forests, and an active semi-professional theatre group, the Ferndale Repertory Theatre.

The playhouse itself was built in 1920 to show new-fangled moving picture shows. The rep company came much later, in 1971. The raked proscenium stage looks out on well-padded standard theatre seats. The

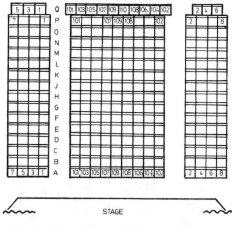

THE OLD VILLAGE PLAYHOUSE, FERNDALE

decor runs from original 1920s art pieces, through Art Deco, to a new wood-stained redwood concession stand in the lobby. The box office is the old under-the-marquee type.

Tickets sell for $5 and $6 to plays that are both contemporary and classic, drawn from the popular American repertory library or the list of British hits. An occasional musical is thrown in. In short, you can see just about anything in the way of theatre at the Ferndale Repertory.

Ferndale is about 17 miles south of Eureka. Take the Ferndale-Fernbridge exit off Highway 101, and in 5 short miles you'll be in the center of town. The Old Village Playhouse is in the center of town on the left side of Main Street.

FORUM THEATRE

---

300 seats (unreserved).
LOCATION AND BOX OFFICE
Tompkins Hill Road
Eureka, CA 95501.
BOX OFFICE-BUSINESS TELEPHONE
(707) 443-8411, extension 530.
MANAGING-ARTISTIC DIRECTOR Jane Hill.
HANDICAPPED ACCESS There is a specially marked parking area for the handicapped. Wheelchair access is easy, with seating locations in the rear. The theatre is small, and sight and sound are good from these positions. The restrooms are fully equipped for the handicapped.

I haven't included many academic facilities in this guide, but, because of its accessibility to the Eureka community and its active schedule, I'm making an exception for the College of the Redwoods' Forum Theatre.

This facility is available, regular scheduling having precedence, for theatrical events other than college productions, such as touring shows and locally produced presentations. The collegiate season (early December, late March, early June, and early August) includes classics and musicals, along with student-written and -mounted originals.

The theatre, like the campus, was built in 1966 and blends into the contours of the landscape they share. The building materials are native to Humboldt County. The theatre itself is warm and intimate, with the redwood theme carried through in the wall paneling. The technical facilities are modest but adequate for the productions offered, and the acoustics are better than average.

Take the College of the Redwoods exit from Highway 101 eight miles south of Eureka. Pack a picnic, because there are public picnic areas with spectacular views of this luscious country.

Ashland, Oregon

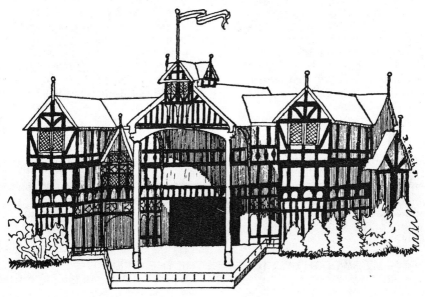

THE ELIZABETHAN THEATRE

THE OREGON SHAKESPEAREAN FESTIVAL

BOX OFFICE-BUSINESS ADDRESS
P.O. Box 158
15 South Pioneer
Ashland, Oregon 97520.
BOX OFFICE TELEPHONE (503) 482-4331.
BUSINESS TELEPHONE (503) 482-2111.
EXECUTIVE DIRECTOR William W. Patton.
ARTISTIC DIRECTOR Jerry Turner.
HANDICAPPED ACCESS There are wheelchair access and special seating arrangements for the handicapped in all three theatres. Requests for this consideration should be made in advance, when the tickets are purchased. All restrooms are equipped for the handicapped.

BABYSITTING SERVICE Since children under three years of age are not permitted in any of the theatres, babysitting is available through the Tudor Guild Babysitting Service. Arrange in advance by writing P.O. Box 1210, Ashland, OR 97520, or phone (503) 482-0940.

Have you ever found a place that suits you to a T? A place that could be the end of your rainbow? A place where you could settle down and travel no more? If you've been to Ashland, Oregon, you may, like me, think you've found that special place. If you've never been—have I got a pot of gold for you.

Ashland is in Jackson County, Oregon, nestled in the Siskiyou Mountains. The area also contains the marvelous wilderness lands of the

Rogue River. The forests gave Ashland its first industry, lumber, back in 1852. Two Ohioans (from Ashland County) gave up on the California Gold Rush and struck out for the north. Californians have been doing that in increasing numbers ever since. The Ashland-Medford area is growing at a phenomenal, and to many, a shocking, rate. Medford is proud to be called the Pear Capital of the World, and being just twelve miles north of Ashland, it also shares in the tourist business.

By the way, if you feel strangely tranquil on your visit to Ashland, it's the water. Drink it! It contains lithium, used extensively in medicinal calmatives. The word *Lithia* is used in the names of several streets and parks in Ashland. And there is no record of a single case of Banquo's revenge as a result of imbibing this mineral-rich liquid.

A BRIEF HISTORY OF THE FESTIVAL
The late Angus Bowmer, founder and director of the Oregon Shakespearean Festival, was a teacher at Southern Oregon College in Ashland. In 1935 he decided that the abandoned Chautauqua shell overlooking lovely Lithia Park would be an ideal setting for an Elizabethan theatre. Lithia Park, by the way, was designed by John McLaren, famed creator San Francisco's Golden Gate Park. With a little help from local businesses, Bowmer's idea became a reality. As part of the Fourth of July celebration that year, audiences were treated to William Shakespeare's *Twelfth Night* and *The Merchant of Venice*. The acting company was asked to share the stage with boxing matches, so that the surefire sporting event would pick up the losses expected on the plays. In fact, the plays covered the deficit of the boxing matches.

Every summer since, with the exception of six years while the nations of the earth staged the real-life tragedy of World War II, Shakespeare's people have trod the boards at Ashland. A tradition of presenting four of the Bard's plays per season evolved and is still the rule.

More recently, other great works of stage literature have shared the annual bill, and new plays are often staged as part of the scheduling. The season, extended over the years, now runs February through October.

In addition to the regular festival activities in the three theatres, a summer course for students in the Institute of Renaissance Studies is offered. This is focused not only on Shakespeare, but also on other Elizabethan writers, and on the culture, art, and music of the time. Preshow musicales are staged by these young performers, who play authentic Elizabethan instruments and dance to old English aires.

THE THEATRES
The present Ashland theatre complex has grown to three facilities. All the theatres are located in the immediate vicinity of East Main and Pioneer streets, with the Elizabethan and Bowmer theatres overlooking Lithia Park. The old Elizabethan structure burned in 1957, and the current outdoor replica of the Fortune Theatre of Shakespeare's London opened in 1959. It seats 1,173 persons, and there's standing room for an additional 115. The seats are comfortable, if not luxurious, and pillows are available for those without sufficient natural cushioning. If the night air is just right, and the play a little slow, you may find yourself an unwitting snoozer.

The $1.8-million-dollar Angus Bowmer Theatre, an impressive, ultra-modern indoor house, opened its doors in 1970. It seats 599 patrons and was built for flexibility in staging and the maximum use of technical effects. Shakespearean plays as well

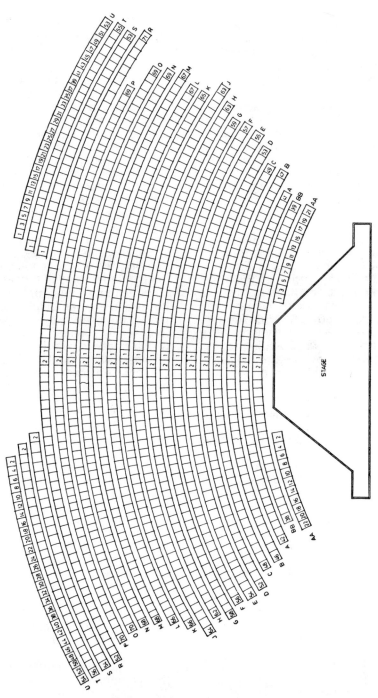

THE ELIZABETHAN THEATRE

as plays by other authors, modern and classic, are presented here. It lacks the charm of the outdoor setting but makes up for it with marvelous sets and lighting.

The newest facility is the intimate and amazingly versatile Black Swan Theatre. Built in 1977, it not only has a completely changeable stage area, but the seating layout switches about as well. It usually allows for 130 to 140 viewers of the more offbeat and experimental of the festival offerings.

TICKET PRICES AND POLICIES
Ticket prices for the Oregon Shakespearean Festival are subject to change, season by season. For instance, two seasons ago the scale was from $4.50 to $8.50. At this writing that has indulged in upward mobility to $5.50 to $10.50. The accompanying seating diagrams show you the breakdown. Standing room, at the Elizabethan Theatre only, is $3.50 and available only on the day of the performance when the performance is sold out.

Refunds and exchanges are made until twenty-four hours before curtain time. There is a $1.00 resale service charge. Mail orders and phone orders are accepted, but there are no credit card sales on phone orders. Mail orders must include payment in full and a stamped self-addressed envelope. Payment for phone orders must reach the box office within four days of the placing of the order. Group, student, and senior citizen discounts are available on request.

THE ELIZABETHAN THEATRE

The theatre complex at Ashland is tied together by a series of walkways and bricked patios. Rising up against the blue sky and lush green forest behind it is the Elizabethan Theatre. It might well be sitting on a plot of land somewhere in England. Surrounded by a high, ivy-covered wall, the buff plaster and dark-brown–beamed facade of a typical Tudor mansion, with its various gables, tells you instantly that this is the outdoor theatre devoted to the works of Shakespeare, Marlowe, and Jonson. The only modern touches are the tall lighting frames that hold the stage lighting. The control booth is housed in a green blockhouse in the rear of the seating area. The roof of this facility is a flat stage upon which dancers, jugglers, mimes, clowns, instrumentalists, and singers present Renaissance entertainment prior to the play of the evening.

The stage is faithful to Elizabethan design, with a center thrust platform, side stages, an inner-below area, and multilevel balconies and windows in which scenes may be played. The entire stage is faced with a low hedge, and the platform edge is topped with a short wooden railing. This may have originally been intended, in the Bard's day, to make a clear definition between the aristocrats, seated on the stage, and the groundlings who crowded the common ground. Now the actors use it to sit on, and it's a pretty touch to the decor. Shields are mounted on the front walls and all around the perimeter with the names and dates of plays performed here in the past. The restrooms are located outside the compound walls to the rear, below the gift shop.

ANGUS BOWMER THEATRE

Back across the courtyard from the Elizabethan Theatre is the ultra-modern house containing the Bowmer Theatre. Tall windows and glass doors mark the entrance to this memorial to the founder of the Festival. Inside the spacious lobby a portrait of the late Angus Bowmer holds a place of prominence against the wooden wall. The carpeting is a gold hue, reflecting the outdoor sunlight entering through the many windows. On display are photos of the present season's productions and those that have played the theatre since its opening. Large prop pieces are featured in special areas and displays of costumes often share the lobby spotlight.

Entrance to the auditorium is gained through doors located on many levels, depending on where in the Continental-style seating area your tickets lead you. The seats themselves are plushly cushioned in a deep-blue fabric. The walls blend in with a dark-gray tone. There is no stage drape, but a proscenium staging is possible on the thrust stage, if such is desired. The control booth is to the rear and at the top of the indoor arena. The Bowmer is the most conventional of the three theatres, but it has been designed for total technical versatility.

THE BLACK SWAN THEATRE

When you leave the Bowmer and head across the plaza to Pioneer Street and the Black Swan Theatre at the corner of East Main Street, you will pass the main box office that handles the tickets for all of the plays and special programs. Bulletin boards in the area will give you

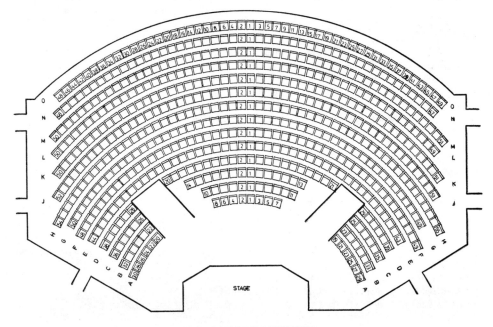

ANGUS BOWMER THEATRE

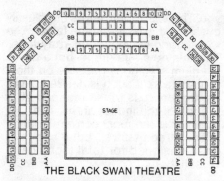

THE BLACK SWAN THEATRE

important and interesting information as to what is going on.

The Black Swan Theatre is housed in what used to be an automobile dealership. That accounts for the modern storefront appearance of the building. A wooden rail with black iron supports acts as a crowd control barrier and a place to rest while you wait for the theatre to open. Once inside, you're surrounded by golden mirrors that follow your progress through the L-shaped lobby and into the theatre. This is a "black-box" room, with all of the walls draped in black fabric. Seating is usually just four rows deep on leveled platforms. The seats are standard theatre types covered in brown fabric. The gray carpeting that cushions the lobby floor ends at the entrance to the performance space. There is a casualness to this facility that is common to experimental theatres and small off-Broadway houses, nicely balancing the Elizabethan and the Bowmer theatres and completing Ashland's broad representation of theatre styles.

ASHLAND

GETTING THERE
Ashland is located twelve miles south of Medford, Oregon, and approximately 350 miles north of the San Francisco Bay Area. If you're determined to drive, it couldn't be easier.

Just follow Highway 5 all the way. If you fly, take United or Air Oregon to the Medford-Jackson County Airport, then take a cab or rent a car for the twelve-mile journey south. And let me throw this idea into the hopper. You can take Amtrak—that's right, a train trip—to Klamath Falls and then bus around the mountains or rent a car, and you're there.

Another travel option is to take either Continental Trailways or Greyhound. Both buslines offer Ashland service, and in both cases San Francisco and Sacramento are the connecting points for the rest of the state.

ACCOMMODATIONS
There are plenty of motel rooms available in Ashland. However, in the summer months it's advisable to make reservations at least a month in advance.

Rates for a double begin at around $25 and climb to the $65-per-night category, depending on the opulence of the establishment. Close into town, about a ten-minute walk from the theatres, is the Bard's Inn. It looks like the run-of-the-mill roadside motel, but it's actually very comfortable and as friendly as all get-out. It's also on the lower end of the cost scale. Out at the other end of town is the plusher Ashland Hills Inn. It's on the upper end of the lodging fee graph. In between, literally, is the Marc Anthony Hotel, right in the center of town. All around these three are plenty of choices in price and style.

If you're going with the family, or if you're just the outdoorsy type, reserve space in one of the numerous campgrounds and sleep under the stars. The Ashland summer climate is perfect for this kind of adventure.

FOOD
As though the scenery and the remarkable congeniality of Ashland weren't enough, wait until you start

eating. Starting is easy; it's the stopping that's a problem. The food is beautifully prepared, charmingly served, and more than fairly priced. The sizes of the portions border on sinful. Here are some names to remember when your stomach alarm goes off: Jasmin's for Greek Cuisine (and fine jazz late at night); the Dahlia Restaurant for Chinese delicacies. The Banbury Cross for crêpes (and a lovely view of the creek), and the Lithia Grocery Restaurant for great delicacies (but whatever you have, finish up with the blueberry cobbler). Omar's on Siskiyou Boulevard is the place for beef and seafood. Mexican dishes, more than you can politely eat, can be had at Casa Feliz on East Main Street in town, or travel a couple of miles north to Talent and give Gallec's a try.

Delicious Eastern European dishes are the specialty of a converted house just outside the city limits, called Chata. For elegant French dining downtown, visit Chateaulin Restaurant Français.

I can't end this section without mentioning breakfast. Don't skip it. Again, you can take your pick without risk. There's Geppetto's, the Brothers, or Hamlet's Roost, all fine. Here's where the blueberries (seasonal) win the day. Ashland has the world's biggest, tastiest, finest blueberry pancakes. Enough, enough! If I keep on this way I'll be on a plane to Ashland before I complete this chapter.

The foregoing list is only partial but, to paraphrase Will Rogers, I never had a meal in Ashland that I didn't like. Dress for dining, as well as for theatregoing, is always casual.

OTHER ACTIVITIES AND SIDE TRIPS
Theatres are traditionally "dark" (closed) on Mondays. To fill the void, the festival is presenting a Monday matinee and evening summer schedule of Hollywood musical films (the subject matter may change from year to year). In the Elizabethan Theatre, Monday evenings are for summer concerts, though not on a regular basis.

Every performance day except July Fourth you can reserve space on a backstage tour led by members of the festival company.

Check with the Chamber of Commerce for the most all-American time you'll have this or any summer: They'll give you the times and dates of the band concerts in the shell in Lithia Park. The band is first-rate, and the feeling you'll go to bed with is worth the trip to Ashland.

The Rogue River is too close not to enjoy. Whether you just walk the banks or ride the whitewater, there are activities for all tastes.

For a day of wandering through history, see Jacksonville, located midway between Medford and Ashland. It's a Gold Rush town that didn't die when the vein petered out. The movie, *The Great Northfield, Minnesota Raid* was shot here, and *Paint Your Wagon* could have been. If you're here in August, enjoy the Britt Music Festival: classical concerts on a wooded hillside under the stars.

CONCLUSION
It's possible to spend a lot more money and travel many more miles from home for a theatre tour or a week or two in the country, but excesses are unnecessary with Ashland so near. Special tour packages are available through your local travel agents, or you can make arrangements for an individual tour package through Ashland Central Reservations—telephone (503) 488-1011. I've visited very few events that have left as positive and as lasting an impression on me as the Oregon Shakespearean Festival. Just a brief qualifier: As with any other theatrical season, some of the plays are excellent, others aren't. But, after all, isn't that part of the magic of going to the theatre?

The San Francisco
International Film Festival

THE PALACE OF FINE ARTS

PALACE OF FINE ARTS THEATRE
CASTRO THEATRE

BUSINESS ADDRESSES AND TELEPHONES
San Francisco International
  Film Festival
3320 Bank of America Center
555 California Street
San Francisco, CA 94104.
Telephone: (415) 391-6881.

San Francisco International
  Film Festival
3501 California Street
San Francisco, CA 94118.
Telephone: (415) 221-9055.

CABLE ADDRESS Filmfest, USA.
EXECUTIVE DIRECTOR Peter Buchanan.
FESTIVAL DIRECTOR Albert Johnson.
ASSOCIATE DIRECTOR Thomas Luddy
(special programs).
ASSOCIATE DIRECTOR Mel Novikoff
(public relations).
OPERATIONS Lorena Cantrell.
MANAGEMENT Patricia Peyton.
OPERATIONS COORDINATOR
Eric Whittington.

A BRIEF HISTORY

It all started like a neighborhood block party, then, like Topsy, it just grew and grew. That's about as apt a description of the San Francisco International Film Festival as anybody is likely to come up with. It began in 1955 as a part of Italian Week, and today ranks with the major film festivals of the world: Cannes, Berlin, and New York. Where it places in the top four depends on whom you ask.

Back in 1955 Irving M. "Bud" Levin, son of a film industry pioneer who operated nickelodeons when San Francisco was a much younger city, and a member of a prominent movie house–owning family, was asked to put together an Italian Film Festival to tie in with a city-wide celebration. With a lot of help from his friends and sponsorship by names such as Magnin and Zellerbach, the festival was a smash hit. An unknown film called *La Strada* was the big attention getter. That one-week event was held at the Alexandria Theater on Geary Boulevard. At the same time a film by an unknown film director named Antonioni was going begging for a commercial exhibitor in the United States.

Levin, not willing to let so much ground work go for naught, decided to make the film festival an annual affair. The deal he got from the Art Commission was that he could mount the San Francisco International Film Festival (the high-falutin new name), and he could also be responsible for any annual deficit. The still-prominent Levin recalls, "I was younger then, and I had the nerve of a thief. I took the deal." Such a deal!

Still tending to his bouncing baby with his professional know-how, the official "director" of the unofficial festival (as far as Hollywood was concerned) relied more and more on local philanthropists and business persons to support the financially losing program. Major hotels donated the rooms where visiting stars and dignitaries signed the tabs and had a great time in San Francisco. All the while, the reputation and the creditability of the film festival was growing.

Part of the problem that Hollywood had with the festival to the north was that prizes were given. Could this grow into competition with the Oscars? Probably not, but such is the nature of the insecurity of Tinseltown that films entered in the San Francisco fest could not have been shown anywhere else in the United States and could not have had a commercial run anywhere in the world. These proved pretty stiff prerequisites for some. As the festival grew, so did the squabbles.

The social side was the icing on the cake for most volunteers involved in this glamorous experiment. You couldn't buy an opening-night ticket. Those seats, a precious 500 of them, were given as rewards for services rendered in getting the festival into shape. Besides, the before-and-after bashes thrown by Levin could only accommodate 250 at a time in his home.

After eight years of eating losses and getting more and more guff from bureaucratic snippers, Levin threw in the towel and took on the safest role in the now nationally renowned spectacle, that of spectator. A couple of years later a few thousand dollars found their way in his direction as reimbursement for all that he had spent on the festival in its formative years.

From 1964 on, the San Francisco International Film Festival took new, giant strides. No longer in the hands of one man and a jury of filmwatchers who gave prizes, the festival took on a more culturally oriented format. The new prime mover, Mel Swig, and his committee of policy molders, decided that the practice of prize-giving should go. Films would be honored instead simply by the distinction of being presented in the City by the Bay during those two exciting weeks of the festival —an event now watched by the world cinema community.

Levin had moved the event to the Metro Theater, which he owned, on Union Street in the Marina District. But the new presenters needed even more room. The festival climbed up Nob Hill to the Masonic Auditorium. Later, a new regime, headed by former child star and Oscar winner Claude Jarman, would headquarter in the Palace of Fine Arts and then annex a beautifully renovated historical landmark, the Castre Theatre (the *tre* spelling is theirs).

Controversy has never been far from the surface of these cinematic doings, but that's normal in so high-profile an event. More important, the two-week celebration of world movie-making has expanded, so that world premieres share the giant screen with already-acclaimed films from America and abroad.

Perhaps the most popular features of the festival are the film retrospectives of the careers of great stars and directors accompanied with personal appearances of these stellar beings. Ironically, Michelangelo Antonioni, who couldn't peddle his flick in the United States back in 1955, turned up as an honored celebrity in 1968.

Some of the other luminaries that have appeared here include Gene Kelly, Walt Disney, Busby Berkeley, Fred Astaire, George Cukor, Jack Warner, Lillian Gish, Edward G. Robinson, Bette Davis, Mike Nichols, Rita Hayworth, Francois Truffaut Jeanne Moreau, Truman Capote, Jane Fonda, Burt Lancaster, Liv Ullmann, Mel Brooks, Sir Alec Guinness and Akira Kurosawa—and that's only a fraction of the list. Folks like that don't show up at second-rate film festivals. Even better where the audience is concerned, a great many of these up-close looks at the great and near-great are free of charge.

The year 1980 saw another major changeover in the administration and thrust of the SFIFF. An energetic new combine, made up of both professional film people and avowed cinema buffs, is now at the helm. and expansion is still the name of the game.

The most far-reaching change in the festival is the alteration of its basic format from a two-week-a-year event to an all-year happening. This is to be partly accomplished by staging small festivals in the city's ethnic centers, presenting films of national origin unique to those centers throughout the twelve-month period. In keeping with this plan, there has been a major Chinese film festival cosponsored by the Chinese

Cultural Center and accomplished with the support of the Chinese and other Asian neighborhood and business communities of the Bay Area.

The spring segment of the festival spotlights the Bay Area Filmmakers' Week. During this period local film directors, animators, and others who have made it (such as George Lucas and Francis Coppola), as well as those yet to attain such status, show and discuss their works at a major San Francisco theater. Another film series, cosponsored with the Pacific Film Archives at the University of California at Berkeley, links the festival with that nationally respected repository of domestic and foreign films.

SAN FRANCISCO FILM SOCIETY

In a move to involve the general public in a more tangible and direct way, the festival has created the San Francisco Film Society. It provides a source of revenue for the funding of the expanded festival, which will help to wipe out an inherited deficit (shades of the pains of the early days).

What's offered to Film Society members? Well, there's a heavy emphasis on fun, with dances, formal dinners, and other shindigs that let sponsors and patrons rub elbows with film personalities on a one-to-one basis. Added to this are sneak previews of yet-unreleased films and a quarterly newsletter to let the membership stay close to what's current in the film business.

The ultimate point of all this, and it's a commendable one, is to involve not just the San Francisco area, but all of northern California in the International Film Festival.

INDIVIDUAL MEMBERSHIP $25 Discounts at all Film Society events. Advance notice of all Film Society events. Free Film Society poster. Free subscription to Film Society newsletter. Free Film Society button.
DUAL MEMBERSHIP $40 All the privileges of Individual Membership for two.

SUSTAINER $40 All the privileges of Individual Membership plus: Free Film Society T-shirt. Discounts on film publications.
DUAL SUSTAINER $55 All the privileges of Sustainer for two.

CONTRIBUTOR $50 All the privileges of Sustainer plus: Free admission to monthly sneak-preview screenings.
DUAL CONTRIBUTOR $80 All the privileges of Contributor for two.

SPONSOR $250 All the privileges of Contributor plus: Free admission to Silver Anniversary Opening Night. Film and Dinner Ceremonies. Invitation to special film and social events.
DUAL SPONSOR $450 All the privileges of Sponsor for two.

PATRON $500 All the privileges of Sponsor plus: Reserved seating admission to all year-round Society-sponsored events.
DUAL PATRON $900 All the privileges of Patron for two.

SENIOR (65) $15 All the privileges of Individual Membership.
DUAL SENIOR $20 All the privileges of Individual Membership for two.

BUSINESS ADDRESS
San Francisco Film Society
San Francisco International Film Festival
3501 California Street, Suite 201
San Francisco, California 94118

GENERAL INFORMATION

Give or take a day or two, the main events of the film festival take place during the second and third weeks of October. All facts and program information should be checked before you make plans to attend. Schedules for each year are available from the festival office.

TICKET INFORMATION

(These specifics are subject to change, year to year.)

Tickets for evening film programs are under $5.00 per seat, usually $4.00 or $4.50. Tickets for special daytime programs, tributes, retrospectives, and so on, range from $2.00 to $4.00.

There are several programs during each film festival that are shown free of charge: the Best of Documentary series, the showing of obscure or forgotten films of a given director, and some new films not entered in the regular festival schedule.

Tickets may be purchased at the Palace of Fine Arts box office, the Downtown Center Box Office in San Francisco, and at the Castro Theatre approximately two weeks prior to the opening of the festival and/or at screening time, depending on ticket demands. Many films and events sell out.

PROGRAMS

Examples of typical events include special programs devoted to new directors, animation, short subjects, television specials and documentaries, film technicians, costumers, makeup artists, stars, character actors and actresses, stuntmen and stuntwomen, and special-effects specialists fill the giant stage with celebrities.

The program day begins at eleven in the morning and continues until late afternoon. For the two-week period of the festival, every day is like a holiday in a world film center, a marathon of movie-watching.

THE FILMS

Films shown at the festival come from almost every nation in the world. Emerging African states, the Eastern European block, the Soviet Union, both Chinas, Bermuda, Central and South America, the United States, Canada, and on and on. Stick a pin in a map with your eyes covered, as in a game of pin-the-tail-on-the-donkey, and chances are that the festival is, has, or will show a short subject, a documentary, or a feature film from the place your pin lands.

Given all of the other merits of this splendiferous event, the one that impresses me most is that no dubbed films are allowed on the screen—foreign films have subtitles only. Occasionally a renegade print will get through and be shown because it didn't clear customs until three minutes before showing time, but that's rare. It is more disappointing when a long-awaited feature from a much-heralded director, a film that promises to be a high point of the festival, is lost somewhere between Addis Ababa and Trenton, New Jersey, and never arrives at all. The substitution, no matter how well intentioned, never fills the breach. That's one of the dangers that both plague and add to the excitement of any international film festival.

IN CONCLUSION

October is doubtless the most pleasant month of the year in San Francisco: The air is clear, the temperature is moderate, and the seasonal breezes are full of the scent of autumn. The grounds surrounding the Palace of Fine Arts are ideal for autumn picnic lunches on the grass beside the duck-inhabited pond. You might give it a try if you're spending the day.

Within a few blocks of the Palace are fine restaurants of all persuasions. One of my favorites is Liverpool Lil's, at the main entrance to the Presidio at Lombard and Lyon. There is no scarcity of good eateries in the Castro District either, so "bon appetit" and good viewing at the Film Festival.

PALACE OF FINE ARTS

1,000 seats (reserved).
LOCATION AND BOX OFFICE
3301 Lyon Street (at Bay Street)
San Francisco, CA 94123.
BOX OFFICE TELEPHONE (415) 921-9968.
BUSINESS TELEPHONE (415) 563-6504.
HANDICAPPED ACCESS The theatre is accessible to wheelchairs. Chair-confined patrons will probably be limited to the forward rows, because the main portion of the auditorium is Continental seating on multiple elevations. The restrooms are equipped for the handicapped.

Bernard R. Maybeck had gained fame as a designer of beautiful homes when he was engaged as the architect for this colossus celebrating the arts at the 1915 Exposition. When it was decided, in the sixties, to rescue the ruins from oblivion, San Francisco architect Hans Gerson was retained to recreate what Maybeck had conceived. Working from original blueprints and drafting new ones, Gerson saw the first phase of his accomplishment opened to public view in 1968. Financing was provided from three sources: a city bond issue, some state aid, and a generous grant from local philanthropist Walter Johnson. There wasn't enough, however, to complete the project. Some of the columns went uncapped until Johnson gave the balance of what was needed, and the Palace of Fine

Arts, as it looks today, was finished in 1975.

Most of the ornamental details of the Palace of Fine Arts are on the outside. The massive Corinthian columns, the graceful arches, the huge urns, and the musing maidens gazing out over the grounds where swans glide on a placid lake are remnants of the 1915 Exposition. The entrance to the lobby is located about half way up the frontage road that parallels Lombard Street. An awning bears the only evidence of the theatre's name. The advance-sale box office is located in the front of the building near the stage door entrance. There is limited parking along this frontage roadway but the spaces are usually gone an hour before showtime. Be warned that the more popular programs will sell out well in advance. Inside, the lobby is large and airy, with concrete-block construction masked occasionally by red draperies. The box office area is to the left. Another set of doors opens into the main lobby. A stone fireplace adds a touch of physical and esthetic warmth to an otherwise plain interior with its chilly, warehouse-style tin ceiling.

The large modern restrooms are located in the long wall between the main auditorium entrances, the women's room on the right, the men's room on the left. This wall is used to display art works or photos. During the festival it features stills from the films and portraits of the stars.

Red carpeting gives way to bare concrete for half of the main lobby. This area contains tables and chairs where patrons may consume the snacks and beverages available at the catered refreshment stands. Other tables hold T-shirts and programs.

On the extreme right and left of the lobby are the entrances to the auditorium, where a wide sea of red theatre seats span the house in an unbroken Continental-style arrange-

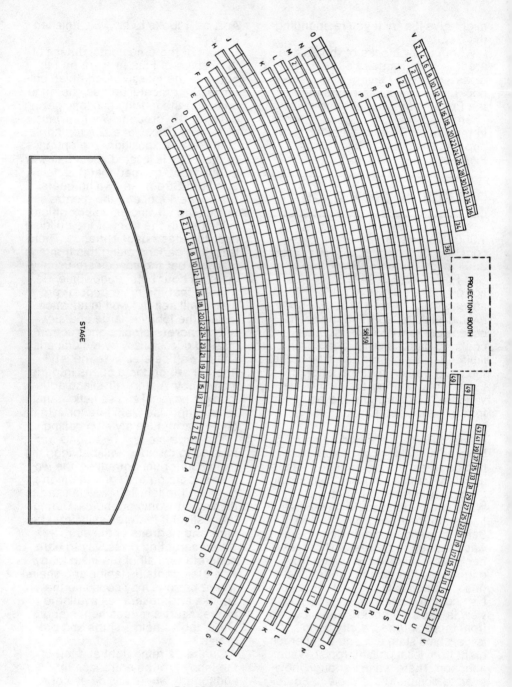

PALACE OF FINE ARTS THEATRE

ment. The elevations carry back to the rear of the house, providing the height for the projection booth that dominates the center rear of the auditorium. The huge crimson-draped stage occupies the entire front of the house, and the orchestra pit is a great spot for international press photographers to snap shots of actors and directors as they grace the stage for seminars and tributes. All the walls are covered with the red draperies that conceal the cement blocks throughout the theatre. Looking up toward the corrugated roof, you'll see a large wrought-iron ring chandelier with white globes. Sound baffle panels have been suspended to aid the acoustics.

Backstage are the conference rooms, offices, dressing rooms, and press meeting rooms. Security is always heavy at the entrances to this rear area, and, without proper passes and credentials, chances are you won't make it past the alert guards and festival staff members.

For the architecture buffs: There is an auto dealership in San Francisco housed in one of Maybeck's masterpieces—a work of art dedicated to the auto touring car, so to speak. In the late 1920s, Packard dealer Earl C. Anthony commissioned the creator of the Palace of Fine Arts to design cathedrals in which to display his cars. There was one in Los Angeles, one in Oakland (torn down in one of Kaiser Corporation's expansion moves) and one in San Francisco. The latter is still standing and has been restored to its original grandeur. Only the chandeliers are not authentic. You can visit it and purchase your next Rolls Royce at 901 Van Ness Avenue (at Ellis) where the current occupant is British Motors.

To get to the Palace from Highway 280 and points south, take Nineteenth Avenue and Park Presidio to Doyle Drive and turn right onto Lombard. You'll see the Palace immediately to your left. Make a left at Lyon into the parking area. From the north, follow the same directions after crossing the Golden Gate Bridge. From the East Bay, take the Broadway exit off the Bay Bridge and follow it to Broadway (North Beach) through the tunnel and right onto Van Ness. Van Ness will take you to Lombard. Turn left on Lombard to Lyon, then right on Lyon into the parking area. From downtown San Francisco, take Van Ness north to Lombard, as above.

CASTRO THEATRE

1,600 seats (nonreserved).
LOCATION AND BOX OFFICE
429 Castro Street
San Francisco, CA 94114.
BOX OFFICE-BUSINESS TELEPHONE
(415) 621-6120.
HANDICAPPED ACCESS The theater is accessible to wheelchairs. The restrooms are not equipped for the handicapped.

The Castro Theatre has been designated a historical landmark by the city and county of San Francisco. Designed by famed architect Timothy L. Pflueger (who also designed the Top of the Mark, the Pacific Telephone Building, 450 Sutter, and the Oakland Paramount Theatre, among other buildings), it opened on June 23, 1922, under the banner of the Nasser Brothers Theatres. Unlike many houses of that era, it was never a vaudeville theatre. Motion pictures were what it was built for and what it is still used for today. Built at a cost of $300,000, it was, and is again in its restored condition, one of the most attractive examples of an elaborate movie palace in northern California.

Opening night was a gala occasion at the Castro. Live music was provided by Waldemar Lind and the New

Castro Orchestra. Sharing the orchestra pit was the mighty theater organ, and on the screen Wallace Reed was starring in *Across The Continent.* A comedy titled *Cold Feet* served as the curtain-raiser. In just a few days the Castro would host the biggest feature film of the year, Rudolph Valentino in *The Four Horsemen of the Apocalypse.* But later the theater lost its first-run status and became a second- and third-run neighborhood house. Realizing the value, both historically and commercially, of such a facility, Mel Novikoff and the Surf Theatres organization obtained the lease, closed the theater for complete restoration, and re-opened it, again with gala festivities, on October 27, 1976. It was declared a landmark on March 9, 1978. It now has a policy of first-run features combined with special series and limited play dates for nostalgic favorites and classics. In addition, it is one of the San Francisco International Film Festival's two primary screening theaters.

The ornate marquee has retained its changeable letter tracks, and the underside is illuminated by bare, frosted light bulbs. The box office, centered under the outer foyer overhang, is covered in patterns of white, gold, blue, and yellow ceramic tiles. The windows are of heavy glass set into ornate metalwork frames. The side walls and display cases carry through the same theme. Rich oak doors lead to a small entry chamber (thus soundproofing the lobby from most street noise), and a matching set of doors leads into the long, narrow main lobby. Wood is also used for the old-fashioned concession stand and the massive frames of the Art Deco lounge furniture. The smell coming from the candy stand is irresistible: The Castro pops its popcorn in one of those marvelous old theater machines. It's fresh, not

bagged in a warehouse somewhere in the Tenderloin.

The metal and opaque glass chandeliers are in the Art Deco mode, and urns with potted palms create the atmosphere of the twenties and thirties. Free-standing display cases herald current and coming events, and on the far right you can investigate the secrets of a 1910 Motiograph Deluxe motion picture projector. The lamp housing has a fixture to receive an incandescent bulb, but one suspects that it was originally a carbon arc apparatus. The women's restroom is to the right as you enter, and the men's to the far left and downstairs.

The upper lobby is spacious, with draped windows looking out over the marquee onto Castro Street. Overstuffed davenports (as opposed to more common couches) and classic throne chairs and wooden tables furnish the waiting area for early arrivals. The walls are hung with tapestries, and potted palms are growing in this room, too. The rug has a large gold, black, red, green, and blue pattern until it reaches the ramps leading to the split-level balcony. Midway up the stairs to this lounge are two tall, framed mirrors, so you can look your best for lounging.

The auditorium of the Castro could have come right out of *A Thousand and One Nights.* The Art Deco lamps suspended from the balcony overhang seem almost too modern for the grandeur of the huge interior. The deep wine-colored plush seats fill the floor to the edge of the orchestra pit, which contains a theater pipe organ. Most evenings the instrument is played by noted theater organist Elbert La Chelle.

The two side walls mirror each other in detail: Psuedo-Corinthian pilasters frame two giant murals of scenes that are strangely reminiscent of the columns and arches of the Palace of Fine Arts. Toward the front of the house, two false garden terraces are located under the richly sculpted pipe organ loft. The organ's pipes are clearly visible against the bright gold ornamentation. On the face of the front wall are spotlighted images of idealized young royal figures.

The pilasters of the side walls take on full dimension as columns framing the proscenium arch. A gold grand drape fills the opening, behind which is a shallow stage and the large motion picture screen. The size of the screen is one of the few things in the theater that are different from the original.

The main all-wooden floor has a gentle rake from the rear to the front. The gold, black, and red-rust hegagon-patterned carpet that begins in the main lobby continues down the aisles. But looking at the floor is not the thing to be doing. Look up.

The ceiling of the Castro is a marvel. It is fashioned to look like the woven and painted ceiling of a desert tent palace of some fabulously rich Oriental potentate, complete with golden rope hangings and tassels. I won't try to describe the detailing of the art work other than to say that multicolored designs are laid against the salmon-colored background. Suspended from the center of it all is a silvery chandelier, with indirect lighting that illuminates the wonders above.

The color scheme throughout the Castro is a tasteful blending of rusts, browns, salmons, ivories, and gold. The management could probably get away with charging admission just to browse about the building, but, fortunately, the ticket price gives us all of that and screen entertainment as well.

To get to the Castro from the East Bay, take any of the downtown San Francisco off-ramps. Ninth Street-Civic Center is probably the best. Travel north to Market Street, then west on Market to Castro Street. Turn left on Castro. The theater is in the first block on the left. There are street parking and scattered city lots. From Highway 280, take Junipero Serra Boulevard from the junction with Nineteenth Avenue. Follow Serra to Portola. Make a right turn up the hill on Portola and continue over the top. On the descending side, Portola becomes market Street. At the bottom of the hill, where the trolley tracks emerge from the tunnel, is Castro Street. Turn right. From the north, take the Nineteenth Avenue turnoff after you exit from the Golden Gate. Follow Park Presidio to Nineteenth, and Nineteenth to Sloat Boulevard. Turn left on Sloat to Serra Boulevard. There you will cross Serra to Portola and follow the directions above, over the hill to Castro Street.

Let's Go to the Movies

STRAND THEATER, MERCED

WHY, I REMEMBER WHEN . . .

I could go to a Saturday matinee with a quarter, see the movie, have a box of popcorn, and have a nickel left over for an ice cream cone (double scoop) on the way home.

That sentence tells you four things: (1) admission prices to the movies ain't what they used to be; (2) ditto popcorn; (3) likewise ice cream cones; (4) this Brooks must be some kind of really old guy. All but the last are accurate. My first recollection of going to the picture show must date to around 1942 when I was but a tad of a lad. I remember Nelson Eddy singing "Stouthearted Men" in *New Moon;* I remember *The Wizard of Oz, Snow White and the Seven Dwarfs, Bambi* and *Pinocchio,* and even Atlanta burning in *Gone with the Wind.* The first "naughty" movie I saw (in junior high school) was *Johnny Belinda.* I remember it because when my Catholic girlfriend recalled that it was on the condemned list, she left me there in the dark all alone. I remember shedding tears for *My Friend Flicka* and my friend *Lassie.* I was ever so proud of my friend, John Wayne. Probably due to him I spent several years of my later life in the United States Marines.

I grew up under the influence of movies and I saw them in the typical movie theater of the day. In this case it was in Lorain, Ohio, where we had the Palace (who didn't?), the Tivoli (all of the musicals with Esther Williams played there), the Ohio (local patriotism sent us there regularly) and the Dreamland. As a matter of fact, the only bad theater in my town was the Elvira, and we went there because that's where the B and C grade jungle pictures played.

Rats were rumored to walk the sticky floors, but so what? It was dark, and the good guys (English accents with pencil-line mustaches) chased the bad guys (dirty pith helmets, scarred faces, and German accents) through the crocodile-infested swamps, the quicksand-infested deserts, the octopus-infested South Seas lagoons.

Since then, movie theaters have gone through as many changes as the people who attended them. The slipping began at the end of World War II. Some strong feature entries saved the early fifties, but television was about to cut the artery to the heart of moviedom, the box office line. Cinemas (a term then being used to denote a new phenomenon, the "art houses" that presented foreign films and gave away espresso coffee and a false sense of intellectualism) grew in numbers as more and more of the traditional neighborhood silver screens went dark and the buildings became supermarkets, shoe stores, or vacant lots to park cars on.

Somewhere along the way came a big anti-trust suit against the studios, which proved that, by owning the theaters in which the flicks were shown, the studios had a monopoly. Uncle Sam forced the titans of Hollywood to divest themselves of their holdings, and now a new breed of businessman came to the fore, "the exhibitor": a man, or corporation, who would take over the operation and management of the surviving movie houses. The "hard ticket" movie was revived: reserved seats sold in advance for features the studios gambled on as "blockbusters." Then, to all intents and purposes, the studios, or at least the studio system, disappeared, independent producers flooded the market with movies, and there weren't enough theaters to go around. Voila! A brand new building boom. Old giants were converted to multiple auditoriums, and shopping center complexes featured modernistic domes or up to six viewing rooms under one roof. Another factor contributing to the turnaround was the need to leave home in order to escape the mediocre fare and entertainment dregs showing on the tube.

What, you may ask, has all of this to do with going to the movies? Everything. While all of us were getting older, the prices of popcorn, ice cream, and tickets to movie theaters were escalating. What is more, it seems that the more we pay, the less we get. Ushers used to show us to our seats, flashlight in hand. That's about as rare these days as a Pathe News reel or a cartoon. The problem? The exhibitor is now paying so much to the distributor of the movie, a fistful more to the owner of the shopping mall for rent, and a bunch more in taxes that, according to the exhibitor, he's had to cut back in service personnel, that is, the ushers. Not only that, he's had to look to the candy stand for any profit margin, and that means high-priced chocolate bars and golden-priced golden popcorn. Some theaters have closed portions of the auditorium, like those old romantic balconies, to cut back on the number of janitors and the number of cleaning hours. Automation has pared the number of projectionists required to man those multiple projectors for those multiple screens, which means that one person must often keep tabs on up to six different movies and make emergency repairs in superhuman time. The theater operator is up against some real problems.

But, then, so are you, the customer. Often you are herded about by a staff that is overworked and, by most standards today, underpaid. If the volume of business is heavy and the cleaning staff lean, you may find your shiny loafer adhering to a sticky floor. Worse, you may sit in something on the seat that would have been better off on the floor—or in a trash barrel. And to top it all off, the manager's had a bad day when you go to the lobby to complain. Maybe the candy stand inventory is short and he has to make up the difference. He adds insult to your best outfit's injury.

What can you do? Well, if you speak to the doorman, or the candy attendant, or, if you actually find one, the usher, you can hope that they will courteously tell you that they can't do anything about it and send you to the manager. He may or may not tell you to bring him the cleaning bill. Unfortunately, some managers may operate on the business principle that you pay your money and you take your chances. Dead end? Not necessarily. To the chagrin of many theater owner-operators, the staff at your local theater may not reflect the company policy or attitude. You may be wasting your time and aggravation on the employees.

So that you may be a happier moviegoer and end that feeling of frustration, let me advise that you go to the top. Speak to the person who can do something about your problem. If you have no problem, send a note to the same person telling him or her what a pleasure it was doing business at his or her cinema (the term now covers all movie houses aspiring to class status) and complimenting the efficient, friendly staff.

By the way, the pendulum is swinging back. Home entertainment centers, video discs, cable television—all make it conceivable that all those new theaters may be vacant during this decade. It may also interest you to know that studios, distributors, and exhibitors alike are buying into all of those aforementioned entertainment ventures. They've no intention of being left out in the empty parking lot this time.

What's it all about, Alfie? At the end of this section is a comprehensive list of the major motion picture owners and operators in northern California. That way, you can go right to the top. If your favorite theater's not here, chances are the owner is a neighbor of yours and you can stop by and see him or her personally. (I know that you caught the theater spelling immediately, so I won't point it out. You will also note that the theater chains don't follow my spelling rule.)

Here are a few closing thoughts about movie theaters: Because of the kinds and volumes of food sold in movie houses, cleanliness becomes a real problem, both for the patron and for the management. Some houses just don't seem to care. Happily, most major chains have embarked on a campaign to make things better. Trailers now appear on screens politely pointing your attention to trash receptacles in the lobby. Stacking popcorn boxes and soda cups in a neat pile before disposing of them may also be suggested. Of course, spot pickups between shows should be a must on the part of the theater staff.

Finally, there's little to be done esthetically about movie houses that are designed like hollow super-markets or parking lots waiting to happen. There are conspicuous ex-ceptions. Take, for instance, the Dream Theater, a newly opened movie palace (miniature) in Monterey. Located at Lighthouse and Prescott Avenue, it has recreated, from scratch, the feeling of going to the movies in the 1930s. There's a three-tiered lobby full of movie star portraits and movie magazine collages. The audi-torium is crowned by a thirty-foot chandelier with 180 lights on ten different color circuits. The front section of the house has contoured, low-profile red seats with three feet of leg space each. That's my kind of comfort. The center seats are blue wing-backed rockers. The last section sports purple upholstered loveseats for couples. The whole auditorium is nicely elevated, the draperies are sumptuous velour, and the carpets are luxurious. That's all in the old-fashioned tradition. The projection and sound equipment are the latest technical advances. A second house in the same building seats patrons on pillows. That's imagination.

Big-city theaters have to be more practical than resort-area, slower-life-style cinemas. But they can still be run with professionalism and know-how and offer clean, well-appointed surroundings. My vote for one of the finest metropolitan theaters in Cali-fornia is the Coronet, on Geary Boulevard at Arguello, in San Fran-cisco. Manager Al Levin has been at the front door for almost three decades. Here, as at any movie house, the policy may be set by the owning company, but the day-to-day tone is set by the manager. The Coronet is one of the few big houses (999 seats) that hasn't been carved into a multiauditorium opera-tion. The decor, with King Arthur and his court represented in golden relief on the walls, is tasteful and quietly opulent. The staff is courteous and on the ball, and the housekeeping is as tip-top as can be expected in a house that fills all its seats for big Hollywood hits on a steady basis. The Coronet is my hallmark for movie house excellence. You prob-ably have one of your own in your locale. Write the owner and the manager and let them know. The same goes for your local cinematic pig sty, if you have one.

I can't leave this section without inserting a footnote for fans of all movies. San Francisco has the very commercial Castro and Richelieu theaters that specialize in this kind of programing. There are, however, two other houses that I'd like to mention and recommend to you because of the atmosphere of the theaters and their respect for this film genre. The first is the quaint and authentic setting for antique films provided by the Vitaphone in Saratoga. The second is the Avenue Theatre at 2650 San Bruno Avenue in San Francisco. It features photoplays and concerts. The concerts are performed on the "Mighty Wurlitzer" theater organ. The instrument also accompanies silent-film classics with authentic musical scorings. Enjoy!

CIRCUIT THEATERS

AMERICAN MULTI-CINEMA, INC.
Stanley Durwood, President
106 West Fourteenth Street,
Kansas City, MO 64105
David Pearson, District Manager
2540 California Street,
Mountain View, CA 94040
Telephone: (415) 948-1711
COLMA Serramonte Six
MOUNTAIN VIEW Old Mill Six
SAN JOSE Oakridge Six, Saratoga Six
SUNNYVALE Sunnyvale Six

ART THEATRE GUILD
Les Natali, City Manager
1034 Kearny Street
San Francisco, CA 94133
Telephone: (415) 391-1073
FRESNO Fine Art
SACRAMENTO Towne International
SAN FRANCISCO Centre, North Beach
Movie, Presidio
SAN JOSE Towne

WILLIAM A. BLAIR THEATRES
William A. Blair, Jr.
P.O. Box 6003
Santa Rosa, CA 95406
Telephone: (707) 544-0214
NAPA Kay Von Drive-in, River Park
Cine 1-2, Uptown 1-2

BLUMENFELD ENTERPRISES, INC.
Joseph, Nate, Allen, Robert, and
Max Blumenfeld
1521 Sutter Street
San Francisco, CA 94109
Telephone: (415) 563-6200
OAKLAND Roxie
SACRAMENTO Esquire Cinema
SAN FRANCISCO Alhambra 1-2,
Regency 1, Regency 2, Royal
SAN JOSE Meridian Quad Six
TIBURON The Playhouse

**CINERAMA THEATRES INC.
OF CALIFORNIA**
Neal Meyer, Director of Operations
5710 Paradise Drive, Suite 8
Corte Madera, CA 94925
Telephone: (415) 927-0262
BERKELEY Berkeley, Oaks 1-2
MENLO PARK Menlo
PALO ALTO Palo Alto Square 1-2

CINE WEST THEATRES
John Buckley, General Manager
2101 Bryant Street
San Francisco, CA 94110
Telephone: (415) 285-9448
SAN FRANCISCO Bridge Theatre, Cento
Cedar Cinema

CREATIVE FILM SERVICES
David Cooper
P.O. Box 748
San Carlos, 94070
Telephone: (415) 592-8518
PLEASANT HILL Hillcrest
FAIRFIELD Cooper 1-2
FREMONT Fox
PLEASANT HILL Hillcrest
SAN PABLO Cooper 1-2

DREAM THEATRE
John Harris and Alan Weber, Owners
301 Prescott Avenue
Monterey, CA 93940
Telephone: (408) 372-6993,
372-1331

ENEA BROTHERS THEATRES
Sal and John Enea
P.O. Box 2257, Dublin, CA 94566
Telephone: (415) 828-4401
DUBLIN Dublin Cinemas Five

FESTIVAL ENTERPRISES, INC.
Richard Jeha, William F. Kartozian,
Stan Sperling
1450 North California Blvd.
Walnut Creek, CA 94596
Telephone: (415) 934-8652
FRESNO Country Squre, Festival
Cinema Six, Fig Garden Four
HAYWARD Festival Cinema Six
MODESTO Festival Cinema Six
PLEASANT HILL Regency Cinema Five
STOCKTON Festival Cinema Center,
Regency Four
WALNUT CREEK Festival Cinema Five

MARTIN FOSTER ENTERPRISES
Martin Foster, Philip Harris
582 Market Street, No. 90
San Francisco, CA 94104
Telephone: (415) 989-4776
ALBANY Albany Cinema
BERKELEY Act I-II, California Cinema
Center (3)
OAKLAND Piedmont Cinema

GENERAL CINEMA CORPORATION
Kirk Sessions, Divisional Manager
24115 Southland Drive
Hayward, CA 94545
Telephone: (415) 783-2601
CONCORD Sun Valley Cinemas 1-2
FRESNO Manchester Cinemas 1-2
HAYWARD Southland Cinemas 1-2-3-4
MODESTO Vintage Faire Four
SACRAMENTO Sacramento Inn
Cinemas 1-2-3
SAN FRANCISCO Ghirardelli Square
Cinema
SAN MATEO Hillsdale Cinemas 1-2
STOCKTON Cinema Sherwood Plaza 1-2
VISALIA Sequoia Mall Cinema 1-2-3
SPARKS, NEVADA Reno-Sparks

GENERAL THEATRICAL CO.
Ben Levin, Jesse Levin, Steve Levin
230 Hyde Street
San Francisco, CA 94102
Telephone: (415) 673-2343
SAN JOSE Jose

JACK GUNSKY THEATRES
P.O. Box 6395
San Jose, CA 95150
Telephone: (408) 378-2431
CAMPBELL Plaza 1-2-3
SAN JOSE Almaden 1-2

CENTURY 23, SAN JOSE

ROBERT L. LIPPERT THEATRES
Robert L. Lippert, Jr., President
Pier 32
San Francisco, CA 94105
Telephone: (415) 546-9200
ALAMEDA Southshore Cinemas 1-2
HAYWARD Hayward Cinemas Five
MARYSVILLE Marysville Drive-In
(formerly Sierra Drive-In)
SACRAMENTO Village
YUBA CITY Yuba City Drive-In
(formerly Auto See Drive-In)

MAESTRI MANAGEMENT CORPORATION
Charles J. Maestri, Robert C. Maestri
544 Golden Gate Avenue
San Francisco, CA 94102
Telephone: (415) 771-5900
CERES Ceres Drive-In
MODESTO McHenry Drive-In 1-2,
Prescott Drive-In 1-2-3
YREKA Broadway
MEDFORD, OREGON Cinema Center,
Craterian, Holly, Starlite Drive-In 1-2,
Medford Cinema 4

MANN THEATRES CORPORATION OF CALIFORNIA
R. A. Smith, Divisional Manager
988 Market Street, No. 413
San Francisco, CA 94102
Telephone: (415) 776-8500
CITRUS HEIGHTS Birdcage Walk Three
DUBLIN Mann's Cinemas Six
SAN JOSE Town and Country
VISALIA Fox
RENO, NEVADA Cinema, Old Town Mall
1-2-3

MARIN CINEMAS
Neal Meyer, Director of Operations
5710 Paradise Drive, Suite No. 8
Corte Madera, CA 94925
Telephone: (415) 927-0262
CORTE MADERA Cinema I
FAIRFAX Fairfax
LARKSPUR Festival Four, Lark
MILL VALLEY Sequoia 1-2
NOVATO Ignacio
SAN ANSELMO Tamalpais

SAN RAFAEL Montecito, Northgate,
Rafael
SAUSALITO Marin

RALPH MARTIN THEATRES
1465 Grove Way
Hayward, CA 94596
Telephone: (415) 886-7727
OAKLAND Plaza
SAN LEANDRO Bal

AL MITCHELL THEATRES
33 Oak Street
Red Bluff, CA 96080
CHICO Pageant
RED BLUFF State

RON MORGAN THEATRES
P.O. Box 1209
Roseville, CA 95678
Telephone: (916) 782-2955
CARMICHAEL Madison Square Four
RANCHO CORDOVA Cordova Cinemas
1-2
ROSEVILLE Tower

PACIFIC DRIVE-IN THEATRES
Jerome A. Forman, General Manager
120 North Robertson Blvd.
Los Angeles, CA 90048
Telephone: (213) 657-8420
FRESNO Sunset Drive-In, Sunnyside
Drive-In 1-2, Woodward Park Four
Drive-Ins

PARALIAX THEATRES
Gary Meyer
2302 Fillmore Street
San Francisco, CA 94115
Telephone: (415) 921-8563
BERKELEY U.C.
SACRAMENTO J Street Cinema,
Showcase, Tower 1-2-3

PLITT THEATRES OF CALIFORNIA
Robert McKeehan, District Manager
2290 Powell Street
San Francisco, CA 94115
Telephone (415) 989-6060
CONCORD Capri
DALY CITY Plaza 1-2
RICHMOND Hilltop Mall Four

SACRAMENTO Capitol 1-2, State 1-2
SAN FRANCISCO Northpoint
STOCKTON Sherwood

PREMIERE THEATRES
Ben Myron and Jesse Beaton,
Operations
2193 Fillmore, No. 2
San Francisco, CA 94115
BERKELEY Northside 1-2
NOVATO Novato
PALO ALTO Aquarius 1-2
PETALUMA Plaza
SAN CARLOS Tivoli 1-2
SACRAMENTO Crossroads Cinema

REDWOOD THEATRES, INC.
Richard Mann, George Vogan
544 Golden Gate Avenue
San Francisco, CA 94102
Telephone: (415) 771-5900
EUREKA Eureka 1-2-3, Midway
Drive-In, State 1-2-3
KLAMATH FALLS, OREGON Esquire,
Pelican Cinemas 4
MODESTO Briggsmore, Cinema 1-2
SANTA ROSA Coddingtown Cinemas
1-2-3, Park Cinemas 1-2, Village
Drive-in
UKIAH State Drive-In, Ukiah 1-2-3-4
WOODLAND State 1-2-3

RENAISSANCE RIALTO THEATRES
Allen Michaan
209 Twenty-ninth Street
San Francisco, CA 94131
Telephone: (415) 647-2425
BERKELEY Renaissance Rialto Four
MENLO PARK Guild, Park
OAKLAND Grand Lake Twin
PALO ALTO Fine Arts
SAN FRANCISCO Four Star, York
WALNUT CREEK Cinema

SURF THEATRES
Mel Novikoff, Owner
2302 Fillmore Street
San Francisco, CA 94122
Telephone: (415) 921-9173
SAN FRANCISCO Cannery Cinema,
Castro Theatre, Clay Theatre, Lumiere
Theatre, Surf Theatre

SYUFY ENTERPRISES, INC.
Raymond J. Syufy, President
Jack Myhill, General Manager
150 Golden Gate Avenue
San Francisco, CA 94102
Telephone: (415) 441-3900
ALAMEDA Island Auto Movie
BURLINGAME Burlingame Drive-Ins
1-2-3-4, Hyatt Cinemas 1-2
CAMPBELL Winchester Drive-ins Five
CONCORD Solano Drive-Ins 1-2
DALY CITY Geneva Drive-In
MOUNTAIN VIEW Moffett Drive-Ins 1-2-3
OAKLAND Century 21-22, Coliseum
Drive-Ins 1-2-3
PLEASANT HILL Century 21-22-23-24-25
REDWOOD CITY Redwood Drive-Ins 1-2
RICHMOND Hilltop Drive-in
SACRAMENTO Century 21, Century 22-
23-24-25-26, 49er Drive-Ins 1-2-3-4-
5-6, Sacramento Six Drive-Ins
SALINAS Auto Movies 1-2, Northridge
1-2-3-4
SAN FRANCISCO Cinema 21, Empire 1-
2-3
SAN JOSE Capitol Drive-Ins Six,
Century Almaden Five, Century 21,
Century 22 A-B-C, Century 23 A-B,
Century 24 A-B, Century 25 A-B
SOUTH SAN FRANCISCO Spruce Drive-
Ins 1-2-3-4
SUNNYVALE Sunnyvale Drive-Ins 1-2
UNION CITY Union City Drive-Ins Five
VALLEJO Cine 21-A-B-C, Vallejo Auto
Movies 1-2
RENO, NEVADA Century 21-22-23-24,
Midway Drive-Ins 1-2
SPARKS, NEVADA El Rancho Drive-Ins
1-2-3-4

TEGTMEIER ASSOCIATES INC.
Homer Tegtmeier, President
John Tegtmeier, Vice President
988 Market Street, No. 600
San Francisco, CA 94102
Telephone: (415) 673-4335
FAIRFIELD Fairfield Cinema I, Fairfield
Cinema II, Chief Auto Movies, Chief
Cinemas 1-2
LAKEPORT Lakeport 1-2, Lakeport
Auto Movies

MIKE THOMAS THEATRES
1127 Market Street
San Francisco, CA 94103
Telephone: (415) 552-2396
SAN CARLOS Laurel
SAN FRANCISCO Egyptian, Strand,
Warfield

TOCANN THEATRES
Florence McCann, Judy McCann,
Sue Ellen McCann
199 Petaluma Blvd. North
Petaluma, CA 94952
Telephone: (707) 762-6685
PETALUMA Washington Square
Cinemas 1-2

CINEMA 150, SANTA CLARA

UNITED ARTISTS THEATRE CIRCUIT
Robert A. Naify, President and Chairman of the Board
Marshall Naify, Executive Committee Chairman
Arnold Childhouse, Senior Vice President
Larry Levin, General Manager–Operations
Robert Vallone, Assistant General Manager
172 Golden Gate Avenue
San Francisco, CA 94102
Telephone: (415) 928-3200
ANDERSON Gateway Cinema 4
APTOS Aptos Twin Cinemas 1-2
BERKELEY Elmwood, U A 1-2-3-4, U A Pruneyard 1-2-3
CAMPBELL U A
CAPITOLA Forty-first Avenue Playhouse 3
CARMEL Carmel Center Cinema 1-2, Golden Bough Cinema, Valley Cinema
CHICO El Rey, Senator, Starlight Drive-In, U A Cinemas Three
CITRUS HEIGHTS U A Sunrise Four
COLMA Serra
FRESNO U A Cinemas Four, U A Movies Four
GRASS VALLEY Del Oro Three
MARYSVILLE State 1-2-3
MERCED Merced 1-2-3-4, Starlite Drive-In, U A Cinema, U A Regency
MILLBRAE Millbrae 1-2-3
MONTEREY Cinema 70, U A Regency, U A State 1-2-3, Hill
OROVILLE Mesa Drive-In, State
REDDING Cascade, U A Movies Three
SAN BRUNO U A Tanforan Cinemas Four
SAN FRANCISCO Alexandria 1-2-3, Balboa 1-2, Coliseum, Coronet, Metro I, Metro II, U A Cinema Stonestown 1-2, Vogue
SAN JOSE U A Blossomhill Cinemas 4
SANTA CLARA U A Cinema 150
SANTA CRUZ Del Mar 1-2-3, Rio 1-2, U A Cinemas 1-2
SANTA ROSA Redwood Drive-In, U A Cinema Six, U A Movies Six

YUBA CITY Sutter
RENO, NEVADA Granada A-B, U A Cinema 1-2

VALLEY CINEMAS
Edward M. Fonseca
P.O. Box 967
Manteca, CA 95336
Telephone: (209) 239-3931
JACKSON Valley Cinemas Three
LOS BANOS Crest, Los Banos Cinemas 1-2
MANTECA Valley Cinemas 1-2
STOCKTON Hammer West Cinemas Four, Valley Cinema
TURLOCK Valley 1-2

WESTLAND THEATRES
Rodda W. Harvey, President
Don Babcock, Vice President and General Manager
1829 Pacific Avenue
Stockton, CA 95207
Telephone: (209) 466-4944
STOCKTON Hammer Drive-In, Motor Movies, Stockton Royal 1-2-3-4, Westland Drive-In
VISALIA Mooney Auto Movies East-West
WINNEMUCCA, NEVADA Sage

WEST SIDE-VALLEY THEATRES
Adelaide Cooper, Chairman of the Board
John A. Dobbs, President
Barbara Mannheimer, First Vice President
988 Market Street, No. 711
San Francisco, CA 94102
Telephone: (415) 885-0491
BELMONT Belmont 1-2-3
CUPERTINO Oaks Three
DAVIS Cinema 2, Varsity 1-2
LIVERMORE Vine 1-2
OAKLAND Lux
SAN MATEO Manor 1-2
SONORA Plaza Twin
SUNNYVALE Cinema Hacienda 1-2
TULARE Tower Square Three
VACAVILLE
VISALIA Tower Plaza Three, Visalia

CASTRO THEATRE

Epilogue

I've learned a great deal about northern California theatre (and theater) since I sat down and stared at the blank first page several months (or was it years?) ago. The most striking thing about it is its variety: in architecture, formats, and outlooks. Companies that began with little more than ambition and a minimum of talent have grown prominent in the cultural makeup of their communities. Others have been content to simply survive and do a show now and then, maybe more for the gratification of the players than of the audience. Still others have burst the seams of their original plants, and the sound of the applause of local fans has not been enough. These theatres have expanded their home base and have taken their act on the road.

Professional theatre isn't as strong or as prevalent as it might and should be; the economics in all but the largest metropolitan areas make it impossible to sustain such theatres. But the professional house count seems to hold its own. One theatre may go dark, but somewhere up the pike another one will raise its first opening night curtain. And the big shows are increasing the number of their appearances (and the size of their ticket prices) in the heavily populated centers of the northern half of the state.

I've learned much about the people who make up these theatres: their dreams, their enthusiasm, their biases, their desperation when bill-paying time comes around, their sorrow when Aunt Nellie and Joe the Barber are the only folks who show up, their triumph when the curtain falls and the audience rises to its feet. I've learned that they have more commitment to their cause than nearly any other group of people. There may be some missionaries in Borneo who'd contest that, but I think it's true. Whether for money or for therapy, for glory or for greed, for themselves or for the ticket buyers, it takes an extra amount of intestinal fortitude to walk out on a stage in the belief that someone will be sitting on the other side of the footlights or the orchestra pit waiting to see you.

Being part of an audience takes a like act of faith. Because money is so hard to get and harder to keep, when you plunk it down on the box office counter, it's with a silent hope that, a couple of hours later, you'll be better off for having done so. Of course, if you're Aunt Nellie or Joe the Barber, maybe you don't really care if the show is that good—as long as someone is up there being larger than life. The person up there probably feels much the same about you.

Movies and movie theaters are big business. It's more difficult to get close to your local cinema than to the cop on the beat or the community-theatre stage manager, but give it a try. Just because the flicks are big business doesn't mean that you can't make things a little better by being friendly to the big corporation's human representative. It couldn't hurt. It might even help when you ask for a refund because they showed the film you waited for six months to see with reel six where reel two should have been.

These are some of the things that I've learned. Oh, perhaps I knew them before and this project has just refreshed my memory. Either way, it was worth the effort for me. If it proves to be the same for you, then *Front Row Center* does exactly what I had hoped it would do when page one was blank.

A final word about objectivity and subjectivity. There may have been a time or two in this book when you said to yourself, "There he goes again—once a critic, always a critic!" Sorry, I tried to walk the straight and narrow but every once in a while I slipped. It seems to me that that is bound to happen when two people—you and me—sit down to communicate. And now that we've done it, I hope we're both better for the experience. Enjoy the new-found friends and experiences that await you in the theatre community of northern California (and Ashland). See you at intermission.

Index

BIOGRAPHICAL NOTES

JACK BROOKS

Jack Brooks's career in the theatre—as actor, director, producer, and critic—spans some three decades, from his first acting role at age ten to his current position as entertainment editor for KGO Newstalk Radio in San Francisco. After launching his own professional music theatre in Akron, Ohio, he moved on to Broadway and for six years appeared in, directed, or produced some of the leading hits of the sixties for major stock companies in the East and Midwest. His roles have been as diverse as Nathan Detroit in *Guys and Dolls* and Jason in *Medea*.

For the past dozen years, Jack Brooks has been in the forefront of the Bay Area show business world. His talents as actor-producer-director have enriched a number of local stage presentations. He has also written several musical stage plays as well as radio and TV drama scripts. His theatrical columns have appeared in northern California newspapers and magazines. He has been a regular on KGO Television's "AM-Weekend" and also covers special entertainment events on-camera for Channel 7's "AM San Francisco." Jack Brooks's other activities include motion picture acting and movie theater management. He was an instigator and founding member of the Bay Area Critics' Circle.

DENISE PEACH

A native of Virginia, Denise Peach began her artistic training at home at a very early age as a result of being the daughter of two artists. Her interest and talent grew as she headed art committees and art shows at Dominion University. Denise has taught art to disadvantaged children and, with the publication of *Front Row Center,* is hard at work writing and illustrating her first children's book.